Rebuilding the Nest

A New Commitment to the American Family

Edited by
David Blankenhorn
Steven Bayme
Jean Bethke Elshtain

FSA

Family Service America
11700 West Lake Park Drive
Milwaukee, WI 53224

Library of Congress Cataloging–in–Publication Data

Rebuilding the nest: a new commitment to the American family / edited
  by David Blankenhorn, Steven Bayme, Jean Bethke Elshtain.
    p.   cm.
  Includes bibliographical references.
  ISBN 0-87304-242-5
  1. Family–United States. 2. Family policy–United States.
I. Blankenhorn, David G. II. Bayme, Steven. III. Elshtain, Jean Bethke.
HQ536.R43   1990
306.85'0973–dc20

                                                  90-44116

Contents

85951

Foreword

Dr. Lee Salk

My understanding of the family can be summarized in two propositions, based on my years as a clinical psychologist working with children and as an author of books for parents. First, I believe that becoming a parent is the most important commitment a human being can undertake—that nothing in life is more individually rewarding and socially important than forming families and raising children. Second, I believe that families in our society are under great stress and that the family as a social unit is being threatened by some of our deepest cultural, political, and economic trends.

If both of these propositions are true, the result is alarming: as individuals and as a society, we stand to lose what we need most. This dilemma—its dimensions and consequences as well as what can be done about it—forms the subject of this welcome and much-needed book of essays on the state of the family in America.

This book breaks new ground. It focuses on family well-being rather than on partisan ideological agendas. It rejects the tired political polarizations—left versus right, bigger government versus smaller government—that dominated the family debate in the 1970s and 1980s. Instead, the authors try for something new. The reader can sense their efforts to assert the need for family-oriented cultural values, while at the same time affirming the need for new public- and private-sector policies to strengthen family life and to help families in need.

This book strives, in short, for a new consensus on family values and family policies for the 1990s. The ideas presented here point us in a new direction. It is a direction that I believe our society must follow if we are concerned for our long-term well-being, especially the well-being of our children. I see these essays, then, as an important intellectual resource, not only for scholars, policymakers, and civic leaders, but also for all parents and family members who are concerned about the quality of family life in our society.

Finally, this book comes at an opportune moment. As we enter a new decade, I see all around us a greater emphasis on the family and on family

Dr. Lee Salk is Clinical Professor of Psychology in Psychiatry and Pediatrics at Cornell University Medical College and the author of many books and articles for parents.

values. There is a growing recognition in our society that we must improve the quality of family life and especially the quality of life for children. This new concern is evident in corporate America, as employees and business leaders strive to fashion more family-friendly workplace policies. It is also evident in opinion poll data, popular culture, policy debates, and the media.

Some of this cultural tilt stems from demographics. Our society, for example, is becoming increasingly alarmed about the growing number of children living in poverty. In earlier generations, older people were poorer than any other age group. Today, children are our poorest Americans. One in five children in the United States today is born into poverty. About 40% of all poor Americans are children. We recognize that much of this problem is the result of teen pregnancy, single-parent homes, and family breakdown. The solution, therefore, must lie in large part in strengthening the family unit. This will be a major social and public policy challenge in the coming decade.

There is another demographic reason. The huge baby-boom generation, born in the 15 years following World War II, is now having and raising children in record numbers. In 1989, over four million babies were born in the United States—more than in any other previous year of our history. The birth rate, or the number of children born per woman, is also inching up, in part due to the fact that many couples now in their late 20s and 30s, who had delayed childbearing for a decade or more longer than their parents' generation, are now deciding to have children.

This demographic shift is already causing reverberations in our culture and in our politics. Barbara Whitehead, a social historian, has recently described this emerging change in the baby-boom generation:

> As they step into parenthood, they cross a great cultural divide. . . . They discover that the values that guided them as young adults aren't very useful in raising children. The same culture that supported them as individuals, they are now realizing, is indifferent or even hostile to them as parents and to their children.[1]

In short, for a number of reasons, the family will become a major and growing national focus in the coming years. We thus face a unique opportunity in the 1990s to create a more family-friendly society. The challenge is large and the stakes are high. With the seminal ideas and the challenges to the old thinking presented in this book, we can now declare: Let the new debate begin.

---

1. Barbara Dafoe Whitehead, "The Family in an Unfriendly Culture," *Family Affairs* 3 (Nos. 1–2, Spring/Summer 1990), p. 5.

Acknowledgments

This book has many parents. So many, in fact, that creating it demanded diplomatic as well as scholarly skills. The "What Do Families Do?" conference, held at Stanford University on November 9–12, 1989, was cosponsored by three organizations:

● The *Institute for American Values*, a New York-based organization devoted to research, publication, and public education on issues of family well-being and family policy;
● The *Center for the Study of Families, Children and Youth*, based at Stanford University in Palo Alto, California, which sponsors research and disseminates information, especially research findings that can benefit parents; and
● The *William Petschek National Jewish Family Center*, a New York-based arm of the American Jewish Committee that studies family issues relevant to both the American Jewish community and the broader society.

That conference, chaired by Professor Jean Bethke Elshtain of Vanderbilt University, brought together more than 20 of the nation's leading family scholars. The commissioned papers from the conference form the basis of this book. Conference follow-up, including editorial and publication activities, was coordinated by the Institute for American Values and the William Petschek National Jewish Family Center. In addition to the three sponsoring organizations, financial support for this project was provided by the Joseph P. Kennedy, Jr., Foundation of Washington, D.C. Special thanks are due to Dr. George Zitnay of the Kennedy Foundation for his help and encouragement. Additional support, for which the editors are deeply grateful, was provided by Peter and Betty Heller and the Allstate Foundation. The editors also wish to acknowledge gratefully the insightful advice and invaluable editorial assistance of Vesna Neskow as well as the generous contributions of Ivan Sacks and Melissa Beacham.

Special thanks, finally, are due to each person who attended that conference. The discussions were spirited and frequently provocative, owing largely to the fact that these participants brought with them, in addition to scholarly expertise, a personal commitment to family well-being in our society. That commitment made this gathering much more than the usual academic event. Frequently during the conference—more frequently even than the sponsors had thought possible—those rare and special moments occurred in which one could literally hear the sounds of new ideas being born. Thus, while each author in this book bears sole responsibility for his or her essay, all of these essays were certainly enriched by the entire group.

Conference Participants

Those attending the "What Do Families Do?" conference at Stanford University on November 9–12, 1989, included:

Steven Bayme

Director of Jewish Communal Affairs,
The American Jewish Committee,
New York City

Robert N. Bellah

Professor of Sociology,
University of California at Berkeley

David Blankenhorn

President, Institute for American Values,
New York City

Urie Bronfenbrenner

Professor of Human Development and
Family Studies, Cornell University,
Ithaca, New York

Lynette Friedrich Cofer

Professor of Psychology, University of
New Mexico at Albuquerque

Sanford M. Dornbusch

Director, Center for the Study of
Families, Children and Youth,
Stanford University, Stanford, California

Jean Bethke Elshtain

Centennial Professor of Political Science
Vanderbilt University, Nashville, Tennessee

Shirley Feldman

Associate Director, Center for the Study of
Families, Children and Youth,
Stanford University, Stanford, California

Victor R. Fuchs

Henry J. Kaiser, Jr. Professor,
Department of Economics,
Stanford University, Stanford, California

Norval D. Glenn

Distinguished Professor of Sociology,
University of Texas at Austin

Bruce C. Hafen

Provost of Brigham Young University,
Provo, Utah

Sylvia Ann Hewlett
Visiting Professor of Public Policy,
Sarah Lawrence College,
Bronxville, New York

Robin Smith Jacobvitz
Assistant Professor of Psychology,
University of New Mexico at Albuquerque

Richard Kinch
Program Officer, The Johnson Foundation,
Racine, Wisconsin

Philip Lankford
Economic and Demographic Research,
Allstate Research and Planning Center,
Menlo Park, California

Carol McClelland
Human Resource Research,
Allstate Research and Planning Center,
Menlo Park, California

Lawrence M. Mead
Associate Professor of Politics,
New York University, New York City

Gilbert Meilaender
Professor of Religion,
Oberlin College, Oberlin, Ohio

Dennis K. Orthner
Director, Human Services Research Laboratory,
University of North Carolina at Chapel Hill

David Popenoe
Associate Dean for the Social Sciences,
Rutgers University, New Brunswick, New Jersey

Robert M. Rice
Executive Vice President, Family Service America,
Milwaukee, Wisconsin

Sherry Rosen
Research Associate, Jewish Communal Affairs,
The American Jewish Committee,
New York City

Jan Rosenberg
Associate Professor of Sociology,
Long Island University, Brooklyn, New York

Carol Sanger
Visiting Scholar,
Center for the Study of Law and Society,
University of California at Berkeley

Stephen Szmrecsanyi
Legislative Assistant to the Executive Director,
Father Flanagan's Boys' Home,
Boys' Town, Nebraska

Edward F. Zigler
Sterling Professor of Psychology,
Yale University, New Haven, Connecticut

Introduction

David Blankenhorn

Editors discover many reasons—not all of them necessarily high-minded—to publish books of essays. Such books feed the academic imperative to "publish or perish," for example, by providing respectable homes for scholarly papers that otherwise might remain unnoticed by the wider public. In such collections, moreover, it is the time-honored duty of editors to announce that, despite appearances, the disparate essays contained in the volume are in fact united by a common theme. This is my present task.

Yet in this volume, what possible unity can we detect among such diverse authors? Some are well-known liberals; others are proud conservatives. Some are hard-nosed empiricists; others contend that nothing is more real than pondering life's ultimate purposes. Some focus on policy analysis, others on cultural institutions. Their varying fields of expertise—psychology, sociology, economics, political science, demography, social work, theology, law, education, and philosophy—produce in this book an almost promiscuously interdisciplinary discussion. Sometimes the special language of scholarship gets in the way: where the theologian detects "love," the economist may see "psychic income."

Moreover, these authors come together to address what may be the most emotional and ill-defined topic in today's domestic policy debate—the status and future of the family as a social institution. Few questions in our time are so controversial. Few are so fraught with excess baggage and hidden agendas. Few are less likely to produce consensus in any gathering larger than one person.

Despite these difficulties, I believe I can meet my time-honored editorial duty. These essays do fit together. All of them, from different vantage points, address the same subject. Moreover, they are bound together by a common conceptual framework. Most important, taken as a whole, they contribute something new and vital to our public discourse on the family. These are large claims; let me briefly explain.

THE CONCEPTUAL FRAMEWORK

The arguments in this volume, although diverse and sometimes in conflict with one another, constitute more than a simple free-for-all on the subject of family. Certain values and assumptions were established at the outset. These guiding presuppositions appealed to some people and not to others. Our starting ideas led us, in short, to those scholars who are interested in a certain kind of discourse.

First, *we assume that family is the subject.* This idea is less self-evident than it may sound. Especially since the family has become a potent political theme, many interests and agendas have sought to decorate themselves with family imagery. Moreover, it's hard to imagine a topic—from pollution to housing to public prayer to corporate competitiveness—that does not, in some way, bear upon family life. But we insist here on a more limited definition of our subject—not the universe of issues that may relate to or symbolize the family, but the nature and quality of family life itself.

Second, *we assume that the family is a social institution.* Again, this idea is not universally accepted. Even the key word, "family," is in dispute. Some, seeking to recognize and valorize the diversity of contemporary family forms, always say "families." They argue that there can be no such thing as "the family" and certainly no such thing as the "institution" of family.

Others, however, insist on subjecting families to a more institutional analysis. As a result, they focus on social functions—what families do that society depends on—and on social norms. Just as one can generalize about "public education" rather than simply describe the diversity of "schools," or study "monarchy" as an institution rather than "kings and queens," so in this volume we present more general arguments about the family as a distinctive social unit with distinctive, albeit changing, social functions.

Third, *we assume that the family is a good thing.* A case can be made, of course, that the family is a bad thing—that it oppresses women, abuses children, fosters authoritarianism, stifles individualism, promotes inequality, harbors bigotry, encourages chauvinism, offends democratic principles, bolsters unjust powers, and generally stands in the way of greater freedom and justice for modern societies. Though these charges sting precisely because they contain grains of truth, we leave the case against family life for others to make. In the final analysis, or at least until something better comes along, we are for the family, not against it.

Fourth and finally, *we assume that the current family debate is impoverished by sterile political polarizations:* imprisoned by the ideological categories of left versus right and governed by broader agendas that have little to do with what makes families distinctive social units.

Regarding the family, we are, as a group, politically homeless. We assume, therefore, that new thinking—cutting across both political labels and academic specializations—is far more important than carrying water for any of today's pre-set political or ideological agendas. Our rule of thumb

What Do Families Do?
The Six Social Functions of the Family

1. *Procreation*. Families produce society's children. When functioning well, they produce at least enough children to replace the preceding generation.

2. *Socialization*. The family, more than any other institution, is where core values are taught and learned—where people find out who they are and where parents pass on to children the basic traits of character and citizenship that are essential to both individual and societal well-being.

3. *Affection*. The family is the basis for caring and nurturing relationships—the source, for most people, of life's greatest loves and most enduring commitments. In this regard, the family may be society's most important institution in determining the level of what might be called Gross National Happiness.

4. *Sexuality*. Traditionally, family status is an important governor of sexual behavior. The family unit, in short, regulates the sexual activity of its members. Whether and how this regulation occurs, of course, carries profound personal and social consequences.

5. *Cooperation*. Family members share resources and cooperate economically. Families have been called "oases of socialism," because family relationships are distinctly noncapitalist. They are governed by neither contract nor voluntary agreement, nor are they calculated on the basis of individual financial gain. Yet these relationships have lasting economic consequences for both the individual and society.

6. *Pluralism*. Independent family units constitute one necessary precondition for cultural diversity, free economies, and democratic institutions. As the main mediating structures between the individual and the state, families protect pluralism: they retard the social concentration of power, resources, and loyalties. For this reason, totalitarians have historically regarded the family with deep hostility.

---

has been: if you understand the current family debate as a clear political contest of good versus evil, right versus wrong, then our project is not for you. In that sense, what we sponsor is less a debate than a conversation. It is less a set of answers than a new mode of inquiry.

ORGANIZATION

The book is organized into three sections. Part One is descriptive, focusing on the actual conditions of contemporary family life. It asks the question: Is the family an institution in trouble? Part Two moves from conditions to causes. What is the source of our current dilemma? This section focuses on changing cultural values and changing social institutions. Part Three begins a discussion of solutions. If we have an idea of the challenges we face, what is the agenda for the future?

A NEW CONSENSUS?

Consensus is a big word. As the reader will discover, the authors in this volume do not always agree. Each has his own special perspective, her own main point. Sometimes the disagreements are clear and sharp, but more frequent are differences of emphasis, language, and qualification.

Yet taking the essays as a whole, I find several areas of general agreement that are far more noteworthy—and far more relevant to today's public debate—than any differences. Three in particular stand out.

1. *As a social institution, the family in America is increasingly less able to carry out its basic functions.* The family, in short, is becoming weaker as an institution in our society.

2. *The quality of life for America's children is declining.* On this point, consensus really is the proper word. Scholarship tells us plainly that it is becoming harder each year to be a child in the United States. Surely, such an alarming fact should be widely known in our society. It is not. Surely, it should guide public discourse and policy debate. It does not.

3. *Our family dilemma is not simply one of public policy or economics but it is also one of cultural values and social institutions.* Although to create stronger families will require policy changes, a policy agenda alone is not enough. Ultimately, our crisis is not due only to someone else, or some outside institution, or some economic trend, or some act of government. The crisis is us. The workplace, the school, the church and synagogue, the media, the court, the civic and voluntary association—and most important, the individual citizen and family member—must all contribute to a new cultural ethos of strong family life. To believe otherwise is to misunderstand the challenge of "family policy."

Despite these quite important points of convergence, however, this book provides no final answer to the bottom-line question: What is to be done? Although many of the authors offer specific ideas for action, and although these authors agree more than they disagree about solutions, the book as a whole offers no detailed legislative, private-sector, or institutional agendas for strengthening family life in America. These essays, in short, constitute less a set of answers than a first attempt to think about the family dilemma in a new way.

There are next steps. We expect that this book will contribute to the creation of a larger, multiyear initiative to examine the status and future of the family in America. As one important product of that initiative, we envision a multivolume set of essays that explores in more detail the central themes and questions raised in this book. In addition, we anticipate a Report to the Nation, to be completed over the next several years, that will not only summarize the body of scholarship that has been produced, but will also propose a national family agenda for policymakers, scholars, and the American public—one that addresses the major family-issue challenges facing our society as we approach the 21st century.

Part I

Conditions:
Is the Family
In Decline?

=1=
American Family Dilemmas

David Blankenhorn

Over the past decade, "family" has gone public. Popular opinion is clearly worried about it. Everyone seems to agree that it is changing. Politicians of both parties insist that they care about it. Legislators and lobbyists daily announce their plans to help it. Media commentators increasingly comment on it. Scholars research it. The baby-boom generation, approaching age 40, has now discovered it. Corporations, worried about their future labor force, create new personnel policies in order to accommodate it. Though important exceptions exist, most people today seem to be in favor of it.

Yet what does "it" mean? In Washington "family policy" is a term unburdened by any specific meaning. The words are simply a political Rorschach test, designed to convey whatever anyone wants them to convey. Want to help the poor? Want to cut taxes? Want to support working women? Want children to pray in school? If you do, or do not, then you want "family policy." Similarly, "family" and "family values," although frequently invoked, usually amount to little more than rhetorical Trojan horses, intended to camouflage any number of special interests and hidden agendas.

This dilemma—the confusing, often contentless nature of the family debate—certainly retards and distorts the policymaking process. But more important, it also impoverishes our broader understanding of what may be our society's most urgent social question. To understand how, consider two main dimensions of the problem: first, the public absence of expert knowledge; and second, the clash of basic cultural values.

When Congressional committees seek testimony on Social Security—or on nuclear weapons or any number of issues—they call upon publicly acknowledged authorities. These experts play a key role. They disci-

David Blankenhorn is President of the Institute for American Values, an organization based in New York City that conducts research and public education on family issues.

pline the debate. They cannot eliminate political posturing from policy-making, of course, but they do help to reduce it. They do not agree among themselves on the answers, but they generally do agree on the proper questions as well as on the definitions of the words that govern the debate.

Yet regarding family policy, this discipline is largely absent. Consider the major family issues facing the Congress: child care, parental leave, divorce law, teen pregnancy, changes in the tax code, and others. Have they been framed, or even significantly influenced, by acknowledged experts on the family as a social institution? The answer, I believe, is no.

Congressional staffers, as well as newspaper reporters or television producers, can and do find expert authorities in psychology, poverty, child development, women's rights, aging, education, trends in the labor force, and any number of other areas that seem, somehow, to relate to the family. But they rarely find authorities on the family itself. The reason for this is simple but telling: this category of expertise is still publicly invisible. It is seldom acknowledged or even recognized; the gatekeepers and traffic cops of today's family debate remain unsure even of what constitutes expertise on the institution of the family. As a result, the debate is always open-ended: without definitions, without boundaries, without any baseline understanding of what it means to stray from the subject. It remains, in short, a standing invitation to anyone with an agenda to peddle.

For some, then, "family policy" means helping poor children. For others, it becomes empowering women in the work force. It can also become children's rights. Or redistributing income. Or expanding the welfare state. Or attacking the welfare state. For corporate managers, it becomes a work-force issue: reducing absenteeism and personnel turnover. For most politicians, it literally translates into "my ideas to help people."

But the basic problem extends beyond turf battles, issue boundaries, and the absence of expert knowledge. This same dilemma of incoherence is also apparent on a second and even deeper level: "family policy" constitutes a strategic battleground in the war of cultural values.

Is unwed parenthood morally wrong? Is abortion? Which is the preferred family: the "traditional" family or the modern "working" family? Should unmarried or gay relationships receive the legal protections currently restricted to family relationships? Should an unhappy couple stay together for the sake of their children? Which is more important: individualism and self-expression or commitment and self-sacrifice?

These questions touch our deepest and most private chords of morality and emotion. Moreover, especially in the United States, public discussion of social norms often produces more conflict than consensus. We are a heterogeneous nation. Certainly, few societies celebrate diversity and tolerance as much as ours does. Value issues, therefore, can be sharply polarizing, often along lines of class, gender, race, region, and religion.

They emerge very quickly in the family debate, in part precisely because the debate remains so undisciplined and vague.

Yet these value clashes are also inherent and inevitable. The family, after all, is an institution based on morally defined relationships. Thus family issues, almost by definition, are inseparable from moral issues. In the area of, say, computer science, it may be credible to argue that one's research or policy analysis is "value-free." Regarding the family, that claim is not credible.

Is it possible to imagine a divorce law that does not reflect a normative idea about marriage? Or child-care legislation that is ethically neutral about the role of parents? Or a school-based health clinic that conveys no moral message about teenage sexuality? Or research on family dysfunction that contains no normative assumptions about what is functional? In some respects, indeed, values are what the family debate is all about. In fact, if everyone involved in the debate, including scholars, were to acknowledge this truth more explicitly, much unnecessary fog would clear away.

At the same time, for anyone venturing into the public dialogue about the status and future of the family, these value issues constitute a minefield—always dangerous, sometimes explosive, often forcing the discussion toward the sensational but marginal extremes, yet, in the final analysis, absolutely necessary and unavoidable. To negotiate that minefield requires a blend of intellectual rigor and moral vision that is, at best, an exceedingly difficult task. So it is understandable, yet also profoundly disturbing, that during the past decade, since "family" has gone public, our public discourse has not done well at that task.

The current family debate, in sum, is like swimming in molasses or nailing Jell-O to a tree. It can hardly be done at all. This same set of problems prompted Gilbert Y. Steiner of the Brookings Institution, after the 1979 White House Conference on Families, to write a book with its jeremiad in the title: *The Futility of Family Policy*.[1]

Is Steiner right? Is family policy "futile"? I hope and believe that he is wrong. But his warning is undoubtedly proper. In an examination of "American family dilemmas," therefore, the first dilemma is this: today's debate on the family is fundamentally adrift and riven by competing social values.

A User's Guide for Today's Family Debate

Is it possible, however, in today's jangling public discourse on the family, to discover any underlying clarity? Can we discern, amid the seeming incoherence, an underlying structure and rationale? Certainly a prerequisite for improving the debate is to map the contours and fault lines that now define it and to explicate the implicit competing epistemologies that now govern it. To begin on an impressionistic level, engage in these three thought experiments.

What the Picture Says

First, react to this photograph. What do you see? How do you feel about it? (Stop reading until you finish your contemplation.)

During the past year, I have asked many people—some in the family study business, others not—to participate in this experiment.[2] Of course, these viewers constitute only a random and unscientific sample. Yet I received fascinatingly diverse responses. Here, edited into composites, are the most frequent:

> That's me. That's my family on vacation when I was a child. There's my mother. I love the picture. But of course, I'd be resentful if I were expected to be that mother today.

> It makes me feel sad and guilty. When I got married in the '50s, that's what we thought a family was. I thought I was that kind of mother, married to that kind of father. But what we thought wasn't the way it turned out—at least not for a lot of us.

> That's my dad cooking the hot dogs. Look how perfectly the fruit is arranged on the plate—my mom did it that way. It makes me nostalgic. And it makes me wonder if I'll do as well at this family business as they did.

> I don't like it. It represents people who aren't me. It's too perfectionist, too composed. It's an idealization of a past era, and it's not inclusive. I'm sure that black people weren't allowed on that beach.

What's wrong with this picture? These people look happy to me. That family looks like a great family. Given the family problems we have today, maybe we ought to pay attention to what these people are doing.

It fills me with dread and fear and anger. The sex roles are rigid. Everything is too ordered. The children are too perfect. This is Wonder Bread ideology for middle-class, Protestant, white America. Especially for white men—he's cooking the bacon he brought home; she smiles adoringly at him and his children. Horrible.

What the Nerd Says

The second thought experiment is to react to a line in a 1988 movie, *River's Edge*. The movie—made by young, politically liberal filmmakers in California—is based on a true story.[3] A suburban teenage boy, for no apparent reason, strangles to death a female classmate, leaving her body near a river where he and his friends sometimes congregate. He confesses the murder to his friends, who go with him to see the body. But for days, no one goes to the police. The friends, upset and bewildered, cover up the killing.

The main teenage characters are portrayed as aimless and confused, frequently cynical and listless. Their parents, mostly in their late 30s to early 40s, are, on the whole, pathetic and impotent. When one mother (divorced, with a younger live-in boyfriend) scolds her son for smoking marijuana, he replies, "Don't worry, I didn't take any of yours."

When the guilty boy is finally taken into custody, his friends discuss the meaning of the incident with their high school teacher—a former 1960s firebrand who frequently admonishes the teenagers about their seeming lack of idealism, rebelliousness, and social conscience. In the middle of the teacher's passionate lecture, the class nerd—hopelessly square, barely tolerated by the other students and patronized by the hip teacher—interrupts with this self-righteous importunity: "The whole incident points up a fundamental moral breakdown in our society." The viewer is left to ponder: Is this fellow naive? Or is he, like Dostoevski's Idiot, the unlikely conveyor of the moral of the story?

Regress or Progress?

Consider a third and final experiment. Imagine two infants. You know nothing about them except these facts: one is born in the United States in 1950, and the other is born in the United States today. Now surmise—knowing all of the social and material progress of the past 403 years—which of those two infants will have a better quality of life during childhood.

The Defining Question

Each of these thought experiments invites us, in a different way, to answer the same fundamental question: *What are the dimensions and consequences of changes in the family during the past quarter century?* I believe that this question constitutes the Rubicon—the primary fault line—in the nation's current discourse on the status and future of the family as an institution. Moreover, two seemingly incompatible answers to this question define the underlying boundaries and structure of today's family policy debate.

Do you approve of the photograph more than you disapprove? Do you suspect that the nerd is more right than wrong? Do you guess that, on the whole, the 1950 infant will have the better childhood? This sensibility precisely distinguishes one of the two major schools of thought in today's family debate. If, on the other hand, you dislike the picture, distrust the nerd, and bet on today's infant, welcome to the second school.

I would like to suggest, in short, that today's serious family debate becomes coherent only when seen as the clash of two implicit world views. Moreover, these governing epistemologies do not fit our usual categories of "liberal" and "conservative." As a result, they remain largely obscured in the media and poorly understood even by many who are active in the debate.

Optimism versus Pessimism

Call one school of thought "optimism" and the other "pessimism." Both sides agree—indeed, it has become an almost meaningless cliché—that the family "is changing." But the two schools disagree profoundly on the dimensions and consequences of that change.

To summarize, optimists emphasize the positive (or at least benign) results of those changes, particularly for women, and propose social policies to reflect and accommodate the new realities. Pessimists, on the other hand, see the family in decline as a social institution and emphasize the negative consequences of that decline, particularly for children.

At bottom, the devaluation of children and child rearing forms the heart of the pessimists' analysis: if they lose that debate, their entire argument begins to unravel. Similarly, the new individual freedoms for adults form the core of the optimists' case. Greater adult self-fulfillment, therefore, is the ground they can least afford to cede.

Elite opinion today—in the media, in government, on the two coasts—tilts clearly toward optimism and away from the decidedly more pessimistic cast of grass-roots opinion.[4] Congresswoman Pat Schroeder of Colorado is probably the nation's most prominent and articulate spokesperson for this point of view. Her book, *Champion of the Great American Family*, is an eloquent summary of the optimists' perspective on the changing American family.[5]

Until recently, scholarly experts, like most other elites, have tended to be optimists. For example, Mary Jo Bane's very influential 1976 book on the family delivers a message that is implicit in the book's title: *Here to Stay*. Many ideas of family decline, she wrote, are "more myth than fact."

Her study reported "surprising stabilities" in American families and "the persistence of commitments to family life."[6]

Recent scholarship, however, has become more pessimistic.[7] One important benchmark in this direction is David Popenoe's *Disturbing the Nest: Family Change and Decline in Modern Societies*.[8] Popenoe's conclusions, though carefully nuanced to encompass alternative views, convey an almost Spenglerian mood. It is a paradigmatic example of the current scholarly tilt toward pessimism regarding the state of the family.

It may prove helpful, then, to illustrate the optimist-versus-pessimist dispute (which I propose as the underlying logic of today's public discourse on the family) by examining the Popenoe and Schroeder books together, viewing them as an exemplary case study in the debate between these two basic schools of thought. Popenoe and Schroeder's argument is not, at bottom, an argument between politics and scholarship. Nor is it basically a clash between "liberalism" and "conservatism." Both authors, in fact, are "liberals" in the parlance of contemporary politics. Their dispute is of a different nature: they disagree fundamentally on the social consequences of family change in our era.

For Schroeder, as with many people who write about the family, theory is autobiography. (The subtitle of *Champion of the Great American Family* is *A Personal and Political Book*.) Her optimism about family change is rooted in her own experience. As a young attorney in Denver in the 1960s, she became a local, and later national, leader in the movements to expand opportunities for women in the workplace and in public life. The women's movement, in short, changed her life—for the better.

Along with her pioneering career achievements, Schroeder is also the married mother of two children. She knows well the often formidable challenges facing parents, especially mothers, who seek to balance career and family. She and her own family seem to have struck that balance with notable success, flair, and good humor. But it required change and adaptation.

When her first child was born in 1966, she quit her job only to discover that "I didn't like being a full-time homemaker. The truth is, I failed homemaking. I found it incredibly frustrating."[9] She

> soon learned that children don't care who does their laundry or grocery shopping or makes their bed. In fact, they don't care if anyone does it. . . . In short order I gave up many of my ideas about what was required of a proper wife and mother.[10]

Elected to Congress in 1972, she came to Washington, D.C., determined to "champion women's rights and the American family." Her guiding principle became

> if we get rid of the inequalities that hinder women, we strengthen the family at the same time. For me, building a family policy has meant finding a way to bridge the gap between public policy and the reality of women's lives.[11]

Today, Schroeder is a leading proponent in Congress for what she terms "a national family policy." The main components of her proposed policy include more child-care assistance for working parents; family and medical leave legislation, which would grant working parents the right to unpaid, job-protected leaves in order to care for newly born or seriously ill children; stricter child-support requirements for divorced or separated noncustodial parents, usually fathers; additional services and supports for divorced and widowed women, especially displaced homemakers; pay equity (comparable worth) for working women; greater state efforts to prevent domestic violence and child abuse; and larger tax deductions for families with children, especially two-earner families.

Current policies, Schroeder argues, "lag far behind the realities faced by today's working families."[12] Her proposed family policy, by contrast, would "acknowledge the kinds of lives women really lead"[13] and assist families who are "desperate to find answers that will help them juggle all the chores modern life has laid upon them."[14]

There is much to admire in Pat Schroeder and much to commend in her policy ideas. The particular vantage point from which she assesses recent changes in the family—as a champion of women's rights and of new opportunities for parents to combine work and family—is a fundamentally important one. It is shared by millions of women and men across the country precisely because it reflects the realities of their lives. It is a perspective that will almost certainly, and in my view properly, influence public policy in the 1990s.

Yet Schroeder's analysis of the family as a social institution is seriously flawed. These analytic failures, moreover, are not simply intellectual shortcomings—they distort her policy agenda. Also, especially because her views typify much of today's elite conventional wisdom, they help to impoverish the nation's larger cultural debate on the status and future of the family.

Her basic failure is this: conceptually, she refuses to distinguish between the needs of working women as individuals and those of the family as an institution. Indeed, as shown above, she frequently asserts that these needs are identical—that to understand one kind is also to understand the other. Her entire analysis and policy agenda, in fact, is rooted in this core idea.

Doubtless this concept is comforting. It simplifies things. As if by magic, it solves what otherwise would remain highly difficult issues. And of course, no one would deny the important (if complex) relationships between the status of employed women and the status of the family as an institution.

But employed women do not a family make. The goals of women (and of men, too) in the workplace are primarily individualistic: social recognition, wages, opportunities for advancement, and self-fulfillment. But the family is about collective goals that by definition extend beyond

CATCHING THE RERUNS:
OZZIE, HARRIET, AND THE MEDIA

It used to be so simple, it seems in retrospect. Dad at the office or factory and mom at home nurturing the next generation. . . . But the return of those days is about as likely as a prime time comeback of Ozzie and Harriet. Less than ten percent of U.S. families are "traditional"—father at work and mother at home.
The Detroit News, May 22, 1988

Most of us were raised in a typical nuclear American family. . . . But today, there is no such thing as a typical family. And only a distinct minority (7 percent) of America's population fits the traditional family profile.
John Naisbitt, in his bestseller *Megatrends: Ten New Directions Transforming Our Lives*

Today, less than ten percent of the population lives in the "Ozzie and Harriet" two-parent family where Dad is the sole financial support.
The National Report on Work and Family, Fall, 1989

There are only one in ten American families today where you have mom at home and dad at work—only one in ten. Ozzie and Harriet . . . are gone.
Senator Chris Dodd of Connecticut, March 1989

At a hearing before the Legislature [State Representative Mary Jane] Gibson noted that fewer than ten percent of American families resemble the familiar "Ozzie and Harriet" model of mother as caregiver and father as breadwinner.
The Boston Globe, April 11, 1989

Inspired by [Blankenhorn's] op-ed piece in the *Washington Post*, we sidled up to Nexis the other day and nonchalantly asked how many news stories in 1989 included the phrase "Ozzie and Harriet." Startling answer: 88 stories. Usual context in which those names from the Fifties were being invoked: A politician was on stage reciting the news that the traditional nuclear family—the kind symbolized by the Nelsons during their marathon stint on black-and-white TV—was dead or dying.
Daniel Seligman, in *Fortune Magazine*, July 17, 1989

the individual: procreation, socializing the young, caring for the old, and building life's most enduring bonds of affection, nurturance, mutual support, and long-term commitment. Surely Schroeder's insistence on the idea of full symmetry is almost self-evidently untrue.

There is another, related problem. One of Schroeder's most deeply held beliefs—and a basic tenet of the optimists' view of the changing family—is that people who disagree with her suffer from a disabling "nostalgia" about "the mythical family" of the past. These confused people, she explains, have "based their criticisms on a mistaken and nostalgic view of a family that never (or hardly ever) existed. The Norman Rockwell picture that is dragged out like an icon as our ideal family is not something many Americans have experienced in real life."[15]

On a nationally televised interview in 1988, she repeated what has become her trademark opening comment on the changing family: that "only seven percent" of today's families "fit the old 'Ozzie and Harriet' syn-

TABLE 1: FAMILIES WITH PRESCHOOL CHILDREN

Family type	Number (thousands)	Percent of all families with preschoolers
Traditional: father works, mother at home	4,957	33.3
Working: both parents work full time	4,277	28.8
Mixed: married mother works part time	2,343	15.8
Single in-labor-force mother head of family	1,506	10.1
Single at-home mother head of family	1,089	7.3
Married couple, father not in labor force	402	2.7
Single father head of family	300	2.0
TOTALS	14,874	100.0

Source: Calculated from Bureau of Labor Statistics, unpublished report, March 1987.

drome." To say that our nation's child-care policy must recognize the needs of traditional families, she writes, "is like saying the highway program must recognize people who don't drive."[16]

These ideas—particularly the notion that few of today's families contain homemaker mothers married to breadwinner fathers—are very widespread today. They largely govern the media's treatment of family issues, in no small part due to Schroeder's flair and persistence in marketing them. The "fewer than 10%" idea is probably today's most repeated statistic about the American family. (See "Catching the Reruns," page 11.)

Yet these claims are simply not supported by the evidence. Certainly, for example, maternal employment and family diversity are among the most important family trends of the past quarter-century. Yet more than one-third of all families with preschool children today are "Ozzie and Harriets": homemaker mothers married to breadwinner fathers. They still comprise the nation's largest single category of families with preschool children (Table 1).

Viewed from any reasonable angle, the under-10% claim is flatly wrong. Not just factually wrong in some technical sense, but fundamentally wrong in that it creates a distorted picture of our society.[17] So, of course, does the even wilder exaggeration that traditional nuclear families "never (or hardly ever) existed."

In addition, the "nostalgia" charge only diverts attention from the real question. David Popenoe clearly has Schroeder's type of argument in mind when he remarks:

> Being nostalgic about the past may be in the same class as being optimistic about the future, and it is quite possibly a natural human propensity. But challenging popular nostalgia about families of the past says little about how the family as an institution has in fact empirically been changing, and whether or not that change could be defined as decline.[18]

By defining her most vexing problems out of existence—traditional families don't exist (except as false nostalgia), and working women equal the family as an institution—Schroeder is able to glide into a one-sided, optimistic assessment of recent changes in the American family. We must, she argues, "rise above the doom-and-gloom predictions" of those who "were wrong, of course. The American family was not in danger of extinction. Over the course of our three-hundred-year history it has weathered far-reaching social and economic change by changing itself dramatically."[19] She insists that family decline has been greatly exaggerated:

> The statistics on divorce were high and on the increase, but so were the figures for remarriage. The majority of Americans who divorced did not give up on marriage, they just went looking for a more perfect union. People did not stop having children, they tried to figure out the best way to manage.[20]

Note the straw men residing in these quotes. What serious analyst ever suggested that the family was becoming "extinct"? Who ever said that Americans were "giving up on marriage" or had decided to "stop having children"? These are unserious topics. Whether the family is in decline as an institution, however, remains a serious topic.

On the other hand, is it really true, as Schroeder implies, that marriage and remarriage convey the same good news about the institution of marriage? To again borrow from the Popenoe book, isn't that like saying that America's high rate of residential mobility proves that Americans love rootedness and community? After all, don't we move around in search of stronger roots, better community? Even accounting for the usual hyperbole that we permit our political leaders, the glibness of this style of argument is remarkable.

In some respects, Popenoe's *Disturbing the Nest* is a scholarly jeremiad—a plea for us to recognize the family "as a perishable social institution that is being quietly corroded by some of the social and cultural currents of our time." To him

> the interesting question is not why people believe in the "myth" of family decline, but why so many sociologists think of family decline as a myth and seek to dismiss the idea with such vigor and seeming certainty. The irony of the vigorous promotion by sociologists today of the antidecline position is that it comes precisely at a time when the family has been changing rapidly, far more rapidly than in those previous historical periods when the idea of family decline was pervasive among members of the social-science community.[21]

Popenoe focuses largely on the Swedish family. He does so for two reasons. First, family decline has been greater in Sweden than in any other modern society. Moreover, current family trends in Sweden reflect, in advanced form, trends that are evident today in most modern societies, particularly the United States.

Popenoe defines "decline" analytically rather than pejoratively or morally. The family is "declining," in his view, when it is "becoming weaker" as an institution.[22] This process includes five measurable trends. First, individual members become more autonomous and less bound by the family, which in turn becomes less cohesive. Second, the family becomes less able to carry out its social functions: procreation at a level to replace the population, the regulation of sexual behavior, socializing children, and providing care for its members. Third, as an institution, the family loses power to other institutions, such as schools, the media, and the state. Fourth, families get smaller and more unstable; their members spend less time in them. And finally, familism as a cultural value loses ground to other values such as individualism and egalitarianism.

Guided by these standards of measurement, Popenoe presents overwhelming evidence that family decline is one of the most significant trends in modern societies today. Yet his evaluation cannot be reduced simply to what Schroeder calls "doom-and-gloom." He insists, for example, that "decline" is not synonymous with "bad." It may well be that "many aspects of family decline are 'good,' for the individual, for society, or for both."[23]

Certainly the decline of the family is related to the rise of many of today's reigning cultural ideals: personal autonomy, self-expression, individual rights, sexual freedom, social equality, and tolerance for alternative life-styles. It may be true that people are happier today—despite or even because of family decline—than ever before. Certainly, most people in the West live longer, in better health, and in more affluence than ever before.

Optimists, of course, strongly emphasize these points. Many pessimists also concede, and even celebrate, the advances of modern life. But they also insist that we address different, more troubling issues—that we confront what might be called the dark side of modernity. Most people, Popenoe shows, "agree on the ideal of a strong family." Yet "the family decline in evidence today strikes at the very root of this ideal." [24]

Marriage, for example, is becoming "deinstitutionalized." In Sweden, one of every four cohabiting couples is unmarried and nearly half of all childbirths occur outside of marriage. Yet "in all of human history up to

TABLE 2: FIVE KEY INDICATORS OF THE DEINSTITUTIONALIZATION OF MARRIAGE IN THE U.S., 1960–1985

	1960	1985
Percent of childbirths outside of marriage	5	22
Percent of teenage mothers who are unmarried	15	58
Divorced persons per 1,000 married persons	35	130
Percent of children living with only one parent	9	25
Percent of adult life spent with spouse and children	62	43

Source: Sar A. Levitan, *What's Happening to the American Family?* (1988 edition), pp. 114, 120; "Marital Status and Living Arrangements: March, 1988," (Washington, D.C.: Bureau of the Census, Current Population Reports, P-20, No. 433, March 1988); Sandra L. Hofferth, "Updating Children's Life Course," *Journal of Marriage and the Family* 47 (No. 1, 1985), pp. 93–115; Susan Cotts Watkins, Jane A. Menken, and John Bongaarts, "Demographic Foundations of Family Change," *American Sociological Review* 52 (No. 3, 1987), pp. 346–358.

the present some form of public marriage has been the basis of the family as a social institution." [25]

The deinstitutionalization of marriage is evident in the United States as well (see Table 2). Today, for example, nearly one child in four in the United States is born outside of marriage, and the divorce rate in the United States is perhaps the highest in the world. Although the impact of this trend on adult happiness may be debatable, its impact on children's well-being is alarmingly clear—the mounting evidence of the harm done to children by divorce and unwed parenthood in our society has now become virtually unchallengeable.[26]

Consider, in this regard, recent trends in family law. Some courts and localities, for example, are now legally redefining "family" to include a variety of relationships other than those of marriage, blood, or adoption.[27] This radically new legal norm, still nascent in the United States, is now the governing idea of Swedish family law.

This phenomenon, moreover, represents only one manifestation of a broader societal trend that Mary Ann Glendon terms the "dejuridification of marriage," that is, the "withdrawal of much official regulation of marriage." In most Western societies over the past two decades, she concludes, "the legal posture of the state with respect to the family was undergoing its most fundamental shift since family law had begun to be secularized at the time of the Protestant Reformation." Yet the United States ventured "further than any country except Sweden in making marriage freely terminable." This "particular and extreme position" constitutes the legal enshrinement in the United States of "the idea of no-fault, no-responsibility divorce."[28] These new legal norms certainly represent the deinstitutionalization of marriage and family in the most literal meaning of the term.

In Sweden, Popenoe finds, the number of people living alone increased by 50% between 1968 and 1981.[29] Even members of families are becoming less dependent on each other: they spend less time in the role of family member and more time as "clients of a large group of public employees who take care of them throughout their lives."[30] Yet certainly these "non–kin relationships typically lack the special sense of obligations and responsibilities found in kinship ties."[31] Is it not probable that these shifts weaken the "psychological anchorage" of adults in modern societies?

At the heart of Popenoe's jeremiad, however, is the changing "social ecology of childrearing" and the manifest shift in modern societies "from child-centeredness to adult-centeredness."[32] With each year, he concludes, modern societies are "drifting farther away" from what is demonstrably "the ideal child-rearing environment"—a relatively large family headed by two parents who stay married, spend a lot of quality time with their children, and foster a "rich family subculture" of traditions and values.[33]

Is this ideal of family life losing ground in the United States? If so, should we worry about it? My own sense is that, in the final analysis, the pessimists have the better argument—that we as a society are increasingly unwilling, either through public behavior or private action, to value purposes larger than the self, and are especially unwilling to make those sacrifices necessary to foster good environments for children. I suspect that our "family deficit" is at least as dangerous to our long-term well-being as are our federal budget and trade deficits. Perhaps, also, the habits of heart and mind that produce the latter also create the former. In short, the conspicuous deterioration and frailty of contemporary family life, harmful to adults but epitomized most clearly by the cultural tilt away from children's needs, constitutes the second and most serious American family dilemma.

TEN SUGGESTIONS FOR IMPROVING THE FAMILY DEBATE IN THE 1990S

What is to be done? Is it possible to strengthen the family as an institution as we approach the new century? Whether we lean toward optimism or pessimism, few questions in our time are so important. At stake is nothing less than the kind of society we wish to be.

In this essay, however, I have argued that to strengthen the family, we must first strengthen and clarify the terms of our public discussion. I would like to conclude, therefore, not with a full-blown agenda to improve family well-being, but rather with a more limited set of proposals to improve our discourse on the family.

In the underlying debate between optimism and pessimism, I conclude that the evidence tilts toward the pessimistic view. This view, moreover, coincides with what I believe to be the clear, though quite recent, general trend of scholarly opinion regarding the family. In a sense it seems strange to declare oneself a pessimist: the United States is perhaps the world's most optimistic society. Yet the facts of contemporary family well-being, I believe, remain transparent and alarming. I am heartened in this case by Gramsci's famous self-description: "pessimism of the intellect, optimism of the will."

At the same time, I offer two cheers for "optimism of the intellect" regarding the family. Many of the specifics in the optimists' overall argument—the importance of women's rights and of shared authority between spouses, for example, or the need for new public and private-sector policies to help families—are vitally important. They must certainly inform the family debate of the coming decade. These proposals, then, also seek to reflect several of the optimists' basic concerns.

Many people, of course, will disagree with some or even most of these ideas. But perhaps these proposals can contribute to a refined conceptual framework—an analytic and normative perspective on the family that reflects widely held American values, that can help overcome the polarizations of the past decade, and that points toward a new consensus on the nation's family agenda for the 1990s. Call them the Ten Suggestions.

One

Critically evaluate today's prevailing cultural ethos of "adult individualism." Quite simply, this ethos is harmful to family well-being. We are becoming, more than ever before, an atomized, adult-centered society in which expressive individualism—what has been called the "untrammeled self"—has become a governing cultural ideal, overshadowing and to some degree displacing other cultural norms, such as civic virtue, religious belief, and family values.[34] At the same time, dissatisfaction with this ethos is growing in our culture, in part because modern individualism possesses a mixed record, at best, in what is supposedly its strength: increasing the level of overall adult happiness.[35] It seems that our society, or at least much of it, is in fact yearning to reconnect with purposes larger than the self, particularly the family. What would help is a language and an analysis of the family to give voice to that yearning.

Two

Analyze the family primarily through the eyes of children. Not exclusively, just primarily. Child rearing, after all, is probably the family's most important social function. Such an analytic vantage point would help avoid many of the hidden agendas that now attach themselves to the family debate. It would also help to soften, and even perhaps to inform, the inevitable clash between the needs of adult women and those of adult men.

Consider, for example, the current debate over whether single-parent families should be judged as better, worse, or "just as good as" families with two parents. If the children involved were given the choice, which would they choose, and why? Or take the example of corporate day care for sick children, a growing trend in the American workplace that is widely celebrated in the media as "pro-family." Perhaps it is. Certainly it helps the corporation by reducing absenteeism. And it may also help busy parents. But is it an equally unmixed blessing for the sick child? Might it not be better to permit—even encourage—the parents of sick children to take time off from work? I do not claim that we should ignore adult needs. Nor do I claim that these issues—either single-parent families or sick child care—are simple ones. They are not. But I do claim that viewing them through the eyes of children offers an essential perspective that is frequently absent in today's family debate.

Three

Formulate family policy "from the inside out," [36] that is, from the distinctive vantage point of family functions and the family as an institution, rather than from the imperatives of broader policy or political goals. If family policy is to be worthy of the name, if it is to be different from simply ideas to help people, it must derive solely from what might be called "family business": to marry; to bring children into the world, raising them to be healthy, productive citizens; to pass on basic social and moral values to the next generation; to care for aged parents and grandparents; and most fundamentally, to build and maintain those bonds of affection, nurturance, mutual support, and lifetime commitment that form the very definition of family life. Establishing this criterion would locate the family itself at the center of "family policy." It would force many extraneous ideas currently hitching a ride on the family express simply to get off the train and seek their rightful destination. Less baggage and the proper passengers: that would be an enormous blessing.

Four

Recognize that the American family dilemma is androgynous. In particular, it is not reducible to a "woman's problem" or a "woman's responsibility." Thus strengthening family life in the 1990s cannot and should not mean the repeal of the past 30 years of new opportunities for women in the workplace and in public life. Just as today's cultural ethos of individualism affects men just as much as women, so must a revived ethos of family life affect the behavior and priorities of both sexes.

Five

Rehabilitate, for modern conditions, the "good family man." This compliment was once widely heard in our culture, bestowed on those deserving it as a badge of honor. Rough translation: "He puts his family first." Ponder the three words: "good" (moral values), "family" (purposes larger than the self), and "man" (a norm of masculinity). Yet today, especially within elite culture, the phrase sounds antiquated, almost embarrassing. Part of the reason, of course, is the modern gender-role revolution: the "good family man" carries a lingering connotation of "sole breadwinner" and "head of the family." Yet it is also true that contemporary American culture simply no longer celebrates, among its various and competing norms of masculinity, a widely shared and compelling ideal of the man who puts his family first. Especially since some, even much, of today's family dilemma stems simply from male abandonment and male flight from family obligation, surely we must revive for the new century a widely shared conception of the good family man.

Six

Stop the special-interest pleading, ubiquitous in today's family debate, that pits the "working" family against the "traditional" family. Liberals tend to champion the former, conservatives the latter. Each side frequently twists the numbers in an attempt to define the other out of existence; each seems morally dismissive of the other; each acts as if family policy were a zero-sum game in which one family type can gain only at the expense of the other.

But all families deserve support, not just some. Those parents who stay at home with children are not bad, or quaint, or even unusual. Yet these parents, who deserve our praise and support, are frequently told by our culture that they are old-fashioned, outmoded, irrelevant. At the same time, working parents also deserve support with new policies from both government and employers to help them balance the demands of family and work. Any family policy, from the political left or right, that seeks to help one type of family by belittling another is simply not acceptable.

Seven

A rule of thumb: while new government programs and policies will not solve the American family dilemma, they can and should play a role in strengthening family life and, at a minimum, in ameliorating some of the negative consequences of family decline. From the right, we hear that government is the main enemy, because the state inherently erodes family autonomy. We are warned, "Look what government is doing to you!" From the left, we hear that government is the main ally, because public authority can assist families in need. We are entreated, "Look what government can do for you!" This familiar dichotomy—long the dividing line in the politics of the modern welfare state—needlessly polarizes the family debate. The issue is neither the size of government nor some inherent quality (good or bad) of public authority, but rather the relationship of specific policies to family well-being.

Government programs should seldom, if ever, seek to replace private family functions. "Family policies" that simply facilitate the transfer of family functions to public authorities—for example, child-care policies that in effect reduce parental authority and choice—may be desirable on other grounds, but they can hardly be described as strengthening the family as an institution. At the same time, the tools of government can and should be used not to replace families but to empower them and to foster their well-being. Daniel Patrick Moynihan once observed that, in the long run, it is culture, not politics, that determines the health of a society. That is the conservatives' truth. But, he added, politics can influence culture. That is the liberals' truth.

Eight

Encourage, and in some cases require, private-sector employers to recognize that their employees are also family members. Working parents, fathers as well as mothers, need new opportunities to balance work and family: family leave options, part-time and job-sharing opportunities, flexible work hours, and other family-oriented workplace policies.

Nine

Recognize that the family debate, in large part, is a debate about cultural values. Yet an influential current of opinion today, especially within elite culture, views any set of unambiguous norms with suspicion, fearing them to be oppressive and overly judgmental. This belief that norms themselves are the problem, and that the best ethos regarding the family is one of moral agnosticism, is not only historically unprecedented but is itself an important contributor to the American family dilemma. In addition to this valorization of normlessness, there is also a frequent refusal in the family debate to state clearly what our guiding values are. It is unhelpful, for example, for scholars to assert that values do not or should not influence scholarship. If we could, in fact, somehow remove values from the family debate, we would have very little of importance left to say.

Ten

Strive for a new consensus on "family values." Even in our pluralistic and often culturally divided society, surely there exist some broadly shared "family values" of deep social importance.[37] And surely people interested in family policy should understand and debate these values—not in order to legislate or police them, but simply in order to know whether a proposed family policy is supportive of them or undermines them. In this spirit, I propose some beginning definitions.

We value families. The family is society's primary institution for raising children, caring for the elderly, and passing on and developing the values of society. It is usually the source of both our greatest loves and our greatest sorrows. It is the main mediating institution between the individual and the state: the basic social unit of our culture. For these reasons, most of us see the family as our central and most enduring commitment beyond the self.

We value marriage. The marital commitment is a foundation of strong families. Although divorce may be the least bad alternative for a damaged marriage, today's high divorce rate is a troubling sign for families. We value marriage as an equal partnership, based on shared commitment, compromise, and responsibility, not domination or inequality.

We value children. We see in children our hopes for the future. While recognizing the primary responsibility of parents in child rearing, we also affirm that raising children is more than a series of private choices: it is also a social imperative that should be supported by other social institutions, by the workplace, and by public policy.

We value parents. Parents are a child's first and most influential teachers and a child's major providers of love, guidance, and protection. The parental role is socially invaluable and irreplaceable; it should be honored and supported by society. Parenthood is a serious responsibility that should not be entered into lightly or casually. Although many divorced or widowed parents are admirably successful, few would deny that the duties of parenthood are best met by two parents working together in marriage. Moreover, bringing a child into the world outside of marriage, or when parents are too young or unprepared to be real parents, is almost always personally and socially harmful.

We value our elders. Caring for our elders is one of the family's most important functions—one that should be facilitated and encouraged by other social institutions and by public policy. Moreover, we recognize the unique contributions elders can make: to the economy, in child-care and teaching, and to our broader cultural life.

We value community. Institutions that make up community life—the school, the church, the synagogue, the workplace association, the service and charitable organization—are enriched by strong families. The institutions of community also enrich family life by extending our concerns beyond the family to the broader society.

We affirm basic moral values. As part of the heritage we received from our parents and will develop and pass on to our children, we affirm basic moral values. These values of character and citizenship include honesty, the "golden rule," respect for others and for the law, the link between effort and reward, and the benefits and responsibilities of living in a democracy. Other institutions, from schools to the media, should support and reinforce parental efforts to teach and pass on basic values.

We see the need for societal concern. Reflected in public and private sector policies, societal concern will strengthen all families, empowering them to realize and build upon these family values that form a cornerstone of our culture.

NOTES

1. Gilbert Y. Steiner, *The Futility of Family Policy* (Washington, DC: Brookings Institution, 1981).

2. The photograph, *Longboat Key, Florida, 1958,* by Joe Steinmetz, is located in the Photography Archive of the Carpenter Center for the Visual Arts at Harvard University. My use of this photograph as a window on cultural values was inspired and influenced by Benita Eisler, *Private Lives: Men and Women of the Fifties* (New York: Franklin Watts, 1986), pp. 1–26.

3. *River's Edge* (Los Angeles: Hemdale Film Corporation, 1988), directed by Tim Hunter, written by Neal Jimenez, produced by Sarah Pillsbury and Midge Sanford.

4. See "Mass Mutual American Family Values Study" (Washington, DC: Mellman & Lazarus, 1989). In this survey, strong majorities expressed pessimism on questions about the nation's "quality of family life."

5. Pat Schroeder (with Andrea Camp and Robyn Lipner), *Champion of the Great American Family* (New York: Random House, 1989).

6. Mary Jo Bane, *Here to Stay: American Families in the Twentieth Century* (New York: Basic Books, 1976), pp. x–xii, 19.

7. See Norval D. Glenn, "Continuity Versus Change, Sanguineness Versus Concern: Views of the American Family in the Late 1980's," *Journal of Family Issues* 8 (No. 4, December 1987), pp. 348–354. Glenn, who also edits the *Journal of Family Issues*, invited 18 "prominent" family scholars to comment on "the current state of the American family" and to "include value judgments [that you might] not ordinarily include in a paper to be published in a professional journal." To his surprise, he found that "in the contributions as a whole, change [in the family] is emphasized more than continuity, and the authors are more concerned than sanguine." Glenn's own view, moreover, "has shifted in recent years from the 'continuity-sanguine' position to just within the 'change-concerned' cell."

Another family scholar, Dennis Orthner of the University of North Carolina, reacting in a conversation to my proposed ideal types of "optimism" and "pessimism," summarized his own recent evolution from strong "optimism" to a "cautious optimism."

Other examples of the recent scholarly shift toward what I term pessimism can be seen in: Lenore J. Weitzman, *The Divorce Revolution* (New York: The Free Press, 1985); Robert N. Bellah, Richard Masden, William M. Sullivan, Ann Swidler, and Steven M. Tipton, *Habits of the Heart* (Berkeley, CA: University of California Press, 1985); and the 1988 revised edition, as compared with the 1981 original edition, of Sar A. Levitan, Richard S. Belous, and Frank Gallo, *What's Happening to the American Family?* (Baltimore, MD: The Johns Hopkins University Press, 1981 and 1988).

8. David Popenoe, *Disturbing the Nest: Family Change and Decline in Modern Societies* (New York: Aldine de Gruyter, 1988).

9. Schroeder, op. cit., p. 89.

10. Ibid., p. 15.

11. Ibid., p. 114.

12. Ibid., p. 24.

13. Ibid., p. 22.

14. Ibid., p. 9.

15. Ibid., p. 20.

16. Ibid., p. 84.

17. David Blankenhorn, "Ozzie and Harriet, Alive and Well," *The Washington Post*, June 11, 1989, Outlook section, p. 3. Also, see "Counting on Child Care," *Family Affairs* 1 (No. 3, Fall 1988), p. 8; "Ozzie and Harriet: Have Reports of Their Death Been Greatly Exaggerated?" *Family Affairs* 2 (Nos. 2-3, Summer/Fall, 1989), p. 10.

18. Popenoe, op. cit., p. 33.

19. Schroeder, op. cit., p. 20.

20. Ibid., p. 91.

21. Popenoe, op. cit., p. 34.

22. Ibid., pp. 8–9.

23. Ibid., p. 9.

24. Ibid., p. 309.

25. Ibid., p. 190.

26. See, for example, Irwin Garfinkel and Sara McLanahan, *Single Mothers and their Children: A New American Dilemma* (Washington, DC: Urban Institute Press, 1986); Victor R. Fuchs, *Women's Quest for Economic Equality* (Cambridge, MA: Harvard University Press, 1988), especially pp. 104–116; Judith Wallerstein, *Second Chances: Men, Women and Children a Decade After Divorce* (New York: Ticknor and Fields, 1989); Peter Uhlenberg and David Eggebeen, "The Declining Well-being of American Adolescents," *The Public Interest* 82 (Winter 1986), pp. 25–38; Norval D. Glenn and Kathryn B. Kramer, "The Psychological Well-being of Adult Children of Divorce," *Journal of Marriage and the Family* 47 (No. 4, November 1985), pp. 905–912. A 1990 Census Bureau study, "Children's Well-Being: An International Comparison," concluded, according to the *New York Times* (March 19, 1990), that "Children in the United States are more likely than children in 11 other industrialized countries to live in poverty, to live with only one parent or to be killed before they reach the age of 25."

27. "New York Court Defines Family to Include Homosexual Couples," *New York Times*, July 7, 1989, p. A1. See also "Family Redefines Itself, and Now the Law Follows," *New York Times*, May 28, 1989, p. C3.

In New York in July 1989, the state's highest court ruled that an unmarried couple—in this case, a gay couple—could be defined as a family under New York City's rent-control laws. The definition of a family, said the New York State Court of Appeals, "should not rest on fictitious legal distinctions or genetic history" but instead should be based on the functional and psychological qualities of the relationship: the "exclusivity and longevity" of a relationship; the "level of emotional and financial commitment"; the "reliance placed upon one another for daily family services"; and how the couple "conducted their everyday lives and held themselves out to society."

Practical and legal matters aside (for example, who is to decide, and how, whether these new psychological criteria for family relationships have been attained?), one can only wonder at the long-term implications of this mode of thinking. For a court to declare that marriage is now only a "fictitious legal distinction" must surely rank as one of the more astonishing legal opinions of our time.

In addition to court cases, recent legislative and administrative decisions in several cities—San Francisco, New York, and Madison, Wisconsin—have extended to unmarried partners a range of benefits, from family leaves to health insurance, previously restricted to married persons.

These events raise deeply troubling questions that have been virtually ignored in the public discussion and media coverage surrounding them. Surely it is constitutionally permissible as well as socially desirable for our society to promote and privilege traditional family relationships of blood, marriage, and adoption. Surely, without denying individual rights or the ideal of social equality, society may properly make distinctions between relationships that are legally protected and other relationships that are legally permitted. See Bruce C. Hafen, "The Constitutional Status of Marriage, Kinship and Sexual Privacy—Balancing the Individual and Social Interests," *Michigan Law Review* 81 (No. 3, January 1983), pp. 463–574.

28. Mary Ann Glendon, *Abortion and Divorce in Western Law* (Cambridge, MA: Harvard University Press, 1987), pp. 63–64, 104–105. Glendon eloquently describes how

laws are carriers of important social meaning: "the imaginative portrayal of family life and ethics in divorce law reaches deeply into our culture—as the law is transmitted in lawyer's offices; in courtrooms; in television news, documentaries and dramas; in newspapers and popular magazines, and in the cinema. . . . In the United States the 'no-fault' idea blended readily with the psychological jargon that already had such a strong influence on how Americans think about their personal relationships [and] fit neatly into an increasingly popular mode of discourse in which values are treated as matters of taste, feelings of guilt are regarded as unhealthy, and an individual's primary responsibility is assumed to be to himself. . . . The American story of marriage, as told in the law and in much popular literature, goes something like this: marriage is a relationship that exists primarily for the fulfillment of the individual spouses. If it ceases to perform this function, no one is to blame and either spouse may terminate it at will. After divorce, each spouse is expected to be self-sufficient. . . . Children hardly appear in the story; at most they are rather shadowy characters in the background. . . . American divorce law in practice seems to be saying to parents, especially mothers, that it is not safe to devote oneself primarily or exclusively to raising children."

29. Popenoe, op. cit., pp. 326–327.

30. Ibid., pp. 209, 205.

31. Ibid., p. 212.

32. Ibid., pp. 310, 302.

33. Ibid., p. 313.

34. One review of survey data, for example, finds "a general shifting of allegiance from social groups and institutions to the self" in the United States. See Norval D. Glenn, "Social Trends in the United States: Evidence from Sample Surveys," *Public Opinion Quarterly* 51 (1987), pp. S109–S126; Robert N. Bellah et al., *Habits of the Heart*, op. cit. I am grateful to Bruce C. Hafen for bringing the following quotation to my attention:
   "The spirit of emancipation has . . . touched deep nerves of truth [but it also reflects] the blind side of our age. [We are witnessing] the transformation of our society from one that strengthens the bonds between people to one that, at best, is indifferent to them. . . . We are coming to look upon life as a lone adventure, a great personal odyssey, and there is much in this view which is exhilarating and strengthening, but we seem to be carrying it to such an extreme that if each of us is an Odysseus, he is an Odysseus with no Telemachus to pursue him, with no Ithaca to long for, with no Penelope to return to—an Odysseus on a journey that has been rendered pointless by becoming limitless." See "Talk of the Town," *New Yorker* (August 30, 1976), pp. 21–22.

35. See Norval D. Glenn and Charles N. Weaver, "The Changing Relationship of Marital Status to Reported Happiness," *Journal of Marriage and the Family* 50 (May 1988), pp. 317–324; Andrew Greeley, "The Declining Morale of Women," in National Opinion Research Center, *SSR* 73 (No. 2, January 1989), pp. 53–58.

36. I am grateful to Lawrence M. Mead of New York University for coining this phrase.

37. See "Mass Mutual American Family Values Study," op. cit., pp. 15–22.

=2=
Discovering What Families Do

Urie Bronfenbrenner

T oday we are witnessing two revolutions: one in society, the other in science. Although these revolutions are occurring in different domains, both center on the same phenomenon: the dramatic changes taking place in family life across the world and the consequences of these changes for the development of human competence and character, both in present and in future generations. In turn, the results of the social revolution are being newly illumined by today's scientific revolution—the research conducted over the past two decades in the field of human development.

The changes now taking place in contemporary family life are better documented for industrial nations, but they are no less and, indeed, are perhaps even more profound in developing countries. In fact, although differing in appearance, the underlying dynamics and ultimate effects of family change are strikingly similar around the globe. We now know that the stresses being experienced today by families everywhere have common roots and call for common strategies grounded in the basic requirements for the survival and growth of all human beings in all human ecologies.

Yet this knowledge creates an unwelcome paradox. It appears that the more we learn about the conditions that undergird and foster the development of human competence and character, the more we see these same conditions being eroded and destroyed in contemporary societies, both developing and developed. Given this paradox, this essay has three aims.

● First, I shall summarize the main findings of the scientific revolution that has occurred in the study of human development.

Urie Bronfenbrenner is Professor of Human Development and Family Studies and of Psychology at Cornell University in Ithaca, New York. This essay is based on an address, "Who Cares for Children?" delivered to UNESCO in Paris in September 1989.

● Second, I shall indicate the implications of the new research findings for the changes that have been taking place in contemporary family life.
● And third, in light of these widespread changes and of the knowledge we are acquiring about their consequences, I shall suggest some practical implications for both public policy and private social action.

What are the conditions and processes that undergird and foster the development of human competence and character from early childhood onward? The requirements for developing competence and character appear to be universal, deriving from the basic biological nature of the species *Homo sapiens*, thus cutting across culture, nationality, and class.

Note the qualifying phrase "appear to be." The findings of science are tentative by definition. Moreover, in my view, the results of research in this particular sphere should be subject to validation by human experience. For this reason, I confine myself to those findings from systematic studies that also have some support from the observations of professionals and paraprofessionals working in the field as well as from families themselves. I begin with those facts that are most clearly established from both perspectives.

First and foremost, all children require good health care and adequate nutrition. Yet millions of children in today's world lack these essentials.[1] Accordingly, many outstanding organizations and agencies have dedicated themselves to meeting these primary needs.

Assigning top priority to this task is unquestionably necessary and urgent. Indeed, recent research only underscores its importance. At the same time, however, the new findings do call into question a policy that makes the provision of health and nutrition its top and *only* priority. Such a policy appears to assume that nothing else is of comparable importance and that once these basic necessities are made available, the achievement of at least normal development for the great majority of young children is, by and large, a likely outcome.

By contrast, the scientific investigations of the past two decades reveal that basic medical services and adequate diet, while essential, are not enough by themselves to insure normal physical and psychological development, particularly for children of families who have been exposed to biological, economic, and social stress. Beyond health care and nutrition, certain other essential requirements must also be met.

A recent UNICEF seminar on early childhood development summarized the issue:

> It has long been accepted that good health and nutrition support the psychological and social development of the young child. Less widely recognized are the more recent findings that developmentally sensitive interaction with a child, namely interaction which satisfies the child's need to grow socially, psychologically, and cognitively, has a direct and measurable impact on the physical health of the child. While the implications of

these interaction effects are of considerable importance for the health and well-being of children, they have been seriously neglected in development planning.[2]

Although "developmentally sensitive interaction" lies at the heart of the matter, it is not the whole scientific story. Nor is it easy to convey the full scope of that story in a necessarily brief chapter. I shall try to do so in a series of five propositions, each followed by some explication and one or more examples.[3]

PROPOSITION I

In order to develop—intellectually, emotionally, socially, and morally—a child requires participation in progressively more complex reciprocal activity, on a regular basis over an extended period in the child's life, with one or more persons with whom the child develops a strong, mutual, irrational, emotional attachment and who is committed to the child's well-being and development, preferably for life.

Although this proposition has the merit of being fairly compact, it is also complex. Therefore we will examine its key elements one by one.

What is meant by "progressively more complex reciprocal activity"? Perhaps an analogy will help. It's what happens in a ping-pong game between two players. As the partners become familiar with each other, they adapt to each other's style. The game starts to move faster, and the shots in both directions tend to become more complicated, as each player, in effect, challenges the other.

In families, who challenges the other the most—the child or the adult? Research evidence indicates that in the beginning the infant calls most of the shots and, so to speak, "teaches" his or her parents or other caregivers.

Almost all adult human beings are adept learners in this situation—males no less than females—provided, of course, that they are willing and able to pay attention to the teacher and go to school almost every day over a long period of time. And there's the rub! In contemporary societies, it is becoming increasingly difficult to maintain the regular attendance and the high level of alertness that such learning requires. In short, while virtually everyone has the needed aptitudes, the learning process is not easy. Indeed, microphotographic studies of parent–infant interaction reveal it to be extraordinarily and increasingly complex as the process evolves.

This increasing complexity develops in two ways. Not only does the same game become more complicated, but new games are added by both parties. This phenomenon is seen especially clearly in early childhood. For example, a longitudinal study in which children were followed from birth through the eighth year of life revealed a progressive sequence in the young child's responsiveness and initiatives toward others. Thus, at birth, infants are especially responsive to vestibular stimulation (being picked up and held in a vertical position close to the body), which has the effect of soothing the baby so that it begins to engage in mutual gazing. By three months, visual exploration extends beyond proximal objects, and the mother's voice is most likely to elicit responses, especially in the form of reciprocal vocalizations. From about six months on, the infant begins actively to manipulate objects spontaneously in a purposeful way and to rearrange the physical environment. By now, both vocalization and gesture are being used to attract the parents' attention and to influence their behavior. In addition, the child increasingly, across modalities, initiates and sustains reciprocal interaction with a widening circle of persons in the immediate environment. The sequence reaches a new climax with the emergence of language as a medium of social interchange. By the age of two or three, the informal play between child and adult becomes a major vehicle of cognitive, emotional, and social development.

Crucial to the establishment and maintenance of this progressive trajectory is the ready responsiveness by a familiar adult to the young child's initiatives as well as the introduction by the adult of activity-engaging objects and experiences appropriate to the youngster's evolving capacities. In the absence of such adult responsiveness and presentation of opportunities, general psychological development is retarded, particularly for children who have been exposed to biological, economic, or social stress.

By now it should be clear that what is made possible by "progressively more complex reciprocal interaction" is a process of mutual "education." The child "teaches" the adult and the adult "teaches" the child. However, a caveat is critical here:[4] the kind of teaching that takes place in this context is quintessentially informal and even unconscious. The young child is not trying to teach the caregiver to respond in a particular way. He or she is simply expressing an evolving repertoire of behavioral initiatives and reactions. Nor can the adult caregiver foresee what the young child will do and thus plan in advance how he or she will respond to the young child's actions. The most the adult can do is to be ready and willing to react and to act in ways that will attract or hold the child's attention.

In sum, we are *not* dealing here with education in its traditional meaning of formal instruction.[5] Rather, such extended informal activities serve as a necessary prerequisite to formal schooling. This point must be borne in mind when we consider the design of policies and programs for enhancing child development.

Yet as already noted, informal education is no less demanding than its formal counterpart; it too takes a long time. Neither the young child nor the adult caregiver can learn much from each other if they get together only now and then for short periods with frequent interruptions. Hence, the specification, as a second key element in Proposition I, of joint activity "on a regular basis over an extended period in the child's life."

Thus far, it would appear that any person who repeatedly engages in progressively complex reciprocal activity with a child will be equally effective in furthering the child's physical and psychological development. The final clause of Proposition I, however, imposes some restrictions in that regard: specifically, the other person must be someone "*with whom the child develops a strong, mutual, irrational emotional attachment and who is committed to the child's well-being and development, preferably for life.*"

What is "an irrational emotional attachment"? It means that an adult regards a particular child as somehow special—especially wonderful, especially precious—even though objectively the adult may well know that this is not the case. It is the illusion that comes with love. The illusion flows in both directions: for the child, the adult is also special—someone to whom the child turns most readily when experiencing both trouble and joy and whose comings and goings are central to the child's experience and well-being.

What is the relevance of this mutual emotional relationship for processes of "progressively more complex reciprocal interaction" between child and adult? Research evidence indicates that such interaction requires high levels of motivation, attentiveness, sensitivity, and persistence on the part of both participants and that *these requisite qualities are more apt to arise and to be sustained in relationships characterized by strong, mutual, emotional attachment.*

Moreover, once such a strong mutual attachment is established, it tends to endure, thus enhancing the likelihood of a continuing pattern of reciprocal interactions at successively more complex levels throughout the child's life. The two parts of Proposition I also have a reciprocal relationship. Thus, one reason mutual attachments tend to endure is that the recurring patterns of reciprocal interactions that they encourage in turn enhance the intensity of the mutual emotional tie.

In sum, it can be said that human development occurs in the context of an escalating psychological ping-pong game between two people who are crazy about each other.

As implied in the preceding exposition, once the processes stipulated in this first proposition become established, they activate and enhance additional potentials for development. Prominent among these are responsive and active orientations, not just toward persons but toward certain other features of the child's immediate environment. One of the earliest and strongest potentials to become activated in this way is the subject of the next proposition.

PROPOSITION II

The establishment of patterns of progressive interpersonal interaction under conditions of strong mutual attachment enhances the young child's responsiveness to other features of the immediate physical, social, and—in due course—symbolic environment that invite exploration, manipulation, elaboration, and imagination. Such activities, in turn, also accelerate the child's psychological growth.

For young children today, how available are objects and settings that meet the developmental criteria set forth in Proposition II? Consider, from this perspective, the wide array of manufactured toys, games, and play equipment produced in modern technological societies. To name a few: battery-powered play vehicles; automated figures of animals, humans, and monsters; playgrounds with special equipment for children of different ages; graduated series of puzzles, construction sets, and board games; and all manner of audiovisual devices and computer games for successive age levels. Many of these products are quite expensive.

Yet upon examination, many of these items hardly fulfill the requirements stipulated in Proposition II. Specifically, they do *not* invite exploration, manipulation, elaboration, or imaginative activity on the part of the child. They fail primarily because they are so rigidly structured as to allow little opportunity for introducing any spontaneous variation. To be sure, many products of modern technology do meet the criteria stipulated in Proposition II or can be designed to do so. These products should be praised and recommended to parents, professionals, and the public at large.

Objects and settings that meet the specified developmental criteria are by no means limited to products of modern technology. They are as readily found in traditional and transitional cultures as they are in so-called "post-industrial" societies. To cite a few examples: objects in nature—both animate and inanimate, large and small—such as domestic animals, stones and shells, trees and caves; objects that can be put inside one another or used to build things that can be broken down again; anything that can make rhythmic and musical sounds, such as pots, pans, and soup spoons; materials that can be used to draw, paint, or mold shapes and forms. More broadly, whatever induces sustained attention and evolving activity of body and mind, such as songs, dances, stories, dolls and stuffed animals that become friends, picture books, and, of course, books that can be read, then reimagined and retold on one's own.

But some children may not respond, even when provided with a range of objects and opportunities for activity. An obvious prerequisite is that the environment include materials appropriate to the child's developing physical and psychological capacities. In addition, the youngster's active orientation toward the physical and symbolic environment is powerfully mediated by prior and persistent patterns of interpersonal interaction in the context of a strong, enduring emotional relationship with one or more adults, almost always including the child's parents. These ongoing experiences remain a potent liberating and energizing force, not only in relation to the physical environment but to the social world as well. Thus they enable the child to relate to persons beyond the immediate family, including peers as well as adults, and to involve them effectively in meeting the child's own developmental needs. At a broader level, the child's newly acquired abilities make it possible for her or him to benefit from experiences in other settings, most notably to learn in school.

In short, the *informal education* that takes place in the family is not merely a pleasant prelude, but rather a powerful prerequisite for success in *formal education* from the primary grades onward. This empowering experience reaches further still. As evidenced in longitudinal studies, it appears to provide a basis, while offering no guarantee, for the subsequent development of the capacity to function responsibly and creatively as an adult in the realms of work, family life, and citizenship.

This does not mean, however, that the absence of early opportunities for interactive experiences in the context of a mutual emotional attachment precludes the possibility of later achieving adult effectiveness. Other routes to the acquisition of competence and character exist. The problem is that these routes are far less efficient and far more expensive, both in time and money.

Thus, taken as a whole, the research evidence indicates that when the elements stipulated in the first two propositions are provided on a continuing basis, the positive effects on children's development are indeed substantial. Accordingly, a society that seeks the well-being and development of its children is well advised to provide them with the kinds of environments and experiences specified in these two propositions.

But there is a catch. Research findings also reveal that the processes of interaction between child and environment that foster development described in Propositions I and II operate efficiently only under certain conditions existing in the broader environment in which these proximal processes occur. The remaining three propositions deal with the nature of these enabling and disabling circumstances. Thus the next proposition sets a qualifying proviso to Proposition I.

PROPOSITION III

The establishment and maintenance of patterns of progressively more complex interaction and emotional attachment between caregiver and child depend in substantial degree on the availability and involvement of another adult, a *third party* who assists, encourages, spells off, gives status to, and expresses admiration and affection for the person caring for and engaging in joint activity with the child.

It also helps, but is not absolutely essential, if the third party is of the opposite sex from that of the person dealing with the child. Isn't science wonderful? We've rediscovered the wheel!

I am sometimes asked up to what age do the foregoing principles apply. The answer is debatable, but I would say anytime up to the age of, say, 99.

The research evidence in support of the third proposition comes mainly from studies of a phenomenon that constitutes one of the main changes occurring in contemporary family life: the rapid rise in the proportion of single-parent households in both the developed and developing world. The overwhelming majority of such homes are those in which the father is absent and the mother bears full responsibility for the upbringing of the child. A large number of investigations of developmental processes and outcomes in families of this kind have now been conducted across a range of cultural and social class groups, including socialist countries and some developing nations as well. In general, the findings lead to two complementary conclusions.

First, results indicate that, controlling for associated factors such as low income, children growing up in such households are at greater risk for experiencing a variety of behavioral and educational problems, including extremes of hyperactivity or withdrawal, lack of attentiveness in the classroom, difficulty in deferring gratification, impaired academic achievement, school misbehavior, absenteeism, dropping out, involvement in socially alienated peer groups, and, especially, the so-called "teenage syndrome" of behaviors that tend to hang together—smoking, drinking, early and frequent sexual experience, a cynical attitude toward work, adolescent pregnancy, and, in the more extreme cases, drugs, suicide, vandalism, violence, and criminal acts. Most of these effects are much more pronounced for boys than for girls.

More intensive investigations of these phenomena have identified a common predisposing factor for the emergence of such problem behaviors, namely, a history of impaired parent–child interaction and relationships beginning in early childhood.

Not all single-parent families, however, exhibit these disturbed relationships and their disruptive effects on development. Systematic studies of the exceptions have identified what may be described as a general "immunizing" factor: children of single-parent mothers are less likely to experience developmental problems in those families in which the mother receives strong support from other adults living in the home or from nearby relatives, friends, or neighbors; members of religious groups; and, when available, staff members of family support and child-care programs.

Interestingly enough, the most effective agent of third-party support (in the minority of instances in which such assistance is provided) appears to be the child's father. And what counted most was not the attention given to the child, important as this was, but the assistance provided to the mother herself by serving as a back-up in times of crisis, doing errands, spelling her off, sharing responsibility for discipline, and providing needed advice and encouragement. It appears that, in the family dance, "it takes three to tango."

The developmental risks associated with a one-parent family structure are relatively small, however, in comparison with those involved in two other types of environmental context. The first and most destructive of these is poverty. Because many single-parent families are also poor, parents and their children are in double jeopardy. But even when two parents are present, research in both developed and developing countries reveals that in households living under stressful economic and social conditions, processes of parent–child interaction and environmentally oriented child activity are more difficult to initiate and to sustain. Much more effort and perseverance on the part of parents are required to achieve the same effect than are required in families living under more favorable circumstances, particularly when, as is often the case, the mother is the only parent or even the only adult in the home.

To be sure, research also indicates that when the mother, or some other adult committed to the child's well-being, does manage to establish and maintain a pattern of progressive reciprocal interaction, the disruptive impact of poverty on development is significantly reduced. But, among the poor, the proportion of parents who, despite their stressful life circumstances, are able to provide quality care is, under present conditions, not very large. And even for this minority, the parents' buffering power begins to decline sharply by the time children are five or six years old and exposed to impoverished and disruptive settings outside the home.

What is the impact of poverty on children's development? The consequences of economic hardship are similar to those for single parenthood in the absence of a third party, but the risks are substantially higher and the effects more pronounced, typically persisting well into adulthood (except in those as-yet-infrequent instances in which opportunities for continuing rehabilitative experiences become available).

Developmental processes are now at risk not only for poor and single-parent families. During the '70s and '80s, other highly vulnerable contexts have evolved that cut across the domains of class, family structure, and culture. Recent studies reveal that a major disruptive factor in the lives of families and their children is the *increasing instability, inconsistency, and hectic character of daily family life.* This growing trend is found in both developed and developing countries, but has somewhat different origins in each. However, the debilitating effect on child-rearing processes and outcomes is much the same. Let's begin with examples from the so-called postindustrial world, since they may be more familiar. The following description is based on observations of the American scene.

> In a world in which both parents usually have to work, often at a considerable distance from home, every family member, through the waking hours from morning till night, is "on the run." The need to coordinate conflicting demands of job and child care, often involving varied arrangements that shift from day to day, can produce a situation in which everyone has to be transported several times a day in different directions, usually at the same time—a state of affairs that prompted a foreign colleague to comment: "It seems to me that in your country, most children are being brought up in moving vehicles."[6]

Many other factors also contribute to the disruption of daily family life: long commutes to and from work; jobs that require one or the other parent to be away for extended periods; frequent changes in employment; the associated moves for the whole family or those that leave the rest of the family behind waiting till the school term ends or adequate housing can be found; and the increasing number of divorces, remarriages, and redivorces. In this regard, the most recent evidence suggests that the disruptive effects of remarriage on children may be even greater than those of divorce.

A parallel disorganization of family life in Third-World countries has been reported in a number of field studies but was perhaps best described by participants from the developing world at the 1982 UNESCO seminar "The Child and the Family in a Changing World." Experts spoke of the breakdown of family traditions and of the reinforcing role of tribal customs and community life through the disruptive inroads of Westernization and urbanization.

What are the developmental outcomes of the hectic character of family life? Once again, the observed consequences are educational impairment and behavior problems, including long-term effects that now also encompass children of the well-educated and the well-to-do.

Obviously, if we are to deal with such deeply rooted societal phenomena as poverty and the hectic pace of daily family life, we must restructure the social order. Nevertheless, the destructive impact of both these forces on the competence and character of future generations is so enormous that their elimination must be given the highest priority at the national and international level.

But such an undertaking is a long-term endeavor, and children can't wait. Some immediate and practicable short-term strategies, however, can reduce the social disarray and human damage produced by both destructive forces. The general nature of these strategies is indicated in the next proposition.

PROPOSITION IV

The effective functioning of child-rearing processes in the family and other child settings requires establishing ongoing patterns of exchange of information, two-way communication, mutual accommodation, and mutual trust between the principal settings in which children and their parents live their lives. In contemporary societies, these settings are the home, child-care programs, the school, and the parents' place of work.

Why the parents' workplace? Research shows that one of the principal sources of stress and disarray in the lives of families and their children lies in job stress—the conflict between the needs of the family and the demands of the job.

But which parent's job stress has the greater disruptive effect on the child? Although the answer may appear counterintuitive, available evi-

36

dence points to the father. Why? The most apt response to this question was given by the distinguished American sociologist Robin M. Williams. Commenting upon this differential effect of stress on the job, he pointed out, "the mothers absorb it all, and the fathers don't even know that there's anything to be absorbed."

Practically speaking, what kind of mutual accommodations can be made between the two domains of family and work? Particular policies and measures, of course, differ from one society to the next, but here are a few examples:

- Flexible work schedules
- Availability of part-time jobs (for both men and women) without loss of job benefits and opportunities for advancement
- Establishment at each work organization of a family resources office or specialist who serves as an advocate in relation to family–work issues; maintains a file of nontechnical publications and resource materials relating to child development and parenthood; provides referral to family services available in the community; serves as a stimulus and resource for introducing cost-effective policies and practices in the workplace that can reduce unnecessary stress resulting from the conflicting demands of work and family life, with due regard to the primary need of the work setting to fulfill its productive and service responsibilities

What is the *quid pro quo*? Studies indicate that such measures reduce absenteeism and job turnover and lead to improved employee morale and quality of performance.

The fifth and final proposition lays out the principal directions to be pursued in policies and practices aimed at enhancing child development and family life in contemporary societies.

PROPOSITION V

> The effective functioning of child-rearing processes in the family and other child settings requires public policies and practices that provide place, time, stability, status, recognition, belief systems, customs, and actions in support of child-rearing activities not only on the part of parents, caregivers, teachers, and other professional personnel, but also relatives, friends, neighbors, co-workers, communities, and the major economic, social, and political institutions of the entire society.[7]

With Proposition V, I complete my effort to convey the general findings of recent research on factors affecting early child development as they relate to the revolution in family life that has been occurring around the globe. In order to link research to reality, the implications of these findings for policy and practice have been incorporated into the presentation of the five propositions summarizing the principal conclusions indicated by the scientific evidence. These implications deal with priority principles and processes applicable at successive levels, beginning with the child in the family and in other care settings, then proceeding to more distant contexts of the workplace, the community, and the society at large.

Today, new grounds exist for believing that national action based on the foregoing principles may at last be possible. The new element in the picture is the increasing recognition and concern on the part of leaders in both the public and private sector with respect to two escalating economic problems. The first is the enormous cost of providing for, or (alternatively and more frequently) neglecting, the growing segments in the population of so-called "uneducables" and "unemployables." The second relates to the quality and dependability of the available work force in an age of increasing economic competition with both developed and developing nations. But this is neither the preferred nor the most potent dynamic for success. The most powerful force is the new hope for families and nations of seeing children seemingly fated to a life of failure and pain bloom into competent and caring human beings.

NOTES

1. For a recent assessment of the nature and scope of the problem on a worldwide basis, see *Strategies for Children in the 1990s* (New York: UNICEF, 1989).

2. *Innocenti Update*, Proceedings of the First Innocenti Global Seminar: Early Child Development (Florence, Italy: UNICEF International Child Development Center, No. 3, July 1989), p. 1.

3. The research on which these propositions are based is summarized and cited in the following publications by the author: "The Ecology of Cognitive Development: Research Models and Fugitive Findings," in R. H. Wozniak and K. Fischer, eds., *Specific Environments: Thinking in Context* (Hillsdale, NJ: Erlbaum, in press); "Ecological Systems Theory," in R. Vasta, ed., *Six Theories of Child Development* (Greenwich, CT: JAI Press, 1989), pp. 185–246; "Ecology of the Family as a Context for Human Development," *Developmental Psychology* 22 (No. 6, 1986), pp. 732–742.

4. This caveat is signaled by the quotation marks I have placed around each of the traditional pedagogical terms.

5. This restricted connotation of the concept is particularly characteristic of English. In a number of other languages, a broader construct exists that encompasses both formal and informal aspects of childrearing; for example, *éducation* in French, *Erziehung* in German, *vospitaniye* in Russian.

6. Urie Bronfenbrenner, "The Changing Family in a Changing World," unpublished paper delivered at the UNESCO conference "The Child and the Family in a Changing World," Munich, November 1982.

7. Urie Bronfenbrenner, "Family Support: The Quiet Revolution," in S. L. Kagan, D. R. Powell, B. Weissbourd, and E. F. Zigler, eds., *America's Family Support Programs. Perspectives and Prospects* (News Haven, CT: Yale University Press, 1987), pp. xi–xvii.

=3=

Family Decline in America

David Popenoe

s a social institution, the family has been "in decline" since the beginning of world history, gradually becoming weaker through losing social functions and power to other institutions such as church, government, and school. Yet during the past 25 years, family decline in the United States, as in other industrialized societies, has been both steeper and more alarming than during any other quarter century in our history. Although they may not use the term "decline," most family scholars now agree, with a growing tinge of pessimism, that the family during this period has undergone a social transformation. Some see "dramatic and unparalleled changes" while others call it "a veritable revolution."[1]

Agreement about the dramatic nature of family change over the past few decades, together with a pessimistic assessment of it, represent a recent shift of viewpoint on the part of many scholars. In the 1970s, in sharp contrast to the prevailing mood of the general public, the outlook of many family experts was one of complacency. For example, in their 1981 book *What's Happening to the American Family?*, economists Sar Levitan and Richard Belous noted that "currently fashionable gloom and doom scenarios miss the essential process of adjustment and change" and that "a critical analysis of the evidence does not paint such a dire picture, and thus a heartfelt 'hurrah' is in order."[2]

Yet after reviewing the events of the 1980s, their optimistic mood shifted strikingly. The second edition of this book, published in 1988, contains much apprehensive talk of "radical changes in family structure." The authors conclude, with some apologies for the "more sanguine scenario" of the earlier edition, that "American families are besieged from all sides" and "widespread family breakdown is bound to have a pervasive and debil-

David Popenoe is Professor of Sociology and Associate Dean for the Social Sciences at Rutgers University in New Brunswick, New Jersey.

itating impact not only on the quality of life but on the vitality of the body politic as well."[3]

The recent social transformation of the family has been so momentous that, in my opinion, we are witnessing the end of an epoch. Today's societal trends are bringing to a close the cultural dominance of what historians call the modern (I will use the term "traditional") nuclear family, a family situated apart from both the larger kin group and the workplace; focused on the procreation of children; and consisting of a legal, lifelong, sexually exclusive, heterosexual, monogamous marriage, based on affection and companionship, in which there is a sharp division of labor, with the female as full-time housewife and the male as primary provider and ultimate authority. Lasting for only a little more than a century, this family form emphasized the male as "good provider," the female as "good wife and mother," and the paramount importance of the family for child rearing. (Of course, not all families were able to live up to these cultural ideals.) During its cultural heyday, the terms "family," "home," and "mother" ranked extraordinarily high in the hierarchy of cultural values.[4]

In certain respects, this family form reached its apogee in the middle of the 20th century. By the 1950s—fueled in part by falling maternal and child mortality rates, greater longevity, and a high marriage rate—it is probably the case that a higher percentage of children than ever before were growing up in stable, two-parent families.[5] Similarly, this period witnessed the highest ever proportion of women who married, bore children, and lived jointly with their husbands until at least age 50.[6]

FLIGHT FROM THE NUCLEAR FAMILY

In the 1960s, however, four major social trends emerged to signal a widespread "flight" from both the ideal and the reality of the traditional nuclear family: rapid fertility decline, the sexual revolution, the movement of mothers into the labor force, and the divorce revolution. None of these changes was new to the 1960s; each represented a tendency that was already evident in earlier years. However, a striking acceleration of these trends occurred in the 1960s, which was made more dramatic by the fact that during the 1950s these trends had leveled off and in some cases even reversed their direction.[7]

The Decline in Fertility

First (taking up these four trends without reference to their relative importance or causal priority), fertility declined in the United States by almost 50% between 1960 and 1989, from an average of 3.7 children per woman to only 1.9. Although fertility has been gradually diminishing for several centuries (the main exception being the two decades following World War II), the level of fertility during the past decade was the lowest in U.S. history and below that necessary for the replacement of the population. As a percentage of the total population, children over the past 25 years have dropped from more than a third to about one-fourth.[8]

Growing dissatisfaction with parenthood is now evident among adults in our culture, along with a dramatic decrease in the stigma associated with childlessness.[9] Some demographers now predict that between 20% and 25% of today's young women will remain completely childless, and nearly 50% will be either childless or have only one child.[10]

The Sexual Revolution

Second, what is often called the sexual revolution has shattered the association of sex and reproduction.[11] The erotic has become a necessary ingredient of personal well-being and fulfillment, both in and outside marriage, as well as a highly marketable commodity. The greatest change has been in the area of premarital sex: from 1971 to 1982, the proportion of unmarried girls in the United States aged 15–19 who engaged in premarital sexual intercourse jumped from 28% to 44%.[12] This behavior reflects a widespread change in values: in 1967, 85% of Americans "condemned premarital sex as morally wrong," compared with only 37% in 1979.[13]

The sexual revolution has been a major contributor to the striking increase in unwed parenthood. Nonmarital births jumped from 5% of all births in 1960 (22% of births among blacks) to 22% in 1985 (60% of births among blacks). This is the highest rate of nonmarital births ever recorded in the United States.

Working Married Mothers

Third, although unmarried women have long been in the labor force, the past quarter century has witnessed a striking movement into the paid work force of married women with children.[14] In 1960, only 19% of married women with children younger than 6 were in the labor force (39% with children between 6 and 17); by 1986, this figure had climbed to 54% (68% of those with older children).[15]

Increased Divorce Rate

Fourth, the divorce rate in the United States over the past 25 years (as measured by the number of divorced persons per 1,000 married persons) has nearly quadrupled, increasing from 35 to 130. This increase has led many to refer to a divorce revolution.[16] A landmark of sorts was passed in 1974, when for the first time in American history more marriages ended in divorce than in death.[17] The probability that a marriage contracted today will end in divorce ranges from 44% to 66%, depending upon the method of calculation.[18]

Reshaped Family Experience

These four trends signal a widespread retreat from the traditional nuclear family in its terms of a lifelong, sexually exclusive unit, focused on

41

children, with a separate-sphere division of labor between husband and wife. Unlike most previous family change, which reduced family functions and diminished the importance of the kin group, the family change of the past 25 years has tended to break up the "nucleus" of the family unit—the bond between husband and wife. Nuclear units, therefore, are losing ground to single-parent families, serial and stepfamilies, and unmarried and homosexual couples.[19]

The number of single-parent families, for example, has risen sharply as a result not only of marital breakup, but also of marriage decline (fewer persons who bear children are getting married) and widespread abandonment by males. In 1960, only 9% of children in the United States younger than 18 were living with one parent; by 1986, this figure had climbed to nearly one-fourth of all children. (The comparable figures for blacks are 22% and 53%, respectively.) Of children born between 1950 and 1954, only 19% of whites (48% of blacks) had lived in a single-parent family by the time they reached age 17. But for children born in 1980, the figure is projected to be 70% (94% for blacks).[20]

During the past quarter century there has also been a retreat from family living in general. For instance, the percentage of "nonfamily" households (households other than those containing two or more persons living together and related by blood, marriage, or adoption) has nearly doubled, from 15% to 28% of all households. Approximately 85% of these new households consist of a person living alone.[21]

To summarize the state of the family today compared with that of 25 years ago:
- fewer persons are marrying and they are marrying later in life
- those marrying are having fewer children
- more marriages end in divorce

Trends such as these have dramatically reshaped people's lifetime family experiences, that is, their connectedness to the institution of the family. The proportion of an average person's adult life spent with spouse and children was 62% in 1960, the highest in our history. Today it has dropped to 43%, the lowest point in our history.[22]

In the United States, the changing family structure has helped to continue, and in some ways exacerbate, the tragedy of child poverty. Since 1974, the poverty rate among children has exceeded that among the elderly, and 40% of all poor people in this nation today are children.[23] According to a recent estimate, one out of every four American preschoolers in 1987 was living below the poverty line.[24]

In addition to family structural change, the psychological character of the marital relationship has also changed substantially over the years.[25] Traditionally, marriage has been understood as a social obligation—an institution designed mainly for economic security and procreation. Today, marriage is understood mainly as a path toward self-fulfillment: self-development is seen to require a significant other, and marital partners are picked primarily to be personal companions. Put another way, marriage is becoming deinstitutional-ized. No longer comprising a set of norms and social obligations that are wide-ly enforced, marriage today is a voluntary relationship that individuals can make and break at will. As one indicator of this shift, laws regulating marriage and divorce have become increasingly more lax.[26]

As psychological expectations for marriage grow ever higher, dashed expectations for personal fulfillment fuel our society's high divorce rate. Divorce also feeds upon itself. The higher the divorce rate, the more "nor-mal" it becomes, with fewer negative sanctions to oppose it, and the more potential partners become available. In general, psychological need, in and of itself, has proved to be a weak basis for stable marriage.

These family trends are all interrelated. They are also evident, in varying degrees, in every industrialized Western country, which suggests that their source lies not in particular political or economic systems but in the broad cultural shift that has accompanied industrialization and urban-ization. Although scholars do not agree on all aspects of this shift, clearly an ethos of radical individualism has emerged in these societies, in which personal autonomy, individual rights, and social equality have gained supremacy as cultural ideals. In keeping with these ideals, the main goals of personal behavior have shifted from commitment to social units of all kinds (families, communities, religions, nations) to personal choices, life-style options, self-fulfillment, and personal pleasure.[27]

FAMILY CHANGE AS FAMILY DECLINE

Despite the dramatic nature of the recent social transformation of the family, many family experts are still reluctant to refer to the transfor-mation as "family decline." This is unfortunate, because the concept of the family as a declining or weakening institution provides a "best fit" for many of the changes that have taken place. The concept also alerts us to examine the consequences of a rapidly changing institution.

During the past 25 years, the institution of the family has weakened substantially in a number of ways. Individual family members have become more autonomous and less bound by the family group, and the group has become less cohesive. Fewer of its traditional social functions are now carried out by the family; these have shifted to other institutions. The family has lost more power and authority to other institutions, espe-cially to the state and its agencies. The family has grown smaller, less sta-ble, and has a shorter life span; people are therefore family members for a smaller percentage of their life. The outcome of these trends is that people have become less willing to invest time, money, and energy in family life. It is the individual him- or herself, not the family unit, in whom the main investments are increasingly made.[28]

Why, then, are so many family scholars reluctant to speak of family decline? The short answer is that to speak of family decline within the intellectual community in recent years has been to be accused of opposing equality for women.

The dominance of the traditional nuclear family in the 1950s helped to fuel the modern women's movement. Reacting strongly to the lingering patriarchy of this family form, as well as to its separate-sphere removal of women from the labor market, the women's movement came to view the traditional nuclear family in very negative terms.[29] Today, those who believe in greater equality for women—and that includes most academics and other intellectuals—favor an egalitarian family form, with substantial economic independence for wives. With respect to these characteristics, the flight from the traditional nuclear family is regarded as progress, not decline.

To speak of decline under these circumstances, therefore, is perceived as being implicitly in favor of a discredited family form, one that oppressed women. Indeed, the term "decline" has been used most forcefully by those conservatives who tend to view every recent family change as negative and who have issued a clarion call for a return to the traditional nuclear family.

But properly used, the term "decline" should not carry such ideological baggage. To empirically conclude that the family is declining should not automatically link one to a particular ideology of family or gender. Moreover, not all decline is negative in its effects; decline is not necessarily the opposite of progress. All sorts of institutional forms that were once fully accepted have declined: theocracies, hereditary monarchies, imperialism. The results of their decline have been by no means merely regressive. It is important to distinguish an empirical trend, such as the weakening of an institution, from both its positive and negative consequences.

THE SOCIAL CONSEQUENCES OF FAMILY DECLINE

How are we to evaluate the social consequences of recent family decline? At the outset, it must be stressed that the issue is extremely complex. Society has been ill-served by the simplistic, either/or terms used by both the political right and left in the national debate.

Certainly, one should not jump immediately to the conclusion that family decline is necessarily bad for our society. A great many positive aspects of the recent family changes stand out as noteworthy. During this same quarter century of family decline, women (and many minorities) have clearly improved their status and probably the overall quality of their lives. Much of women's gain in status has come through their release from family duties and increased participation in the labor force. In addition, given the great emphasis on psychological criteria for choosing and keeping marriage partners, it can be argued persuasively that those marriages today that endure are more likely than ever before to be emotionally rewarding companionships.[30]

This period has also seen improved health care and longevity as well as widespread economic affluence, all of which have produced, for most people, a material standard of living that is historically unprecedented. Some of this improvement is due to the fact that people are no longer so dependent on their families for health care and economic support; they no longer are so imprisoned by social class and family obligation. When in need, they can now rely more on public care and support, as well as self-initiative and self-development.

Despite these positive aspects, the negative consequences of family decline are real and profound. The greatest negative effect, in the opinion of nearly everyone, is on children. Because children represent the future of a society, any negative consequences for them are especially significant. Substantial, if not conclusive, evidence indicates that, partly due to family changes, the quality of life for children in the past 25 years has worsened.[31] Much of the problem is of a psychological nature and thus is difficult to measure quantitatively.

Perhaps the most serious problem is a weakening in many families of the fundamental assumption that children are to be loved and valued at the highest level of priority. The general disinvestment in family life that has occurred has commonly meant a disinvestment in children's welfare. Some refer to this as a national "parent deficit." Yet the deficit goes well beyond parents to encompass an increasingly less child-friendly society. The parent deficient is all too easily blamed on newly working women. But it is men who have left the parenting scene in large numbers, a phenomenon one scholar has called "A disappearing act by fathers."[32] More than ever before, fathers are denying paternity, avoiding their parental obligations, and absent from home (at the same time there has been a slow but not offsetting growth of the "housefather" role).[33] Indeed, a persuasive case can be made that men began to abandon the "good provider" role at about the same time that many women started to relinquish the role of the full-time homemaker.[34] Thus, men and women may have been equally involved in triggering the recent flight from the traditional nuclear family.

The breakup of the nuclear unit has been the focus of much concern. Virtually every child desires two biological parents for life, and substantial evidence exists that child rearing is most successful when it involves two parents, both of whom are strongly motivated for the task.[35] This is not to say that other family forms can not be successful, only that as a group they are not as likely to be successful. This is also not to say that the two strongly motivated parents must be organized in the patriarchal and separate-sphere terms of the traditional nuclear family.

Regardless of family form, a significant change has occurred over the past quarter century in what can be called the social ecology of childhood.[36] Advanced societies are moving ever farther from what many hold to be a highly desirable child-rearing environment consisting of the following characteristics: a relatively large family that does a lot of things together, has many routines and traditions, and provides a great deal of quality contact time between adults and children; regular contact with relatives, active friendships in a supportive neighborhood, and contact with the adult world of work; little concern on the part of children that their parents will break up; and the coming together of all these ingredients in the development of a rich family subculture that has lasting meaning and strongly promulgates family values such as cooperation and sharing.

As this brief sketch of the changing ecology of childhood suggests, not only the family has been transformed, but also the community environment in which families exist. Children are especially sensitive to their local environments; yet adults, too, have a big stake in the quality of their surroundings.

The family has always been a fundamental and probably essential unit of what some call "civil society"—the local society made up of kin and friendship networks, neighborhoods, religious institutions, and voluntary associations. Civil society provides meaning and attachment for people's lives and helps to protect them from the impersonal forces of market and state.[37] As the market and state "megastructures" grow ever more powerful, the need for the mediating structures of civil society becomes that much more compelling, both for psychic survival and political freedom.[38] Although reasonable doubt can be expressed about the empirical accuracy of the common phrase "as the family goes, so goes the nation," I am not so doubtful about the phrase "as the family goes, so goes civil society."

FAMILY DECLINE AND TODAY'S POLICY DEBATE

What should be done to counteract or remedy the negative effects of family decline? This is the most controversial question of all, and the most difficult to answer.

The problems of purposive social action are enormous. In remedying the negative effects, it is never easy to avoid canceling out the positive benefits. Also, if family decline in fact stems from a broad cultural shift, it will not be easy to modify. The underlying trend may simply have to play itself out. It could be, of course, that the problems we are seeing result not from the intrinsic character of the cultural shift, but rather from its extreme rapidity. From this perspective, as the changes become complete and society settles down, we may be able to adjust without great difficulty to the new conditions.

Let us assume, however, that purposive social action is both called for and can have a useful outcome. Among the broad proposals for change that have been put forth, two extremes stand out prominently in the national debate: (1) a return to the structure of the traditional nuclear family characteristic of the 1950s and (2) the development of extensive governmental family policies.

Aside from the fact that it is probably impossible to return to a situation of an earlier time, the first alternative has major drawbacks. Such a shift would require many women to leave the work force and to some extent become "de-liberated," an unlikely occurrence indeed. Economic conditions necessitate that even more women take jobs, and cultural conditions stress ever greater equality between the sexes.

In addition to such considerations, the traditional nuclear family form, in today's world, may be fundamentally flawed. As an indication of this, one should realize that the young people who led the transformation of the family during the 1960s and 1970s were brought up in 1950s families. If the 1950s families were so wonderful, why didn't their children seek to emulate them? In hindsight, the 1950s families seem to have been beset with problems that went well beyond patriarchy and separate spheres. For many families the mother–child unit had become increasingly isolated from the kin group, the neighborhood, and community, and even from the father, who worked a long distance away. This was especially true for women who were fully educated and eager to take their place in work and public life. Maternal child rearing under these historically unprecedented circumstances became highly problematic.[39]

Despite such difficulties, the traditional nuclear family is still the family of choice for millions of Americans. They are comfortable with it, and for them it seems to work. It is reasonable, therefore, at least not to place roadblocks in the way of couples with children who wish to conduct their lives according to the traditional family's dictates. Women who freely desire to spend much of their lives as mothers and housewives, outside the labor force, should not be economically penalized by public policy for making that choice. Nor should they be denigrated by our culture as second-class citizens.

The second major proposal for change that has been stressed in national debate is the development of extensive governmental programs offering monetary support and social services for families, especially for the new "nonnuclear" families. In some cases these programs assist with functions that families are unable to perform adequately; in other cases, the functions are taken over, transforming them from family to public responsibilities.

This is the path followed by the European welfare states, but it has been less accepted by the United States than by any other industrialized nation. The European welfare states have been far more successful than the United States in minimizing the negative economic impact of family decline on family members, especially children. In addition, many European nations have established policies making it much easier for women (and increasingly men) to combine work with child rearing.[40] With these successes in mind, it seems inevitable that the United States will (and I believe should) move gradually in the direction of European countries with respect to family policies, just as we are now moving gradually in that direction with respect to medical care.

There are clear drawbacks, however, in moving too far down this road. If children are to be best served, we should seek to make the family stronger, not to replace it. At the same time that welfare states are minimizing some of the consequences of family decline, they may also be caus-ing further decline of the family unit. This phenomenon can be witnessed today in Sweden, where the institution of the family has probably grown weaker than anywhere else in the world.[41] On a lesser scale, the phe-nomenon has been seen in the United States in connection with our wel-fare programs. Fundamental to the success of welfare-state programs, therefore, is keeping the ultimate goal of strengthening families upper-most in mind.

A NEW SOCIAL MOVEMENT

Although each of the above alternatives has some merit, I suggest a third alternative, which is premised on the fact that we cannot return to the 1950s family, nor can we depend on the welfare state for a solution. Instead, we should strike at the heart of the cultural shift that has occurred, point up its negative aspects, and seek to reinvigorate the cultur-al ideals of "family," "parents," and "children" within the changed circum-stances of our time. We should stress that the individualistic ethos has gone too far, that children are being woefully shortchanged, and that, in the long run, strong families represent the best path toward self-fulfillment and personal happiness. We should bring again to the cultural forefront the old ideal of parents living together and sharing responsibility for their children and for each other.

What is needed is a new social movement whose purpose is the pro-motion of families and family values within the new constraints of modern life. It should point out the supreme importance of strong families to soci-ety, while at the same time suggesting ways that the family can better adapt to the modern conditions of individualism, equality, and the labor-force participation of both women and men. Such a movement could build on the fact that the overwhelming majority of young people today still put forth as their major life goal a lasting, monogamous, heterosexual relationship that includes the procreation of children. It is reasonable to suppose that this goal is so pervasive because it is based on a deep-seated human need.

The reassertion of this personal goal as a highly ranked cultural value is not a legislative alternative; politics necessarily must respond to the obvious diversity in American life. But it is an alternative ideally suit-ed to the leadership of broad-based citizens' groups. The history of recent social movements in America provides good reason for hope that such an initiative can make an impact. Witness the recent cultural shifts toward female and minority-group equality and the current move toward environ-mental protection, each of which has been led by popular movements focusing on fundamental social values. The time seems ripe to reassert that strong families concerned with the needs of children are, under modern conditions, not only possible but necessary.

NOTES

1. Norval Glenn, ed., "The State of the American Family," *Journal of Family Issues* 8 (No. 4, December 1987), Special Issue.

2. Sar A. Levitan and Richard S. Belous, *What's Happening to the American Family?* (Baltimore: Johns Hopkins, 1981), pp. 190, 15.

3. Sar A. Levitan, Richard S. Belous, and Frank Gallo, *What's Happening to the American Family?* (rev. ed.) (Baltimore: Johns Hopkins, 1988), pp. vi, viii.

4. Carl N. Degler, *At Odds: Women and the Family in America from the Revolution to the Present* (Oxford, England: Oxford University Press, 1980); Lawrence Stone, *The Family, Sex, and Marriage in England 1500–1800* (New York: Harper and Row, 1977); Steven Mintz and Susan Kellogg, *Domestic Revolutions: A Social History of the American Family* (New York: Free Press, 1988).

5. Andrew Cherlin and Frank F. Furstenberg, Jr., "The Changing European Family: Lessons for the American Reader," *Journal of Family Issues* 9 (No. 3, 1988), p. 294; John Modell, Frank F. Furstenberg, Jr., and Douglas Strong, "The Timing of Marriage in the Transition to Adulthood: Continuity and Change, 1860-1975," *American Journal of Sociology* 84 (1978), pp. S120–S150.

6. Susan Cotts Watkins, Jane A. Menken, and John Bongaarts, "Demographic Foundations of Family Change," *American Sociological Review* 52 (No. 3, 1987), pp. 346–358.

7. Andrew J. Cherlin, *Marriage, Divorce, Remarriage* (Cambridge, MA: Harvard University Press, 1981).

8. All data are from the U.S. Census Bureau, unless otherwise indicated.

9. Arthur G. Neal, Theodore Groat, and Jerry W. Wicks, "Attitudes about Having Children: A Study of 600 Couples in the Early Years of Marriage," *Journal of Marriage and the Family* 51 (No. 2, 1989), pp. 313–328; Joseph Veroff, Elizabeth Douvan, and Richard A. Kulka, *The Inner American: A Self-Portrait from 1957 to 1976* (New York: Basic Books, 1981); James A. Sweet and Larry L. Bumpass, *American Families and Households* (New York: Russell Sage Foundation, 1987), p. 400.

10. David E. Bloom and James Trussell, "What Are the Determinants of Delayed Childbearing and Permanent Childlessness in the United States?" *Demography* 21 (No. 4, 1984), pp. 591–611; Charles F. Westoff, "Perspective on Nuptiality and Fertility," *Population and Development Review* Supplement (No. 12, 1986), pp. 155–170.

11. John D'Emilio and Estelle B. Freedman, *Intimate Matters: A History of Sexuality in America* (New York: Harper and Row, 1988).

12. From a 1987 study sponsored by the National Academy of Sciences, reported in *The New York Times*, February 27, 1989, p. B11.

13. Daniel Yankelovich, *New Rules: Searching for Self-Fulfillment in a World Turned Upside Down* (New York: Random House, 1981), p. 94.

14. Suzanne M. Bianchi and Daphne Spain, *American Women in Transition* (New York:

Russell Sage Foundation, 1986); Victor R. Fuchs, *Women's Quest for Economic Equality* (Cambridge, MA: Harvard University Press, 1988).

15. Data assembled from U.S. Census reports by Maris A. Vinovskis, "The Unraveling of the Family Wage since World War II: Some Demographic, Economic, and Cultural Considerations," in Bryce Christensen, Allan Carlson, Maris Vinovskis, Richard Vedder, and Jean Bethke Elshtain, *The Family Wage: Work, Gender, and Children in the Modern Economy* (Rockford, IL: The Rockford Institute, 1988), pp. 33–58.

16. Lenore J. Weitzman, *The Divorce Revolution* (New York: Free Press, 1985).

17. Paul C. Glick, "Fifty Years of Family Demography: A Record of Social Change," *Journal of Marriage and the Family* 50 (No. 4, 1988), p. 868.

18. Robert Schoen, "The Continuing Retreat from Marriage: Figures from the 1983 U.S. Marital Status Life Tables," *Social Science Research* 71 (No. 2,1987), pp. 108–109; Teresa Castro Martin and Larry L. Bumpass, "Recent Trends in Marital Disruption," *Demography* 26 (No. 1, 1989), pp. 37–51.

19. Sanford M. Dornbusch and Myra H. Strober, *Feminism, Children, and the New Families* (New York: Guilford Press, 1988).

20. Sandra L. Hofferth, "Updating Children's Life Course," *Journal of Marriage and the Family* 47 (No. 1, 1985), pp. 93–115.

21. The 20-year downward spiral of family households came to a (temporary?) halt in the 1986–87 period, when the percentage of family households increased slightly, as documented in Judith Waldrop, "The Fashionable Family," *American Demographics* (March 1988).

22. Susan Cotts Watkins, Jane A. Menken, and John Bongaarts, op. cit., 1987.

23. Eugene Smolensky, Sheldon Danziger, and Peter Gottschalk, "The Declining Significance of Age in the United States: Trends in the Well-being of Children and the Elderly since 1939," in John L. Palmer, Timothy Smeeding, and Barbara Boyle Torrey, eds., *The Vulnerable* (Washington, DC: Urban Institute, 1988), pp. 29–54.

24. Report of House Select Committee on Children, Youth and Families, *The New York Times*, October 2, 1989, p. A12.

25. Kingsley Davis, ed., *Contemporary Marriage: Comparative Perspectives on a Changing Institution* (New York: Russell Sage Foundation, 1985).

26. Mary Ann Glendon, *The Transformation of Family Law* (Chicago: University of Chicago, 1989).

27. Robert N. Bellah, Richard Madsen, William M. Sullivan, Ann Swidler, and Steven M. Tipton, *Habits of the Heart: Individualism and Commitment in American Life* (Berkeley, CA: University of California Press, 1985).

28. Victor Fuchs, *How We Live* (Cambridge, MA: Harvard University Press, 1983).

29. Jean Bethke Elshtain, *Public Man, Private Women: Women in Social and Political Thought* (Princeton, NJ: Princeton University Press, 1981).

30. Francesca M. Cancian, *Love in America: Gender and Self-Development* (Cambridge, England, and New York: Cambridge University Press, 1987).

31. *U.S. Children and Their Families: Current Conditions and Recent Trends, 1989* (Washington, DC: U.S. Government Printing Office). Nicholas Zill and Carolyn C. Rogers, "Recent Trends in the Well-being of Children in the United States and Their Implications for Public Policy," in Andrew Cherlin, ed., *The Changing American Family and Public Policy* (Washington, DC: Urban Institute, 1988), pp. 31–115; Peter Uhlenberg and David Eggebeen, "The Declining Well-being of American Adolescents," *The Public Interest* (No. 82, 1986), pp. 25–38.

32. Samuel H. Preston, "Children and the Elderly: Divergent Paths for America's Dependents," *Demography* 21 (No. 4, 1984), p. 443.

33. Frank F. Furstenberg, Jr., "Good Dads-Bad Dads: Two Faces of Fatherhood," in Andrew Cherlin, ed., *The Changing American Family and Public Policy* (Washington, DC: Urban Institute, 1988), pp. 193–218.

34. Barbara Ehrenreich, *The Hearts of Men: American Dreams and the Flight from Commitment* (New York: Anchor, 1983).

35. E. Mavis Hetherington and Josephine D. Arasteh, eds., *Impact of Divorce, Single Parenting, and Stepparenting on Children* (Hillsdale, NJ: Lawrence Erlbaum Associates, 1988); Sara McLanahan and Karen Booth, "Mother-Only Families: Problems, Prospects, and Politics," *Journal of Marriage and the Family* 51 (No. 3, 1989), pp. 557–580.

36. Urie Bronfenbrenner, *The Ecology of Human Development* (Cambridge, MA: Harvard University Press, 1979).

37. Alan Wolfe, *Whose Keeper? Social Science and Moral Obligation* (Berkeley, CA: University of California Press, 1989).

38. Peter L. Berger and Richard J. Neuhaus, *To Empower People: The Role of Mediating Structures in Public Policy* (Washington, DC: American Enterprise Institute, 1977).

39. Betty Friedan, *The Feminine Mystique* (New York: Laurel, 1983, 1963).

40. Sylvia Ann Hewlett, *A Lesser Life* (New York: William Morrow, 1986).

41. David Popenoe, *Disturbing the Nest: Family Change and Decline in Modern Societies* (New York: Aldine de Gruyter, 1988).

=4=
Are Americans Underinvesting In Children?

Victor R. Fuchs

A ccording to many experts, American children are in trouble. Not all children, to be sure. But compared with the previous generation, today's youngsters perform worse in school, are more than twice as likely to commit suicide, and use much more alcohol and drugs. Not only are they are twice as likely to be obese, but they also show other signs of physical, mental, and emotional distress. Experts disagree about the causes of these problems; but one theme surfaces frequently: the adequacy of our investment in children.

Are Americans underinvesting in children? If surveyed, a majority of Americans might answer "yes." But what about those who would answer "don't know"? What kind of information would help them to answer yea or nay? Is underinvestment something like obscenity—difficult to define, but you know it when you see it? Those who think that the underinvestment is obvious might consider some additional questions. Surely not all Americans are underinvesting. Which ones are, and why? Surely not all children are experiencing underinvestment. Again, which ones are, and why? The question could also be addressed in a comparative context, both historical and international. If Americans are underinvesting in children now, was there a time when they did not? If this is so, when did the transition occur, and why? If it exists in the United States, is underinvestment in children observed in other countries as well? If there are international differences, what accounts for them?

Although these questions are too complex to consider fully here, they provide a useful background for the three, more limited, objectives of this chapter:

Victor R. Fuchs is Henry J. Kaiser, Jr. Professor at Stanford University in Stanford, California, and a Research Associate at the National Bureau of Economic Research. The author gratefully acknowledges support from the Andrew W. Mellon Foundation for "The Well-Being of Children" project of the National Bureau of Economic Research. The author is also grateful to Sherwin Rosen, John Shoven, and Michael Wald for helpful comments.

● to sharpen the question of underinvestment by defining terms and discussing several thorny conceptual issues
● to present and interpret some relevant evidence
● to consider several policy options to increase investment in children

CONCEPTS

Investment

Investment, in the most general sense, means present sacrifice for future benefit. Investment creates capital, either in tangible form, such as plant, equipment, and roads, or in intangible form, such as the development of the health and skills of individuals. The latter is usually referred to as "human capital"; its quintessential example is investment in children.

Sacrifices can take many forms, including forgoing consumption of goods and services, losing leisure time, or incurring disutility. For example, one may dislike practicing the violin, but practice is an investment undertaken in order to realize future benefits in the form of greater proficiency. The benefits can take the form of additional resources for consumption or further investment, additional leisure, or enhanced utility. The value of the benefits, the value of the sacrifices, and the time interval between them determine the rate of return on the investment, usually expressed as percent per annum.

Economists typically classify all expenditures as either investment or consumption. This distinction is usually clear-cut; for example, the factors that influence a farmer's decision to purchase a tractor are obviously different from those that influence his or her purchase of a ticket to the movies.

Regarding expenditures on children, however, it may be difficult to say how much is investment and how much is consumption. Education is usually thought of as investment, but what if the child actually enjoys going to school? Expenditures for food are normally classified under consumption, but in the case of a growing child they could also be regarded as investment in future health.

The notion that sacrifice is inherent in investment is also problematic. Consider a parent who gives up an afternoon of leisure to take his or her child to visit a museum. From the child's perspective the visit may be an investment in human capital, with future benefits in the form of increased appreciation of natural or human creations. But what if the parent enjoys the visit and does not regard it as any sacrifice at all? What if the parent would have undertaken the visit even if there were no future benefits? It is often impossible to separate child-centered activities into those that are investment and those that are consumption; in one sense, perhaps, they should all be viewed as investment.

Underinvestment

When the level of investment is "too low," it is characterized as underinvestment. Is there some generally accepted standard for judging whether the level is too low? In order to define underinvestment, it is necessary to deal with the corollary concepts of overinvestment and optimal investment. To think that too much can never be invested in children is to trivialize the concept of underinvestment. But what is the optimal rate? In economics, it is defined by equality between the rate of return on the investment and the rate at which future benefits are discounted relative to present benefits (that is, the rate of time preference or time discount). If a person is indifferent with regard to a choice between having $1,000 today and $1,100 (of constant purchasing power) a year from today, and if an investment opportunity exists that will yield a rate of return over that period of more than 10%, failure to take that opportunity would constitute underinvestment.[1]

It is important to realize that although *under*investment may be correlated with *low* investment, the two are not identical. The level of investment may be low, either by historical or international standards, but the explanation may be that the rate of return is low or the rate of time discount is high. If either or both are true, it may be inaccurate to characterize the situation as underinvestment. As *The New Palgrave Dictionary of Economics* states, "There is a widespread mythology that investment is good, and the more investment the better. But investment may be good or bad, and there may be too much as well as too little."[2]

If the rate of time discount is not known, it may still be useful to make inferences about underinvestment by comparing rates of return on different kinds of investment. If, for example, the rate of return on investment in children (at the margin) is greater than that on other investments, society would benefit from shifting some investment to children because optimal investment requires equal rates of return at the margin (adjusted for risk).

In comparing rates of return, it is important to consider possible deviations between the *private* and the *social* rate. The latter, which should govern resource allocation if the goal is to maximize social welfare, may be greater than the former if *positive externalities* are associated with the investment. For instance, preprimary enrichment programs for disadvantaged children may yield social benefits if these children become better citizens as adults. Such societal benefits must be added to private benefits such as higher earnings.

Sometimes *negative* externalities result from investment; that is, the social rate of return is lower than the private. Offshore oil drilling is considered by many to fall into this category. Questions have also been raised about the social return of investment in higher education. Some observers have argued that one of the reasons earnings rise as years of schooling increase is that completion of additional schooling merely serves as a signal of superior ability rather than because the schooling itself raises the individual's productivity. The individual earns higher pay as a result of the additional schooling, but his or her private return may exceed the social return.[3]

Imperfections in capital markets can also contribute to underinvestment in children, even when the private return is high. Consider, for instance, the case of a child who would realize a large return to investment in an early childhood program. How can the child get command of the money needed to enter that program? The chances that the child can borrow the money are virtually nonexistent. Even when the child's parents can afford the investment, they may not wish to use their money in that way, in part because they have no assurance that the child would ever reimburse them.[4]

Another useful distinction is between underinvestment in general and underinvestment in children specifically. The financial press is constantly telling us that the overall level of investment is too low or—what is really the same thing—that Americans are overconsuming and undersaving. In comparison with other countries, or with this country in earlier eras, we have a low rate of investment in plants, equipment, and most other kinds of physical capital. It may not be surprising that a country that neglects its roads and bridges and has not built a major new airport in 20 years is also neglecting its children. The explanations for general underinvestment range from unwise tax laws to television advertising to the decline of the Protestant ethic. If Americans are underinvesting in general—including underinvesting in children—we would need to consider all the social, psychological, and economic reasons why so much emphasis is placed on the present at the expense of the future.

Misinvestment

Suppose one observes a business firm losing out to competitors and facing bankruptcy. One possible explanation is that the firm has underinvested in plant, equipment, or research and development. Another explanation may be that the total amount of investment was appropriate; it was simply misinvested. The firm's difficulties may result from having bought the wrong equipment or carried out the wrong research. The same possibility must be considered with respect to children. If we observe children entering adulthood with serious deficiencies, the problem may not be one of underinvestment, but of misinvestment. For example, the total amount of investment in child health may be appropriate, but perhaps the return would be greater if more of the investment were directed toward prenatal and postnatal preventive health services and less toward neonatal intensive care. The same questions could be applied to investment in education. Perhaps total spending for education is appropriate, but the objects of expenditure are inappropriate.

To raise the question of misinvestment is to introduce the possibility of differences in values or goals. In the case of the business firm, the goal is relatively clear-cut—to make profits and avoid losses. Failure to reach this goal points a finger of suspicion at underinvestment or misinvestment. In the case of education, however, a clear consensus on values and goals is not apparent. Failure of children to achieve proficiency in mathematics and English may be interpreted as misinvestment by some, whereas others may consider failure to develop the child's personality or to inculcate liberal social attitudes more serious. Almost everyone will agree that some "misinvestment" has occurred but few will agree as to what form it has taken.

Aggregate Investment or Per-Child Investment?

Is the adequacy of investment in children to be judged by the amount per child or by the product of that amount and the number of children—that is, the aggregate investment? The latter criterion makes the fertility rate a critical variable. By historical standards, this rate is low in almost all industrialized countries, resulting in a marked increase in the relative share of national income devoted to adults and a decrease in the share devoted to children. From a biological point of view, any population with a fertility rate below replacement level (2.1 children per woman) is "underinvesting"; in the absence of immigration, that population will eventually disappear. Fertility in the United States has been slightly below replacement level every year since 1973; in many European countries the rate is far lower.

The connection between fertility and investment per child is often close. High fertility makes it more difficult to invest a great deal in each child; low fertility makes it much easier. The economists Becker and Lewis[5] discuss this "quality–quantity" tradeoff. The absence of any consensus regarding what is an optimal fertility rate (or optimal population size) creates additional difficulties for the assessment of the adequacy of investment in children. Because the trends in U.S. fertility are well known, this chapter focuses primarily on investment per child.

Who Is Underinvesting?

This chapter is not the first attempt to address the question of underinvestment in children, but my emphasis on *Americans* may differentiate it from the usual approach. Most often the responsibility for underinvestment is laid at the door of "America" or "society" or "the public sector." The impression is often created that underinvestment is the result of some vague, impersonal forces rather than the consequences of the decisions of individual Americans in their roles as parents, consumers, workers, stockholders, taxpayers, and the like.

Although it is important to focus attention on the behavior of individuals, categorizing them in various ways can help to sharpen the analysis. One of the most useful distinctions is between adults who are parents and those who are not. Either or both of these groups must be responsible for any underinvestment in children. If underinvestment is a relatively new phenomenon in the United States, it must be because parents as a group are now less willing to invest in children or because those who are not parents are now less willing to transfer resources to households with children. If the former explanation is significant, it can result from a decline in parental investment in their own children, or from changes in income distribution and redistribution among households with children.

Which Children?

Even those who are most convinced that Americans are underinvesting in children do not believe that the term applies to all children. The conventional wisdom seems to be that many, if not most, children receive adequate investment but that a substantial number do not. These children are often referred to as "disadvantaged." The principal characteristics used to describe children in this group are low family income, minority status, and living with only one parent.

Parental investment in children is undoubtedly correlated with parental income. Inequality of investment across children will, in part, reflect inequality in income among households that have children. It may also reflect shifts in income shares between households with children and those that are childless as well as changes in redistribution through tax-supported services (such as education) for children.

When some children receive much more investment than others, the rate of return at the margin is probably higher for those receiving less investment, but this need not always be true. Suppose a family had two children, one of whom would benefit much more from investment in education than would the other. The parents might invest differentially in the two children according to their potential to benefit; this would be an optimal investment strategy. But it would be unequal. The parents could try to rectify the inequality by giving money to the child who received less education.

The problem for society is more complicated. Children probably do differ in their potential to benefit from investment. For instance, there is no reason to believe that providing the same amount of education for each child (e.g., 14 years) would be an optimal investment strategy. But provision of unequal amounts of education contributes to inequality in income and to other inequalities as well. If equality of outcome is an important objective, it may be necessary to overinvest in some children and underinvest in others.

In studying underinvestment, children can also be categorized by age. Numerous studies of services for preschool children suggest that investment in such programs is relatively much greater in many European countries than it is in the United States. On the other hand, Americans invest far more in higher education than do the people of any other country. Thus, an assessment of investment levels based on international comparisons will result in very different answers, depending upon the children's age. When one measures investment up to age 22, the level of investment in the United States is very high. On the other hand, when one cuts off the measurement at a much younger age, investment levels are relatively higher in many European countries.

At present we do not know whether the European or the American investment strategy yields a greater social return. We do, however, have a fairly clear view of the distributional implications of the two alternatives. Public subsidy of higher education tends to favor families with average and above-average income because they account for the great majority of college students. European-style support for preschoolers is more egalitarian because low-income families benefit at least as much as others.

UNDERINVESTMENT: EVIDENCE

Several kinds of evidence shed light on the question of underinvestment, but none provides a definitive answer. The most relevant would be measures of rates of return, although these are extremely scarce. Other evidence includes measures of child well-being and measures of inputs to children.

Rates of Return

Rates of return are the data most relevant to judging the appropriateness of investment, but they are extremely difficult to calculate. Even for large corporations with elaborate accounting systems, it is frequently unclear whether the reported figures overstate or understate the true economic rate of return.

The rate of return on investment in human capital is even more difficult to calculate than is that on a firm's investment in plant and equipment. There are three main problems. First, it is often difficult to assess the cost of the investment because it probably involves time and effort and disutility, as well as direct outlays of money. Indeed, some of the most important investments in children require no monetary outlays at all. Second, it is often difficult to attribute specific benefits to specific investments. If, some years after an investment in a child is undertaken, we observe an improvement in health or reading ability or a decrease in antisocial behavior, how accurately can these results be traced to the particular investment? Third, valuing the benefits is problematic. In the case of the business firm, the benefits (in the form of profits) already have a dollar value, but no such easy standard is available for many of the benefits of investment in human capital.

Of the many kinds of investment in children, schooling has received the most attention from a rate-of-return perspective. And the benefit of schooling that has been studied at great length is increased earnings. The correlation between higher earnings and increased schooling is well established; since about 1960, there have been numerous attempts to estimate the rate of return implicit in the correlation. In general, the calculations show that the private rate of return is at least as high as it is on investment in the private business sector. However, to the extent that students do not bear the full cost of their education, the private rate of return is higher than the social rate.

Considerable controversy revolves around the correct way to calculate rates of return on investment in schooling. Virtually all methods rely on earnings differentials as a crucial variable. These differentials have varied during the past several decades for a variety of reasons, including changes in the relative size of entering cohorts and shifts in the industrial and occupational distributions of employment. For white men the earnings differential between college and high school graduates rose in the 1950s and 1960s, dropped in the 1970s for young workers, and then rose sharply in the 1980s. For the entire period since World War II, the differential has averaged approximately 45%.[6] The percentage differential between female college and high school graduates has usually been somewhat higher than for white males; the absolute differential has been smaller.

Some analysts believe that reliance on the earnings differential leads to an underestimate of the rate of return on investment in higher education. They claim that other benefits flow from increased schooling (e.g., improved health) that have a value to the individual apart from any effect on earnings. On the other hand, some believe that earnings differentials overstate the return on schooling because they implicitly assume that the college and high school graduates are identical in all other respects or that differences between them have been controlled for in the statistical analysis.

An example of how schooling can inappropriately be credited with a favorable result is the correlation between schooling and cigarette smoking. All recent research on smoking finds a strong negative relationship between years of education and the probability of smoking. But is the additional schooling the cause of the decrease in smoking? Probably not. A study of individuals at age 17 who had the same amount of schooling found that the probability of smoking at that age was strongly related to the amount of schooling the individual would eventually attain.[7] But at age 17, the additional schooling could not possibly be the cause of the difference in smoking behavior.

Rates of return on investment in health care are much scarcer than for schooling, but several attempts have been made to evaluate the relative effectiveness of different programs aimed at children's health. One review of the literature[8] concluded that prenatal care and dental care are much more effective than is pediatric care (except for immunizations). A more recent study addressed the cost-effectiveness of various programs designed to reduce neonatal mortality.[9] The authors concluded that the early initiation of prenatal care was the most cost-effective intervention, particularly for blacks. The Special Supplemental Food Program for Women, Infants, and Children (WIC) also scored well in the cost-effectiveness calculations. The least cost-effective intervention was neonatal intensive care, with costs per life saved running into the millions of dollars in some hospitals.

Although support for the idea that prenatal care is a good form of investment is widespread, a panel of medical experts sponsored by the U.S.

Public Health Service recently recommended that less prenatal care be provided to the approximately 40% of pregnant women whose fetuses are at no apparent risk of health problems. This recommendation was tied to another recommendation urging that more care be given to women whose fetuses are at risk.[10] For low-risk pregnancies, the panel recommended that the usual 13 prenatal visits be cut to seven or eight, that pelvic examinations should be done only on the first visit, that routine urine tests for protein be eliminated in the early months, and that Pap tests are unnecessary if the woman has had such a test within the past year. The panel apparently believes that the rate of return on these services is very low.

The Well-Being of Children

Some of the most suggestive data concerning possible underinvestment in children come from trends in measures of well-being. To be sure, not all the trends are unfavorable. The infant mortality rate, for instance, has been cut in half since 1970. But several measures indicate a deterioration in the well-being of children during the past few decades.

Probably the most highly publicized evidence of an unfavorable trend is student performance on standardized tests. Scores on the verbal and mathematical parts of the Scholastic Aptitude Test declined substantially in the 1960s and 1970s, and this decline is not just an artifact of an increase in the proportion of students taking the test. Scores declined in all types of schools, among all socioeconomic groups, and in all parts of the country. The decline was almost twice as large for the verbal as for the mathematical scores. Test results leveled off around 1980 and since then have risen slightly.

Approximately 25% of all children fail to complete high school, and their command of English, mathematics, and other basic intellectual tools is usually very weak. Unfortunately, much the same can be said for a substantial fraction of students who do graduate from high school. Business firms in large cities committed to hiring substantial numbers of high school graduates for their work force have found that many of these graduates cannot pass tests of basic reading and reasoning skills.[11]

Another indicator of decreased well-being of children during the 1960s and 1970s is the rise in suicide in the 15- to 19-year-old age group. This rate more than doubled during a period when the rate among prime-age adults (25–64 years of age) remained stable. The total number of teenage suicides is relatively small, but it is important to note that many more young people attempt suicide or kill themselves slowly through substance abuse. The teenage suicide rate leveled off in the 1980s, albeit at a high level.

Surveys of obesity also point to a decline in the well-being of children. This major nutritional disorder, which raises the risk of hypertension, psychosocial problems, respiratory disease, diabetes, and orthopedic problems, was much more prevalent in the late 1970s than it was in the 1960s.[12] Among children aged 6–11, the proportion found to be obese jumped from 18% to 27% in 14 years, while the proportion found to be superobese doubled, from 6% to 12%. Similar increases were observed among children 12–17 years of age. The increases were greater among black children than among white children and greater among boys than among girls at young ages, but greater among girls than among boys at ages 12–17. Most notable was an increase in superobesity among adolescent girls from 6% to 11% between the late 1960s and the late 1970s.

Other measures, based on less reliable data, also indicate worsening conditions for children in recent decades. Most disturbing is a tripling of the number of maltreatment cases reported per 10,000 children between 1976 and 1985.[13] It is possible that more thorough reporting contributed to this result, but it is also likely that increased use of alcohol and drugs by parents and the fragmentation of households have resulted in a real increase in child abuse and neglect.

Inputs

If the well-being of children is declining, are these changes the result of decreased inputs of resources to children? Absolute declines in such inputs, or declines relative to other economic trends, would suggest the possibility of underinvestment. To be sure, stable or rising trends would not prove that the level of investment is appropriate, but they would suggest that, if there is underinvestment, it is not a new phenomenon.

Despite frequent expressions of concern that Americans have abandoned their commitment to public education, the data on inputs do not support the notion of a downward trend in this area. Between 1975 and 1987, expenditures per pupil in public elementary and secondary schools rose at the rate of 9.4% per annum. This rate is appreciably faster than the rate of growth of gross national product per capita (7.7%) or disposable personal income per capita (7.6%). Moreover, not all of the increased expenditures per pupil were needed to cover higher prices of inputs. During that same period, the input price index for education rose by 7.4% per annum, indicating a substantial increase in real inputs to the schools.[14]

The data on teachers' salaries tell a similar story. Compensation per public school employee grew at 7.6% per annum between 1975 and 1987, while the average hourly earnings of all private nonagricultural workers rose at the rate of only 5.8%. Moreover, women who teach in elementary and secondary schools earn approximately 20% more than do women in other occupations. This result is based on an analysis of the hourly earnings of more than 100,000 women who worked at least 20 hours per week; the study controls for years of schooling, age, marital status, presence of children, and several other socioeconomic variables.[15]

High average levels of spending on education do not, however, refute the claim of underinvestment in some children. In Texas, for instance, the 100 poorest school districts spend less than $3,000 per year per student, whereas in the 100 richest districts the average expenditure per student is more than $7,000. One cannot be certain of the effects of such disparity, but the presumption is that the shifting of some resources from the rich to the poor districts would increase the social rate of return on investment in schooling. In order to achieve this redistribution, the state would probably have to enact an income tax, and the effects of such a tax on work and saving would also have to be considered in an overall assessment of the economic impact of such a policy.

Health care is another major investment in human capital. Per-capita expenditures on adults are much greater than on children, but there is no evidence that children's share has been declining over time. Indeed, Table 1 shows that the rate of growth between 1977 and 1987 for children exceeded the rate for adults aged 20–64 by a large margin and that growth was almost as rapid as that for the elderly. Surprisingly, the rate of growth of public expenditures on personal health care for children was equal to that for adults 65 years of age and older.

TABLE 1: PER-CAPITA PERSONAL HEALTH CARE EXPENDITURES (1987) AND RATE OF CHANGE (1977–1987), BY AGE

Age	< 19	20–64	≥ 65	All ages
Per-capita expenditures, 1987 (dollars)				
All sources	745	1535	5360	1776
Private	547	1139	2004	1079
Public	198	1395	3356	696
Rate of change, deflated[a] per-capita expenditures, 1977–87 (% per annum)				
All sources	1.9	0.3	2.3	1.6
Private	1.9	0.5	2.9	1.5
Public	2.0	−0.3	2.0	1.8

[a]Deflated by the medical care component of the Consumer Price Index.

Source: Daniel R. Waldo et al., "Health Expenditures by Age Group, 1977 and 1987," *Health Care Financing Review* 10 (No. 4, Summer 1989), pp. 114–117, Tables 2 and 3.

Parents are usually the most important source of investment in children; they provide two kinds of inputs: those that are produced in the market and purchased with money and those that are produced at home. The latter can take a wide variety of forms, including health care, help with homework, love, discipline, and so forth. The amount of market inputs to children is determined primarily by family income. Recent trends in that measure have been very unfavorable for children, resulting in a rise in the proportion of children living in poverty in the 1980s, despite an increase nationally in real per-capita personal income. By the mid-1980s, the poverty rate among children (21%) was almost double the rate among adults (11%), a situation without precedent in American history.

Several factors contribute to this result. One is the sharp improvement in the income of the elderly, largely because increases in Social Security retirement benefits have outpaced changes in earnings. A second factor is the increase in the percentage of children living in female-headed households. This factor is particularly important in explaining the growth in poverty among black children, whose poverty rate is more than 2.5 times that of white youngsters. But even if female-headed households are excluded from the analysis, the gap in poverty between children and adults is still substantial, 14% versus 8%. Again, excluding female-headed households, the poverty rate among children showed a 3.3 percentage point increase between 1979 and 1984. The primary explanation for this phenomenon is the slow growth or actual decline of real income among young adults. Children are highly dependent on the labor income of young adults, and the downward trend in this measure (adjusted for inflation) over the past decade is probably the principal reason that more children are living below the poverty line.

The problem of underinvestment in disadvantaged children has probably grown worse in the past decade, largely because of widening inequality of income and the reluctance of households without children to make transfers (via the tax system) to households with children. The weak economic position of children becomes readily apparent when households are grouped according to the presence of children (Table 2). Money income per person is twice as high in households without children; and the more children in the household, the lower the income on average.

To be sure, a comparison based on money income per person tends to overstate the disparities in economic well-being. One reason for this overstatement is the omission of nonmarket production of goods and services; a second is the failure to take into account the size and composition of households and especially the potential for economies of scale that work to the advantage of larger households. I have, therefore, calculated a second measure, "total effective income per person," for each household. This measure includes money income and the imputed value of housework and child care and it adjusts the sum of money and imputed income to take account of the size and composition of the household. To capture the effects of

64

TABLE 2: ANNUAL INCOME IN HOUSEHOLDS WITH AND
WITHOUT CHILDREN, BY AGE OF HOUSEHOLDER AND
NUMBER OF CHILDREN, 1986 (DOLLARS)

	Type of Household				
	With children	Without children	With 1 child	With 2 children	With 3 or more children
Householder any age					
Percent of households	39	61	16	15	9
Money income per household	31,536	26,815	32,735	31,950	28,575
Money income per person	7,833	14,792	10,297	7,890	5,121
Total effective income per person[a]	26,905	33,496	30,906	27,541	20,977
Householder age 25–44					
Percent of households	65	35	22	26	16
Money income per household	31,234	30,821	32,538	31,955	28,305
Money income per person	7,793	18,748	10,895	8,057	5,189
Total effective income per person[a]	26,661	34,500	31,597	27,775	20,877
Percent in poverty	16	7	10	14	27

[a]Includes imputed value of housework and child care and adjusts for economies of scale based on size and composition of household (see text).

Source: Calculated from March 1986 Current Population Survey.

economies of scale and the presence of children, the number of "adult equiv-alents" for each household was assumed to vary in proportion to the official poverty threshold for each type of household. For instance, the poverty threshold for a household with two adults and two children is 1.95 times the threshold for a single adult. Thus the total income for a two-adult, two-child household was divided by 1.95 to obtain total effective income per person.

Even with this adjusted figure, however, it is still true that persons in households without children have a higher level of economic well-being. Moreover, the disparity increases as the number of children per household increases. This result holds regardless of whether one looks at all house-holds (regardless of the age of the householder) or restricts the analysis to those households with a householder aged 25–44. It is important to note that although only a small proportion of households have three or more children, close to half of all children live in these households.

No hard data are available that measure changes in the nonmarket inputs of parents to their children, but there are good reasons to believe that these crucial inputs have declined. Calculations based on Bureau of Census data show that parental time potentially available to children (total time minus time in paid work) fell appreciably between 1960 and 1986. On aver-age, in white households with children, parents had ten hours less per week of potential parental time; the decrease for black households with children was approximately 12 hours per week. The principal reason for the decline was an increase in the proportion of mothers holding paid jobs. An increase in one-parent households was also important, especially for black children.

It is theoretically possible that the potential parenting hours lost by mothers taking paid jobs was offset by fathers providing more child care, but this seems unlikely. Paid hours of work by fathers remained about the same; thus any increase in paternal child care would have had to come out of the father's leisure or reductions in other work around the house. The large increase in the proportion of households with children in which the father is absent all or nearly all the time has probably offset any increase in parenting by fathers in two-parent households.

Not only are today's parents probably spending less time with their children than they did a generation ago, but time spent with them by grandparents, especially grandmothers, has almost certainly declined as well. Three strong trends suggest this result. First, the labor-force participa-tion of older women has increased greatly. Second, the proportion of elder-ly widows who live with their children and grandchildren has decreased immensely. And third, the increased geographic mobility of the population, especially the elderly, suggests that many more grandparents now live at a considerable distance from their grandchildren. Inputs to children from adult siblings have probably also declined over the past quarter century because fewer of them continue to live in their parents' homes after age 21.

One other source of investment in children that is rarely discussed is the children themselves. Especially in high school, boys and girls often make large investments in themselves by doing homework, engaging in extracurricular activities, and the like. We don't know whether this type of investment has increased, decreased, or stayed the same. One clue that suggests a possible decrease is the large rise in the proportion of high school students who also have a paid job. Employment can be a form of investment in itself, but if the principal purpose is to earn money to spend on leisure activities, it is not unreasonable to infer that the time committed to paid employment and to the spending of the extra money come at the expense of investment in education. The increase in employment is particularly evident among white middle-class high school students.

UNDERINVESTMENT: POLICY OPTIONS

To increase investment in children, it is necessary to divert resources marked for other purposes. In some ways the simplest reallocation would be for parents to spend more time with their children, but it is difficult for public policy to force such a change. Most policy interventions, therefore, seek to change spending patterns in order to reduce consumption or to reduce other forms of investment.

The mechanisms for achieving reallocation of resources are well known. The government can use tax revenues to provide child allowances, direct services, or subsidies for services in the private sector. Child allowances provide the maximum degree of choice for parents; some observers believe this is an advantage, whereas others prefer to tie the aid directly to a specific child-centered service.

The government can reduce taxes (and expenditures for other services), leaving more money in the hands of parents to be spent, at least in part, on investment in their children. These reductions in tax revenues can be achieved by increasing deductions from taxable income or by providing tax credits. The deduction approach tends to favor high-income families because the deduction increases their after-tax income more than it does for a low-income family. Indeed, for families with income too low to pay taxes, the deduction is worthless. Tax credits are more egalitarian, especially if they include equivalent payments to families that do not have to pay any income tax. Finally, the government can mandate child-investment activities on the part of employers. Whatever methods are chosen, the most important questions are:

● To what extent does the policy actually result in greater investment in children?

● What are the implications for efficiency?

● What are the implications for equity?

One useful way of thinking about particular policies is to ask: If more money is being spent on children, who is spending less on what? This question is not always easy to answer, as can be seen if we begin to think through the consequences of a policy that requires employers to provide child-care benefits for their employees in the form of, say, subsidized child care or paid parental leave. These programs are often euphemistically described as "employer provided," as if the costs of the programs were coming out of the pockets of the chief executive and his or her companions in the executive suite. Yet this is certainly not the case. Where does the money come from?

The cost of the program may fall in a variety of directions. First, the employees who benefit directly from the program might bear the cost in the form of lower wages or a loss of other fringe benefits. In the short run this seems unlikely, but over time the compensation of the beneficiaries might be adjusted. A second possibility is that the cost would be borne by all the employees, regardless of whether or not they benefited from the program. We see this kind of adjustment occurring frequently at collective-bargaining tables. An employer offers a compensation package increase of, say, 60 cents an hour, and then the union says how much of it the employees want to take in the form of wages and how much in the form of benefits. A third possibility is that at least some of the cost is borne by stockholders in the form of lower profits. Finally, some of the cost is likely to be passed on to the firm's customers in the form of higher prices. In many respects the cost of a mandated benefit is similar to a tax on the company. Inasmuch as the incidence of business taxes is not known with precision, it is not surprising that there is no clear-cut answer to the question of who bears the cost of a mandated benefit.

It does not follow, however, that the efficiency and equity implications of a mandated benefit are identical to those of a tax-supported program. Indeed, compulsory employer-specific programs are usually less equitable than are tax-supported ones because the transfer burden is not as widely diffused and is not geared to ability to pay. It weighs more heavily on the consumers of particular products and on workers in particular industries—those who employ relatively more women of child-bearing age. If the cost is borne entirely by the beneficiaries of the program, their only gain is a substitution of tax-free compensation for taxable income. The same objective could be accomplished by allowing a tax deduction or a tax credit for the child care.

The distributional implications of mandated paid parental leaves are particularly troublesome. The higher the parent's wage, the higher the value of this benefit—an extremely regressive feature. Furthermore, because eligibility is conditioned by employment, it distorts parental choice. In particular, it denies any benefit to families in which one parent chooses to work exclusively at home. Child-care allowances (or tax credits) given equally to all parents of infants would be more egalitarian. They would not bias the choices parents make between caring for their own children or purchasing child care from others.

These points are not meant to detract from employers' voluntarily providing child-care benefits because they believe it helps attract and keep good employees. Similarly, it may be excellent business policy for employers to offer more flexibility in hours of work, including shared jobs, part-time jobs, and flextime. The question is whether society gains or loses by the government trying to force employers to do what they believe is contrary to their best interests when other options are open to government to achieve the same objectives with greater equity and efficiency.

Another kind of policy exists that would reallocate resources to children, although nominally it is not child-related at all. If income were distributed more equally in the United States, children would be the main beneficiaries because they are overrepresented in low-income households and underrepresented in more affluent ones. When households are ranked by income per person, the ratio of children to adults rises steadily as income falls.

The highest tenth percentile consists almost entirely of adults. Only 6% of the individuals in those households are children. By contrast, children account for 50% of those in households at the 90th percentile. The increase in income inequality that the United States experienced in the 1980s has undoubtedly contributed to a worsening of the position of children.

In the final analysis, resources for children can come from only two places: adults who are parents or adults who are not parents. Public policy can do very little to force parents to reallocate resources to their children. Parental investment in children is determined almost entirely by the willingness and ability of the parents.

The government can, however, through taxes, bring about some transfer of resources from high-income to low-income households (with children) and from childless households to those with children. Consider that among the approximately 40 million households that are headed by someone between the ages of 25 and 44, approximately 14 million have only adult members. These adults are, on average, better educated than are the adults in households that have children. They are also more affluent, primarily because each household has fewer persons to feed, clothe, and shelter. Any program that directed resources toward children (whether for child care, education, or health) that was financed by broad-based general taxes would, in effect, be transferring resources from the childless households.

Those who oppose such transfers can argue that adults who choose to have children do so knowing the financial and other implications of parenthood. Why, then, should those who are unwilling or unable to have children share in those costs? The answer is that children are, to some extent, a public good and that the entire society has a stake in the potential of the next generation. If Americans do not invest enough in children so that they become healthy, well-educated adults, the country's future is bleak, regardless of progress with other issues.

NOTES

1. This discussion assumes a world of perfect certainty. Inclusion of uncertainty in the analysis makes it more complicated but does not significantly alter the basic concepts.

2. Robert M. Coen and Robert Eisner, "Investment," in John Eatwell, Murray Milgate, and Peter Newman, eds., *The New Palgrave Dictionary of Economics* (London: Macmillan, 1987), p. 981.

3. A. M. Spence, *Market Signaling: Information Transfer in Hiring and Related Processes* (Cambridge, MA: Harvard University Press, 1973).

4. Gary S. Becker, *A Treatise on the Family* (Cambridge, MA: Harvard University Press, 1981).

5. Gary S. Becker and Gregg Lewis, "On the Interaction between the Quantity and Quality of Children," *Journal of Political Economy* 81 (March–April 1973, pt. 2), pp. S279–S288.

6. Mary Lydon, "Accounting for Movements in the Earnings/Education Relationship: 1940–1986" (Unpublished paper, Stanford University, 1989).

7. Phillip Farrell and Victor R. Fuchs, "Schooling and Health: The Cigarette Connection," *Journal of Health Economics* 1 (December 1982), pp. 217–230.

8. Gilbert R. Ghez and Michael Grossman, "Preventive Care, Care for Children, and National Health Insurance" (mimeo) (New York: National Bureau of Economic Research Working Paper No. 417, 1979).

9. Theodore Joyce, Hope Corman, and Michael Grossman, "A Cost Effectiveness Analysis of Strategies to Reduce Infant Mortality," *Medical Care* 26 (No. 4, April 1988), pp. 348–360.

10. Gina Kolata, "Less Prenatal Care Urged for Most Healthy Women," *New York Times*, October 4, 1989, p. A-1.

11. Jane Perlez, "Banks' Job Program Fails to Find Enough Qualified Students," *New York Times*, June 29, 1987, p. B-1; Janice C. Simpson, "A Shallow Labor Pool Spurs Businesses to Act to Bolster Education," *Wall Street Journal*, September 28, 1987, p. 1.

12. Steven L. Gortmacher, William H. Dietz, Jr., Arther M. Sobol, and Cheryl A. Wehler, "Increasing Pediatric Obesity in the United States," *American Journal of Diseases of Children* 141 (May 1987), pp. 535–540.

13. U.S. Department of Commerce, *Statistical Abstract* (Washington, DC: U.S. Government Printing Office, 1989), p. 172 (Data section, well-being of children).

14. Ibid., p. 172 (Data section, well-being of children).

15. Victor R. Fuchs, work in progress, Stanford University.

Part II

Causes:
What Are American
Family Values?

= 5 =
Family Time, Family Values

Mark Mellman, Edward Lazarus,
& Allan Rivlin

In 1989 the Massachusetts Mutual Life Insurance Company commissioned from our firm, Mellman & Lazarus, Inc., a comprehensive investigation of family and family values in America. We sought answers to a number of questions. What do people mean when they talk about family? What are "family values" today and how important are they? What are the threats to the American family? What can be done to strengthen family values in America?

In both focus-group discussions and in a major national survey, we found general agreement with the view, put forward by countless politicians in recent elections, that declining family values are at the heart of our nation's major problems. When asked, "Which of the following do you think best explains the incidence of crime and other social problems in the United States today?" the top two answers were "parents failing to discipline their children" (20%) and "declining family values" (17%). Thus, approximately 37% of respondents located the causes of social problems in the family. The next largest number of respondents (13%) cited "poverty," followed by "the influence of TV and movies" (12%) (see Table 1).

Other major findings included the following:

● Family is the central element in the lives of most Americans.
● There is a high degree of consensus on those values that can properly be called family values: love and emotional support, respect for others, and taking responsibility for actions.

Mark Mellman, Edward Lazarus, and Allan Rivlin are with Mellman and Lazarus, Inc., a Washington, D.C.-based consulting firm whose clients include corporations, public interest organizations, and political candidates. The authors are grateful to Katherine B. Rohrbach and Leonard H. Ellis, Vice Presidents at Fleishman Hillard of New York City, for their contributions to this essay.

TABLE 1: CAUSES OF SOCIAL ILLS

Which of the following do you think best explains the incidence of crime and other social problems in the United States today?

Parents failing to discipline their children 20%
Declining family values 17
Poverty 13
The influence of TV and movies 12
Judges who are too soft or lenient 10
Increased greed and materialism 9
Problems with our educational system 6
Too many government social programs 4

Survey respondents picked lack of family discipline and declining family values as the principal causes of crime and other social problems.

● Opposition to abortion and support for prayer in schools do not rank among the top family values.
● The values Americans call "family values" are the most important values to most Americans.
● Americans see a dramatic decline in others' families but do not report a decline in their own family. In other words, when it comes to families, Americans are saying, "I'm O.K., but you're not."
● Lack of time together is recognized as the greatest threat to the American family.
● Americans say they need help from outside institutions to cope with stresses on the family.
● Americans have little faith that government and other institutions, as they exist today, can help them.

These findings are based on a series of four focus-group discussions in Baltimore, Maryland, and Denver, Colorado, and on a survey of 1,200 respondents.[1] The focus groups were used to explore attitudes toward family values without interviewer preconceptions. The range of opinions expressed in the focus groups were then presented to the survey respondents as options in many of the questions.

THE CENTRALITY OF THE FAMILY

Family is central in the lives of most Americans; it is both the source of our greatest joy and the cause of our greatest worries. When asked what gives them the greatest pleasure, 64% of our sample said family. Another 17% identified family as the second greatest joy. Friends were the next most frequently mentioned. However, only 7% said friends were their greatest source of pleasure; another 23% said friends were their second greatest source of happiness. Furthermore, more than three-quarters (77%) of parents said that their children were "the main satisfaction in my life."

More than half (51%) said providing financial security for themselves and their families was one of two things they worried about most. Another 17% cited declining family values as a major concern. Thus,

---

COMMENTS OF SOME FOCUS-GROUP PARTICIPANTS

"When I think of family, I like to think of things like support and love and guidance."

"One thing about my family and my family's values is that my parents love me no matter what."

"[I think of] an ideal family as being one in which there's love, mutual respect, and communication. I don't care if there's one parent, two parents, etc. If those things are there, that's an ideal family. On the other hand, where the children don't feel love and they don't communicate with each other, that's not a very ideal situation. I think you need to define it in those contexts, not just the physical structure of who and where."

"I have the best memories of my childhood. When I was younger, every night my mom would come in after I was put to bed and she'd kiss me good night and she'd sit there for a couple of minutes and we'd talk a little bit and she would leave. Then my dad would come in and kiss me and we'd talk a little bit and he'd leave. And I used to look forward to their coming into my room for those few minutes. I remember that like it was yesterday. I know my parents love me. I know that. They've said it. And I feel comfortable telling them that, and I think they feel comfortable telling me."

"Self-confidence comes from emotional support, because if you've got someone who's always putting you down, you're going to have this much [very little] self-confidence and you're not going to be worth anything to anybody, but if you get support from the family, that helps."

TABLE 2

How well does each describe your family? (Rank ordered by mean)

Positive Attributes

Caring	3.73
Loving	3.72
Honest	3.63
Provided me with good ethical values	3.57
Can always be counted on to help when needed	3.57
Taught me responsibility	3.56
Taught me respect for authority	3.55
Fun to be with	3.55
Respectful of each other	3.53
Taught me discipline	3.52
Provides emotional support	3.51
Close	3.50
Understanding	3.47
In touch with each other	3.44
Lets me be myself	3.36
Helps me financially when necessary	3.33
Spends time together	3.30
Tolerant	3.26
Doing things together	3.26
Communicates well	3.25
Is a place to get away from the pressures of the outside world	3.22
Has traditions	3.17
Makes decisions democratically	3.14
Religious	2.95
Financially secure	2.93
Financially well-off	2.74

Negative Attributes

Argumentative	2.35
A source of frustration	2.18
A source of guilt	1.80
Meddles too much in my life	1.71

the worries of approximately two of every three Americans revolve around family.

This family-centered perspective permeates every segment of the American public. Although older people are less concerned about financial security for their families than are younger people, their families' financial security is still the single most important concern among older people. Moreover, family was by far their greatest joy. Almost all married people (90%) find their greatest joy in family, but so do 56% of single Americans and 74% of those who are currently divorced.

WHAT DO FAMILIES DO?

In the eyes of our respondents, the family performs two principal functions. First, the family is the base for caring and nurturing. Second, the family is the place where values are taught and learned.

When we asked respondents to tell us how well various words and phrases describe their families, some common denominators quickly emerged. Table 2 displays the average score for a range of phrases and terms. A score of four means that the phrase describes the respondent's family "very well," whereas a score of one means "not at all well." Thus, a score of three suggests that the average response was "pretty well."

People see words like "caring" and "loving" as being most descriptive of their families. Interestingly, respondents are less inclined to believe that their families provide emotional support, are close, or communicate well. Although one might think that these latter items are prerequisites for being caring and loving, the public does not seem to see it that way. It seems that in many families members have the positive feelings but lack the skills to express these feelings to one another. They feel love and concern but do not communicate it well or report actions that are associated with these emotions.

The other primary function of family is teaching family values. More than nine of ten (95%) agree with the proposition that "family is the place where most basic values are instilled" (61% agree strongly). This sense of family is also reflected in respondents' descriptions of their own families. Items such as "provided me with good ethical values" and "taught me responsibility," "respect for authority," and "discipline" tend to be at the top of the chart. Indeed, families seem to be as much about teaching as they are about support and closeness.

Many analysts have focused on the family as a haven from the outside world. Although the public does focus on the emotional bonds that tie families together, they do not see their families as being a refuge from "the pressures of the outside world" in any substantial way.

Respondents' biggest complaint was that their families are "argumentative." But none of the negatively loaded terms were seen as more descriptive of respondents' families than even the least descriptive positive term; that is, people tend to see their families in a positive light.

WHAT ARE FAMILY VALUES?

The term *family values* is often used but rarely explicated. Politicians and pundits of various stripes have attempted to co-opt the term in pursuit of their own agendas. To date, no one has asked the American public what "family values" mean to them. We presented respondents with 28 value statements and asked how well the term "family value" described each one. The value statements were based on responses of the focus group participants. The value items represent a sampling of the things people told us are important personal values to them.

Table 3 displays the average score for various terms. A score of 4 means that "family values" describes this term "very well," whereas a score of 1 means "not at all well." A score of 3 would indicate that the average response was "pretty well." The higher the score, the more that particular value is thought of as a family value.

We found significant agreement among respondents on the values that can be properly called "family values." When Americans talk about family values, they tend to think in terms of the nature and quality of relations with others. Providing emotional support, offering respect—for parents, others, children, and authority—and being responsible for one's actions top the list of family values. Self-oriented values—being free of obligations, being well-educated and cultured, having a rewarding job—and material values are much less likely to be thought of as family values.

Religion falls toward the middle of the list. The items "having faith in God" and "following a strict moral code" received a comparable score to "being married to the same person for life" and "leaving the world to the next generation in better shape than we found it." The number of respondents who felt that these traits defined family values "pretty well" was about equal to those who picked "very well."

Some in the political community have tried to define family values in terms of opposition to abortion and support for school prayer. The public does not accept this construction. These items rank near the bottom of this list.

It is important to note that family values are not just about "family," as narrowly or legalistically defined. "Respecting other people for who they are" is as much a family value as is "respecting one's parents." Similarly, "being responsible for your actions" is more of a family value than is "having good relationships with your extended family."

To push deeper and understand what people have in mind when they respond to these value items, we return to the focus groups for a richer explanation of the values Americans call family values.

Love, Caring, Nurturing, and Emotional Support

In the focus groups, a great deal of discussion revolved around the emotions that exist within a family. Love was given primary importance as the key element in a healthy family. Many of the comments about love and support took the form of fond reminiscences about past family rituals.

TABLE 3

How well does the term "family value" describe each particular value? (Rank ordered by mean)

Being able to provide emotional support to your family	3.67
Respecting one's parents	3.66
Respecting other people for who they are	3.65
Being responsible for your actions	3.64
Being able to communicate your feelings to your family	3.61
Having a happy marriage	3.59
Respecting one's children	3.59
Respecting authority	3.52
Living up to my full potential	3.46
Having faith in God	3.45
Leaving the world to the next generation in better shape than we found it	3.40
Being married to the same person for life	3.39
Following a strict moral code	3.37
Having good relationships with your extended family, including aunts, uncles, and cousins	3.31
Being physically fit	3.30
Being married	3.28
Having a rewarding job	3.28
Having children	3.28
Being well educated and cultured	3.27
Being independent	3.25
Earning a good living	3.23
Being financially secure	3.19
Having leisure time for recreational activities	3.14
Helping your community or neighborhood	3.14
Being in favor of prayer in school	2.92
Having nice things	2.75
Opposing abortion	2.72
Being free of obligations so I can do whatever I want to do	2.33

The view of the focus groups seemed to be that when children grow up in a family in which little love is expressed, they will carry feelings of self-doubt rather than self-worth into adult life.

Respect for Others

The issue of respect was raised continuously throughout the focus groups. Three broad themes emerged. The first is respect for authority. In

---

COMMENTS OF SOME FOCUS-GROUP PARTICIPANTS

"You were taught at home when you were spoken to, you did it. You knew it wasn't asked a second time. And you knew to say "yes sir" and "no sir" or "yes ma'am" and "no ma'am" to your elders. You better not step out of line. It taught us respect. It didn't kill us. In fact, it taught us respect. It taught us that you don't do that next time."

"Many children today are not brought up with respect. Parents used to say, 'This is the way it is and that's the way it's going to be.' Well, I kind of raised my kids that way, and all three of them turned out to be an asset to the community. No dope. They don't even smoke cigarettes. They're great. Just drive into a parking lot today. Watch your car. As soon as somebody pulls in next to you, the door opens and crash. That all goes to respect."

"I think the children should have respect for each other; so often you'll find conflicts between each other, where there should be some way to instill respect for their siblings."

"I think you have to respect your children's opinions sometimes, and not always be right, but you got to give them their chance. Sometimes they're right. Sometimes they're wrong. Just because you're older, don't make you right. People are not listening to their children."

"You respect your children, you want your children to respect you. They have to feel they're someone without having a convertible. That has to be reinforced in the family."

"How you manage your money and how you treat other people, and that sort of thing. You don't walk in others' flowers. You don't hurt their dog. You be nice to each other. Respect is part of a real family."

"We are uniquely individual human beings and because you think certain things are right, doesn't mean that everybody is the same way. I think we have to respect individual differences."

---

this view, young people learn to avoid punishment by showing the proper respect for parents, teachers, their elders, and others with the authority to command respect. In the view of some of the older participants, there is far less of this type of respect today than there was in the past.

The second view is mutual respect, which takes the form of parents respecting their children as much as they expect respect from their children.

The third view is a generalized respect for all other people. In this view, all people are due the sort of respect described in the Golden Rule:

COMMENTS OF SOME FOCUS-GROUP PARTICIPANTS

"Responsibility in a family means you have to think about somebody besides yourself. You've got people waiting for you. You've got people to make money to pay the bills for. Those are family responsibilities that you have."

"I'm the one who's working, and if I don't work, and just take off work with no pay—I've got responsibility both financially and to be there to help her with the kids. My wife and I are equal, but it's on me to make sure I bring home the paycheck."

"Responsibility to me would be a person who has a child, they have to be responsible to bringing that child up. A responsible person is—when you do something, you have to stick to what you're going to do. You make a decision that you're going to try to make it the best way you can."

"I think before, your responsibility was to the family, now it's making the money to pay for everything. They're pushing it more toward money to pay for the house. They worry about the house payments before they worry about the kids."

"It goes both ways too. It's not just parent–child, it's every member of the family. As a part of a family, you've got a responsibility and obligation to each member of that family. My sister and I grew up and we couldn't stand each other. We still can't in a lot of ways. But I know that if my sister ever had a problem, [snap] I would be there like that. If she asked, I'd be there like that."

"Responsibility really has an impact on everybody. Everybody's responsibility has an impact on somebody else. If I don't get up and go to work tomorrow, I know some guy in my squad can't get off because I didn't feel like going to work. It affects everybody."

"Do unto others as you would have them do unto you." Many focus-group participants seemed to believe the second and third views of respect are connected. Teaching either one is the same as teaching both.

Living up to Responsibilities

For many, living up to responsibilities means going to work each day to earn money to support a family. Others cited the responsibility of family members to be there when needed to provide emotional support.

In many ways the discussions of responsibilities mirrored those concerning respect in that several common subthemes emerged: traditional responsibility that flows from authority, mutual responsibility among family members, and generalized responsibility to co-workers and society at large.

An interesting generational difference became clear in Americans' views of respect and responsibility. For older participants, one is exchanged for the other: parents are responsible for providing for their children. In return, their children respect them. Younger participants see more mutuality in both areas; for example, parents give respect to children in order to receive it back from them. Similarly, younger participants spoke of the responsibilities that all family members have toward one another.

FAMILY VALUES ARE AMERICANS' MOST IMPORTANT PERSONAL VALUES

Believing that a particular value is a family value is not the same as considering that value to be personally important. In practice, though, we see a strong correlation. A comparison of Table 3 with Table 4 shows that items defined as family values also tend to be the most important values in people's personal lives.

For this question, a five-point scale was used, in which "one of the most important values" is awarded 5 points, "very important" 4 points, "somewhat important" 3, "not too important" 2, and "not at all important" gets 1 point. Thus a mean score of 4 indicates that, on average, respondents found it to be "very important." The higher the score the more important the value.

People's highest values are family values. From top to bottom, the two lists are quite similar. We see responsibility, respect, and the ability to provide emotional support and communicate emotions within the family at the top of both lists. These are Americans' highest values, and they are the values that Americans tell us they regard as family values. Figure 1 illustrates this point dramatically. Here, values that are thought to be family values are toward the right-hand side. (Values that are not seen to be family values are toward the left.) Values that are the most important are found at the top of the chart. The fact that the points fall close to a line sloping up indicates that the more a value is thought to be a family value, the greater its importance to most Americans.

Another interesting finding emerges from Figure 1. The emotional quality of family relationships is felt to be more important than the formal

TABLE 4	
How important is each of the following values to you? (Rank ordered by mean)	
Being responsible for your actions	4.35
Being able to provide emotional support to your family	4.32
Respecting one's parents	4.32
Respecting other people for who they are	4.30
Having a happy marriage	4.30
Respecting one's children	4.27
Being able to communicate your feelings to your family	4.23
Having faith in God	4.15
Respecting authority	4.13
Leaving the world to the next generation in better shape than we found it	4.12
Living up to my full potential	4.11
Being physically fit	4.02
Being married to the same person for life	4.00
Following a strict moral code	3.99
Being independent	3.97
Having a rewarding job	3.95
Being well educated and cultured	3.94
Earning a good living	3.92
Having good relationships with your extended family, including aunts, uncles, and cousins	3.84
Being financially secure	3.83
Having children	3.81
Helping your community or neighborhood	3.75
Having time for leisure activities	3.73
Being married	3.60
Being in favor of prayer in school	3.39
Having nice things	3.21
Opposing abortion	3.11
Being free of obligations so I can do whatever I want to	2.67

status of those relationships. Psychological criteria, in short, outweigh formal criteria. Having a happy marriage is more highly valued than is being married. Respecting one's children ranks higher than does having children. The inner qualities of relationships are valued more than is the simple existence of the relationships.

This emphasis on psychological gratification as a central—perhaps the central—rationale for the family should be recognized, in historical terms, as a relatively new direction for our culture. Moreover, this trend contains profound and multiple consequences for the family as a social institution. People increasingly believe, to take just one example, that divorce is a better solution for an unhappy marriage than is staying together for the sake of children. On the other hand, it may be true that today's marriages that do not end in divorce are in fact happier than were marriages in earlier eras.

THE POLITICS OF FAMILY VALUES

Ever since the emergence of the conservative "pro-family" movement in the late 1970s, as epitomized by the Moral Majority, the Eagle Forum, and other religious and grass-roots organizations, the debate over family values has been divisive and often confusing. Many people feel that they are being asked to choose between two polarized sets of values, neither of which they fully endorse.

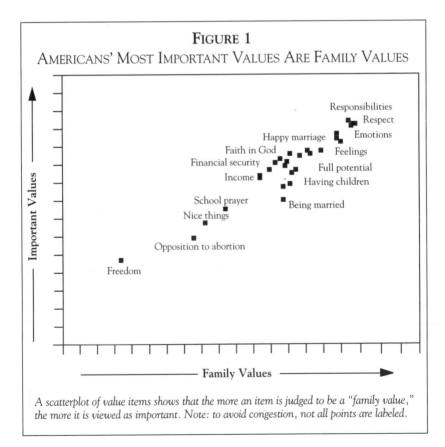

FIGURE 1
AMERICANS' MOST IMPORTANT VALUES ARE FAMILY VALUES

A scatterplot of value items shows that the more an item is judged to be a "family value," the more it is viewed as important. Note: to avoid congestion, not all points are labeled.

The Moral Majority criticized self-centered values, condemning the materialism, sexual freedom, and drug use that they see harming American society and that are featured in television, magazines, and movies. The alternative they proposed emphasizes strong faith in God, opposition to abortion, and support for prayer in the public schools.

Many people are uncomfortable with these choices. Though they reject drug use and other self-centered excesses and feel a strong commitment to their family and often to religious institutions, they are not interested in what was the Moral Majority political agenda. In our poll, the majority believe in family values without accepting the prescriptions of many of today's most outspoken moralists. To understand American family values in the 1990s, therefore, we must leave behind the old polarizations and political symbols of the 1970s and 1980s. We need, in short, a better framework for understanding the choices people make and the issues about which they are concerned.

Toward this end, we sought to elicit people's attitudes toward various values by applying multivariate statistical procedures to the data from the survey. This exercise resulted in a new values "map"—one that we believe to be far richer than the traditional dichotomies of left versus right, conservative versus liberal.

A *Values Map*

The map, displayed in Figure 2, was made with a standard multidimensional scaling routine[2] in two dimensions. All of the results are based on responses to the question: "How *important* are each of the following?"

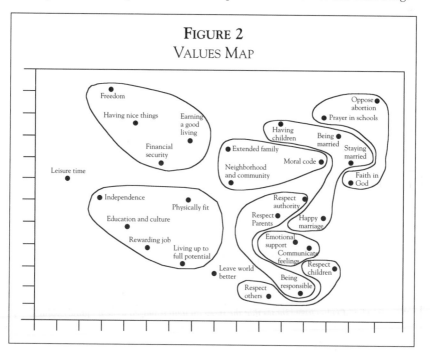

FIGURE 2
VALUES MAP

The map was constructed by a computer program that looks for patterns in the importance different people place on each of the value items. Distances on the map between any two items represent the level of similarity of the items in the minds of the respondents. If two items are close together on the map, like "being married" and "having children," then we know that people who placed a high value on "being married" also placed a high value on "having children." In addition, we know that people who placed a low value on "being married" also placed a low value on "having children."

For two items that are far apart in the map, such as "being married" and "independence," we know that responses to the items tended to go in the opposite direction. If someone said that "independence" was "one of the most important" values to them, they were not likely to place a high value on "being married." Similarly, from the distance in the map we know that people who placed a high value on "being married" probably placed a low value on their "independence."

We added lines that group several of the items together. These groupings are based on a separate statistical routine that clusters items that engendered similar responses.[3] The two procedures use different statistical methods to achieve similar, though not identical, results. Two items that are close in the map may not be in the same cluster. Some rather strange shapes had to be drawn to twist around some items and their labels. (The shape of the clusters has no significance.) The simple explanation for this is that several clusters may occupy the same region of the map. If we were to expand the model to three dimensions instead of two, the model could allow more room for some of the overlapping clusters.

How do we interpret the map? First, we must label the axes (see Figure 3). To the left, or west, we find a series of items that address personal self-interest: "leisure time," "freedom," "independence," "having nice things," "a rewarding job," and "living up to my full potential." On the right, or east, we find other-oriented concerns: "opposing abortion," "staying married," "having faith in God," "respecting one's children," and "being able to communicate feelings within the family." Accordingly, we label the east–west axis "self" and "others."

As described above, many of today's moralists claim the entire east side of the map as their territory and condemn those who find the other values important. However, this is not the whole story.

The significance of the north–south axis becomes clear when we consider some pairs of items. For example, in the north we find "having children"; in the south, "respecting one's children." In the north we see "being married"; in the south, "having a happy marriage." On the "self-oriented" side, in the north we find "earning a good living"; in the south, "having a rewarding job." In all these cases, the northern item describes objective status: one is either married or not, has children or does not. Perhaps to a lesser degree, we can say that the level of one's salary is far more objective than is the level of one's job satisfaction.

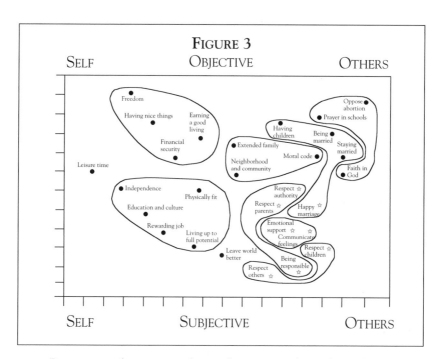

FIGURE 3

By contrast, the items in the south—"a rewarding job," "a happy marriage," and "respecting one's children"—are subjective or psychological goals. The values in the southern part of the map address the quality of life and include words that are more statements of feelings than statements of fact.

Several conclusions emerge from careful study of this map. First, the family cannot be found on the western side of the map. Respondents are clearly indicating that there is a trade-off between personal freedom and family commitments. Those whose primary values are career, leisure time, and material well-being are fundamentally different from those whose primary values are faith in God and emotional closeness in family and children.

But on the east side of the map, we find the family in both the north and south quadrants. In the northeast quadrant, flanked by "a strict moral code," "faith in God," and "prayer in schools," we find "having children," "being married," and "being married to the same person for life" (shortened to "staying married"). Again these are the more objective, descriptive aspects of family. These aspects of family—children and marriage for life—are most closely associated with morality and religion.

In the southeast region of the map we find those who value the family but not the Moral Majority's political positions. Here, the view of family involves mutual respect, emotional sharing, and the quality of family life. These are the items that respondents describe as "family values."

Nationally, the eight items that top the list of values that people call "family values" are all located here in the southeast corner. These are also the values that are most important personally to respondents. At the center we find "being able to provide emotional support to your family," "being able to communicate your feelings to your family," and "having a happy marriage." Arrayed around this emotional center, we find respect and responsibilities, the key concepts that were thought to be most important by the focus-group respondents. Here, we find "respect for others," "respect for one's parents," "respect for one's children," "respect for authority," and "living up to one's responsibilities." This constellation of eight stars represents the ideal family—the norms of family life—for which the majority of Americans are searching.

IMPROVING FAMILY LIFE: TIME IS THE KEY

Americans do perceive threats to the family. The most important threat is lack of time. In particular, American families suffer from a lack of time together as a family. In the focus-group research, we heard a consistent story. In recent years, the number of single-parent families and two-career families has increased dramatically. These changes mean that people, especially parents, have less time for family. The survey results support this assertion.

The deeply felt need for more family time is clearly evident in Table 5, in which most respondents favor "spending more time with family" as the most effective way to strengthen family values. Eighty-six percent agree with the view that "families seem to spend less time together than they did 30 years ago"; 52% agree strongly.

Respondents indicated that during a normal week they spend an average of 47% of their waking time with their families. Not surprisingly, there are important demographic differences. Men spend an average of 41% of their waking time with family compared with 53% for women. Among women younger than 45, the average is 55%, whereas among men younger than 45, it is only 38%.

Married persons spend an average of 53% of their waking hours with family compared with 35% for singles and 36% for divorced persons. The time pressure on single-parent families is particularly evident from the fact that married couples with children spend an average of 52% of their time with family compared with 41% for single parents. That difference is exaggerated further when one recognizes that with two-parent families, the percentage represents 52% of two individuals' time compared with 41% of a single parent's time.

Americans clearly feel this time pressure. Forty-six percent of our respondents state they do not spend enough time with their families. Forty-seven percent believe they spend the right amount of time with family, and 5% say they spend too much time with their families.

The amount of time one spends with the family is related to personal satisfaction with family. Those who are satisfied with their family life spend an average of 50% of their waking time with family. Those who are dissatisfied spend only 39% of their time with family. More to the point, 32% of those who say they spend the right amount of time with family are "extremely" satisfied with their family lives compared with only 18% of those who feel they spend too little time with family. Americans see the need for more family time not only within their own families, but also in families generally. When asked to identify the most important reason for the decline in family values, the largest number (35%) selected "parents having less time to spend with their families." (The reason selected next most frequently was lack of discipline, at 22%.)

The reported family-time shortage is related, people believe, to economics. Nearly eight in ten believe that "it is getting to be impossible to support a family on just one income." More than half (52%) agree strongly with this statement.

Today, the average working wife contributes 28% of her family's income. Wives who work full time fill 40% of the family purse. The median income for families with married partners and a working wife is 50% higher than that for families with married partners in which the wife does not work.

Approximately half (46%) of respondents say that employed married mothers are working "because their families need the money to afford basic necessities." Another third (36%) say married women with children work "to enable their families to afford some of the nicer things in life." Approximately 15% take the view that these women work "because they find it personally satisfying."

TABLE 5: EFFECTIVENESS IN STRENGTHENING FAMILY VALUES (% EXTREMELY)

Spending more time with family	54%
Providing better role models on TV and in movies	32%
Teaching family values in church and synagogue	30%
Full-time parent raising kids	28%
Teaching family values in school	23%
Improving financial situation of families	21%
Allowing more flexible work schedules	18%
Providing day care	18%
Teaching kids about their ancestors and family tree	18%
Full-time relative raising kids	15%
Living closer to other family members	13%
Allowing workers to do more at home	10%

A MAN IN DENVER EXPRESSED A COMMON THEME OF ALL FOUR GROUPS:

"I think the thing that affects family values, currently, is the fact that there are no more full-time parents any more. The economy is forcing more two-income families, there is a lot more single parents, a 50% divorce rate. You're going to have a lot of kids that aren't getting any parental guidance. They're getting all their guidance from a video game or TV."

LIKE MANY OTHERS, A MAN IN THE BALTIMORE GROUP BELIEVES THERE HAS BEEN A CHANGE IN VALUES:

"I think before, your responsibility was to the family, now it's making the money to pay for everything. [People] worry about the house payments before they worry about the kids."

In sum, a majority of Americans believe that economic pressures cause more family members to work harder. This pressure has taken time away from the family, which in turn has caused a decline in the quality of family life, a weakening of family values, and a diminution of satisfaction with one's own family.

On the other hand, few of our respondents indicated that they would refuse a job that offered more money and/or more prestige but entailed less time with the family. All of our respondents were asked to imagine that they were 38 years old and had just been offered a new job in a field they enjoyed. The downside is that "the new job would require you to work more hours and therefore keep you away from your family more often." Three different "upside" scenarios were given, each one to a random third of our total sample. One group was told simply that the new job was "more prestigious than the one you hold now." Another third of the sample were told the job was more prestigious and would result in a 15% raise. The last group was told that the job was more prestigious and carried a 35% salary increase. All respondents were then asked whether they would take the new job.

Among all three groups, nearly two-thirds said they would be at least somewhat likely to take the new job. Overall, 63% said they would be likely to take the job. Only about a third said they would be unlikely to take it. Even among those who would get no raise, approximately 65% said they would be likely to take the job, whereas approximately 35% said they would be unlikely to take it. Thirty-eight percent said they would be very likely to take the new job, but not one person reported she or he would be very unlikely to accept it. Respondents with high incomes were a bit more likely to take the job. These results suggest an apparent conflict between stated values and actual behavior—between generalized ideals and real-life decisions—and illustrate the financial pressure that seems to play such an important role in contemporary American families.

OTHER WAYS TO IMPROVE FAMILY VALUES

Although a majority of Americans do not place primary blame for family problems on the media, the data point to an undercurrent of dissatisfaction with the images presented in the movies and on television. When asked to cite the major causes of crime and other social problems, a small but significant minority (12%) chose "the influence of television and movies." This was the fourth most popular response to the question presented. These data are presented in Table 1. Nearly a third believed that "providing better role models on television and in the movies" would be an "extremely effective way to strengthen family values." Women seem more convinced than men of the value of better role models, with 39% of women as opposed to 26% of men choosing "extremely effective." Similarly, blacks seem particularly conscious of the importance of role models, with 46% of this group choosing "extremely effective."

Educating people about family values, particularly through religious institutions, is also seen as valuable. Those who are most satisfied with their own family lives are particular partisans of this approach.

When asked to identify the major reason for the weakening of family values, the second highest number (22%) said, "parents are not disciplining their children enough." (The most frequent response was not enough time with families.) Moreover, an overwhelming 84% agreed that "parents today are too lenient and permissive with their children." Nearly half (47%) agreed strongly, whereas only 13% expressed any level of disagreement.

CONCLUSIONS

We live in a family-centered society. At a personal level, family is the source of Americans' greatest joys and most significant worries. At a societal level, Americans locate the root causes of our most pressing social problems in the family. The family is the base for caring and nuturing. It is also the place where values are taught and learned. Disrupting either of these functions can produce individuals and societies with serious pathologies.

There is a high degree of consensus as to which values can properly be called "family values." These center on love and emotional support, respect for others, and taking responsibility for one's actions. The same values that Americans call "family values" are also the values that the public holds most dear.

An analysis of Americans' underlying value preferences reveals two central fault lines. The first is self versus others; the second is objective status versus psychological feelings. Most Americans profess values that are other-oriented and concerned with subjective feelings.

To perform family functions, families must have time together. A lack of time is seen as the core threat to American families. Finding ways for families to spend more time together is a central challenge to preserving the family and strengthening family values in our society.

NOTES

1. Interviews were conducted between June 20 and 27, 1989. Respondents were chosen by means of random-digit dialing techniques, such that each telephone household in the nation had an equal probability of being called. The margin of error for the sample as a whole is less than plus or minus 3.5%; however, the margin of error for subgroups is larger.

2. The scaling routine was Kruskal's stress formula 1 in two dimensions, on a Pearson correlation matrix.

3. The clustering procedure was hierarchical clustering of stimuli, based on a matrix of Pearson correlations, with "centroid" linkage.

=6=
The Family in Transition
Dennis K. Orthner

E veryone agrees that the American family is changing. Divorce rates are rising, women are entering the labor force in record numbers, children are more likely to be left unattended or in group day-care arrangements, nonmarital cohabitation is increasingly common, and the number of single persons in the population is rising. All of these trends are quite familiar to the public.

But there has been less agreement on the meaning of these changes. Is the family system in America falling apart or reorganizing? Are we seeing institutional decline or change? Are families losing their ability to foster healthy individuals or are they gaining the freedom to customize their patterns? Are family values no longer important or have new beliefs and values begun to replace outdated ones? If it is possible to do so, we must find policies that will: (1) mitigate the negative impacts of change and (2) foster emerging family patterns and values that help the family adapt to contemporary cultural drifts.

The fundamental question is not how to stop family changes from occurring, but rather how to shape family change in a direction that minimizes the disruptions of these changes on potentially vulnerable groups, such as children and the poor, and maximizes the effectiveness of other organizations in society, such as businesses and community services.

I believe that the family changes now occurring are connected to, and perhaps rooted in, fundamental shifts in norms and values in American society. Much of the current discussion of the family focuses on changes in family structures and functions. However, these are but behavioral manifestations of what is occurring in the soul of our society. The

Dennis K. Orthner is a sociologist and Professor in the School of Social Work at the University of North Carolina at Chapel Hill, where he is also Director of the Human Services Research Laboratory.

beliefs that used to form the basis for relational stability are being reexamined. No longer are people clear about what is expected of them. The sanctions that used to place boundaries around inappropriate behaviors have been crumbling. We can no longer easily define the required duties and obligations associated with such critical roles as husband, wife, mother, father, grandparent, or neighbor.

Too much attention has been focused on the structural properties of families. Not enough attention is being paid to the underlying processes of families, including their ability to handle new stresses, reach out for assistance, adopt new roles, alter patterns of courtship and sexuality, and satisfactorily adapt to the changes that are occurring in other systems outside themselves.

True, it is easier to count the number of divorces or to determine whether a mother is employed or not, but these structural characteristics by themselves are weak predictors of the consequences that most of us really care about: personal and family well-being, economic mobility, educational attainment, children's health, and antisocial behavior.[1]

Norms of family behaviors—and the values that underlie those behaviors—are in transition. The result: unstable and widely varying interpretations of appropriate and inappropriate behavior. During major transitions such as these, any organization (e.g., family, corporation, or government) will find it difficult to establish firm rules for organizational formation, maintenance, and dissolution. The family system is not alone in this struggle: we can see similar organizational stresses and redefinitions being deliberated in businesses,[2] in schools,[3] in governments,[4] and in communities.[5] Nearly all social systems are currently renegotiating their fundamental bases for order. The oft-noted "crisis" of reorganization is much broader than the family, but it is within the family that we can see both the seeds for new organizational patterns and the high costs of failing to achieve a new level of stability.

CHANGING FAMILY VALUES AND BELIEFS

The beliefs and values that undergird any social organization help chart the course for the behavior of system members. The family system is no exception. These rules of behavior can and do vary among societies and also among subgroups within a society. Thus, it is not surprising that the values and expressed beliefs regarding premarital sexuality, for example, can be quite different in Sweden, China, and the United States. Likewise, subcultures within the United States may also vary in this respect.

Cultural values have changed significantly over the past century. In his discourse on "New Rules," Daniel Yankelovich refers to the "giant plates of the culture" that have been shifting dramatically over this century.[6] Like the geological theory of plate tectonics, these cultural plates sometimes shift position, grind against each other, and promote instabilities in basic values and beliefs—creating, in short, the cultural equivalent of an earthquake. According to Yankelovich,

> we now need a new social ethic. Without one we are disoriented, lacking a firm basis for choice. We need new rules to define the epochal tasks that must be accomplished in our era to bring about that minimal harmony between individual and society that is the mark of a successful civilization.[7]

Many of the core values that have been changing are related to the family, including the high priority given to independence instead of marriage, to individual freedom over collective interests, to personal pleasure instead of nurturance, and to instrumental commitments instead of intrinsic commitments.

The Value of Marriage vs. Independence

Those who speculate that the family system is declining claim that marriage as an ideal is less important today. They suggest that positive values associated with voluntary singleness have become more common, making marriage more of a choice than a necessity among those who traditionally have been in the marriage market. If this is true, marriage as a valued institution is indeed in trouble and other forms of nonmarital living arrangements may replace marriage in the future.

Evidence to support this thesis comes from several sources, including the increased proportion of unmarried persons in the population and the rising number of nonmarital cohabitants. Clearly, the decision not to marry is no longer considered a disgrace, and delaying marriage is less likely to foster predictions of spinsterhood. More adults in America today (33%) are ambivalent about whether it is better to be married than single for life, and a minority (16%) even disagree with that assumption.[8] Likewise, the acceptance of nonmarital cohabitation is growing, with 33% of adults considering these relationships "O.K." in 1989 compared with 22% in 1986.[9]

But this concern can be overblown. A consistent 96% of the American public during the past 30 years has expressed a personal desire for marriage.[10] Only 8% of adult women consider remaining single an ideal; this has not changed in the past two decades.[11] More than 80% of the high school classes of 1972 and 1980 said it was "very important" to marry and have a happy family life, and these beliefs increased after graduation.[12] Surveys of college freshman have also remained consistent: 70% of those surveyed in 1970 and 1985 expressed a strong desire to rear a family.[13]

These statistics suggest a greater tolerance for independent living but a stable personal preference for marriage. Although the percentage of adults who are single and cohabiting has increased, this appears to be the result of marriage delays and the increased use of cohabitation as a testing phase in courtship. The overall marriage rate may have declined from the 95% pinnacle of the 1970s to an 85% to 90% rate, but this percentage is still high by world standards. Somewhat more traditional societies than our own, such as Ireland and Australia, have considerably lower marriage rates,[14] but they are not usually considered in "decline." If anything, the value of marriage as a preferable living arrangement appears to be holding its own during this time of institutional transition.

Individualism vs. Collectivism

A second concern is that individualism has become so strong in America that interest in the collectivities of family and community has declined. Robert Bellah and his colleagues note that "individualism lies at the very core of American culture. . . . We believe in the dignity, indeed the sacredness, of the individual. . . . Our highest and noblest aspirations, not only for ourselves, but for those we care about, for our society and for the world, are closely linked to our individualism."[15] David Popenoe worries, however, that "cultural trends associated with the growing importance placed on 'self-fulfillment' . . . could be regarded as another important contributor to the high family-dissolution rate."[16]

Historians generally regard American society as being highly individualistic over its entire course. Early observers of American community and family patterns frequently commented on the strength of individualistic ethics, not just on the frontier, but in cities as well.[17] Carl Solberg stated, "The oldest dilemma that has afflicted American society from its founding in the New World has been the ceaseless conflict between its often unbridled individualism and its fitful and inadequate sense of community."[18] Indeed, American communities have never been characterized by the sense of what the German sociologist Toennies[19] called *Gemeinschaft*, a collective sense of primary relationships that dominates all aspects of community and kin life.

If individualism has been such a dominant feature of American life, how has it manifested itself in the family? One way is through what has been called the development of "modified extended families."[20] Without a strong tradition of extended-family households in America,[21] we created from the very beginning a pattern of relatively independent households with quite strong helping networks across kin and friend lines. If these helping networks have been eroding, then we can assume that individualism has indeed triumphed over collective interests, at least in the family arena.

Studies conducted during the 1950s[22] found a strong sense of obligation among family members to help other family members. This finding surprised some researchers, because they too had come to believe that familism had declined in favor of individualism.[23] These researchers discovered frequent visitations between families, financial help being given to younger and older families, help with child care and other household tasks, and frequent exchanges of advice. In fact, though most people admitted that they preferred to prove their independence by not always seeking help, few were reluctant to accept help when it was offered.[24]

The situation today is not that different. Visits among relatives, especially with parents, have not declined significantly since the 1950s.[25] More than half (53%) of adults with living parents see them at least once a month, and a similar percentage (51%) agree that aging parents should live with their adult children. Among the sample of families participating in the National Survey of Families and Households,[26] the majority (55%) believe that they can call on their relatives in the middle of the night if they have an emergency, and two out of three (66%) say they can borrow $200 from a relative in an emergency.

This is not a gloomy picture of rampant individualism. Rather, it suggests that collective interests remain strong in American families, even within the context of a culture that promotes individual interests. There is little evidence that Americans are giving up on familism.

Commitment vs. Autonomy

Autonomy is often prized because it reflects a level of competence typically associated with adulthood and maturity. Although commitments imply reciprocal obligations, autonomy promises the freedom to enter and leave obligations based solely on self-defined interests. Peter McDonald explains,

> The dilemma faced by families today is the same dilemma that occupied the minds of the Enlightenment philosophers: the reconciliation of the goal of personal autonomy with the conviction that man is irreducibly social. . . . In a heavily structured society, roles are prescribed and the individual has little scope for self-direction. The Enlightenment was a reaction to such structure, and for the past 250 years we have been following a topsy-turvy path towards the goal of individual autonomy.[27]

From a developmental vantage point, childhood has been described in a similar fashion. Many of the developmental activities of children are associated with increased autonomy,[28] culminating in adolescence and young adulthood when this freedom reaches its apex. After that, adults once again seek a balance between the security of attachments and the freedom to pursue individual interests.[29] Indeed, the level of maturity of adults is often defined not by their ability to pursue personal gain, but by their ability to sacrifice individual interests in favor of commitments to others.

One commonly used framework in family theory and family therapy is built on the assumption of balance between autonomy and commitments. In their "circumplex" model of family behavior, David H. Olson and his colleagues[30] assume that extremes in either family-member autonomy (disengagement) or cohesion (enmeshment) have negative consequences. Their research suggests that families whose members have balanced interests in separateness and togetherness are the most likely to report being satisfied and the most likely to stay married.

The inability of many couples to sustain lifelong commitments is often taken as evidence that family commitments are not as strong today as they once were. Furthermore, a large proportion of youth and adults worry that this trend will continue. In a recent survey, only 39% of those polled believed that people who get married today expect the marriage to last forever.[31] Nevertheless, it is difficult to sort out this general sense of pessimism from a personal sense of optimism about their own relationships. The vast majority of adults (71%) believe that "marriage is a lifelong commitment that should not be ended except under extreme circumstances."[32] Even more Americans (85%) say they would remarry their spouses if they had to do it all over again.[33] Even the divorced and separated hold positive ambitions: most people who can do so will remarry and 81% still believe that marriage is a commitment for life.

These statistics do not indicate that Americans are running away from marriage and commitment. Instead, they indicate an underlying search for meaningful commitments and a healthy fear of the negative consequences if these do not last. Perhaps social scientists have been all too successful in pronouncing the decline in commitments: the fear of marital failure has continued to rise through the 1980s even though divorce rates have stabilized, even declined, in the past decade and a half.

Social scientists have not been as successful in marketing (to others or themselves) the understanding that commitment is a process, not a stable product. Social psychological research tells us that a commitment is inherently unstable, "something that grows and changes over time."[34] Long-term commitments are more uncommon than common, and commitments have rarely been for life, unless external constraints made no other option available. For example, divorce may have been uncommon in the 19th century, but marital desertion was a serious problem.

Unfortunately, we know much less about the processes of commitment than we do about the consequences of its absence. We understand its instrumental aspects much better than its intrinsic aspects, based on weighing expected costs and rewards. It is true that the balance between autonomy and commitment in American society continues to shift. But the shift is not away from commitments, as some have alleged, but rather toward different types of commitment—those that provide mutual and balanced gratifications for all family members.

Nurturance vs. Narcissism

Have Americans lapsed into a narcissistic binge, retaining little concern for anyone other than themselves? This fear reached epidemic proportions in the 1970s and early 1980s as an increasingly vocal humanistic-psychology movement placed considerable emphasis on the reification of the self.[35] The search for intimacy, a basic human need, was pushed into new frontiers. This search was directed toward personal awareness and away from lasting relationships.[36] A cultural drift toward narcissism was announced by many observers.[37]

Have we lost any of our capacity to nurture other adults or children? Has the basic social value of supporting others been eroded? This question is crucial; indeed, if the modern family has shifted its primary functions away from meeting instrumental needs toward meeting expressive needs, then its ability to provide nurturance for its members has become the mainstay of its existence.

One fundamental maxim is not debated: the human psychological need for nurturance is innate. Unlike lower animals, humans are born with the need to be dependent and with few, if any, instincts to guide their development. The earliest dependent relationships formed by humans are based on the physiological processes, including feeding and body comfort. These forces transform themselves in adulthood, but the needs for nurturance remain. The basic psychological need for interdependence is considered fundamental to personal well-being and is equally strong in both women and men.[38] As Ashley Montague once observed, "It is probable that sexual activity, indeed the frantic preoccupation with sex that characterizes Western culture, is in many cases not the expression of sexual interest at all, but rather a search for the satisfaction of the need for contact."[39]

The evidence that modern men and women are no longer interested in nurturing others but only themselves is scanty. The data supporting this claim are largely impressionistic and qualitative. Expressed desires for intimate relationships have not decreased. Nor have persons who have left unsatisfactory relationships turned against the search for intimacy with others. Summarizing the results of their landmark study of divorced men and women, Mavis Hetherington, Martha Cox, and Roger Cox state:

> The divorced individuals wanted sustained, meaningful relationships and were not satisfied with a series of superficial encounters. The formation of lasting intimate relations, involving deep concern and a willingness to make sacrifices for the partner, as well as a strong attachment and desire to be near the person, was a strong factor in happiness, self-esteem, and feelings of competence in sexual relations for both divorced men and women.[40]

But what about the children? If the nurturance needs of adults are largely being met, are the needs of children being sacrificed? If public perceptions are any guide, it would appear that they are. Nearly three out of four adults (74%) believe that the problems affecting children are worse than problems they had when they were young. This is especially true for women (79%) and blacks (84%). On this issue, the perceptions of parents and nonparents are similar. Much of the blame for the problems of children is laid on parents; only 53% of adults believe that most children have loving parents. As for the larger society, 63% think that too little effort has been directed toward the problems of children.[41]

Studies of children themselves present a much more mixed picture. Some indicators have improved over the past few decades, especially children's physical health, but others have declined over this period, especially social misconduct and suicide. Still others have both risen and fallen, especially indicators of economic well-being and academic achievement; others yet have remained the same, notably measures of psychological well-being.[42]

On balance, the lives and circumstances of children have not declined to the extent that the public perceives. But there is little question that most adults feel collectively guilty about their lack of attention to the nurturance needs of children. Yet, when parents were asked if they wished they could be free from the responsibilities of child rearing, only 8% agreed and 71% disagreed.[43] This is not the picture of parental and societal neglect that some would like to paint, but it does suggest that more attention must be focused on the needs of children.

Overall, the data suggest that needs for adult and child nurturance remain strong in our society. The issues being raised over the rearing and nurturance of children reflect an undercurrent of concern that is now being transformed into more support services for parents and their children. The increased emphasis on narcissism and selfishness that has been suggested by some does not appear to be a strong cultural value at this time, although it may reflect heightened opportunities for personal freedom during adolescence and young adulthood.

Values Revolution vs. Evolution

The values revolution, which has been discussed extensively in the media, is a bust. This is not to say that changes have not occurred. But most of these changes can be described as extensions of cultural drifts that have been occurring for decades, even centuries. Like the imagery of change in Yankelovich's "giant plates of culture,"[44] this so-called values revolution has not been a revolution at all, but rather a slow and grinding process. Call it values evolution.

Contrary to the general assumption that American culture in the past several decades has tilted toward individualism and autonomy and away from marriage and nurturance, the data suggest that few changes have occurred in the basic tenets of family organization. There has been too much comparison of today with the 1950s, which was only a brief period when considered in the context of the broad historical march examined in this essay.

At the same time, the cultural drift toward increased autonomy and less understanding of the nurturant needs of children may have gone too far. Recent surveys suggest that the American public wants to see renewed attention to fostering commitments and caring for children, both within the family and in public and private institutions. This public concern is echoed by a growing number of commentators who believe that we need to chart a new course. Nevertheless, the route of this new course must be bounded by the values that have been evolving in America since its inception.

CHANGING FAMILY NORMS

Although basic family *values* have not changed dramatically, the *norms* of family behavior have, in fact, undergone dramatic transformations. Family norms, as I define them here, refer to the behavioral expectations associated with the statuses and roles of family members. Whereas values are attached to beliefs, norms are attached to and directly guide behavior. (Also, behavioral changes can change norms.) Thus, norms guide our actions; they serve as cues to appropriate and inappropriate behavior.

Many contemporary family problems are not tied to value transitions at all. Instead, they represent norm transitions. To a large extent, family processes today are confused by conflicting, incongruent, and absent family norms. The rules of family behavior have changed so dramatically in some areas that many men, women, and children do not know how to respond to one another's expectations. With so many alternative cues to guide behavior, confusion is more the rule than the exception in intimate relationships.

Joan Aldous refers to this confusion as a period in which *role making* is dominating the process of *role taking*.[45] During an earlier era, family roles were firmly defined. Expectations for the socialization of children were clear, as were the qualities one looked for in a mate. Most women and men simply adopted the roles of their parents and got the cues for their behavior from relatively well-defined norms. This is not the case today. Although traditional roles remain the norm in some subsets of society, most men and women are unsure of others' expectations of them and of their own expectations of themselves.

This ambiguity in norms leads to confusion and stress in many families. Several studies have found that couples with congruent role expectations are much more likely to be satisfied and stable in their marriages than are couples with incongruent expectations.[46] Other studies show that congruency between norms and behaviors have important psychological consequences. For example, a study of depression in married women found that the least depressed women were those who were employed and preferred to be as well as those who were not employed and preferred not to be. The wives who were employed, but not by choice, were significantly more depressed; the most depressed were those who were not employed but who wanted to be.[47]

Another normative change is the shift away from ascribed family roles toward achieved family roles. Family roles—mother, father, son, daughter—are no longer defined by larger societal norms. Instead, each role is customized; it is defined within the context of the particular family system. My role as a father, for example, is defined more by the expectations my wife and children have of me than by society's notion of what a father should do for his family. Although this gives me more freedom to develop a father role that is rewarding and personally enjoyable, it also increases the level of anxiety associated with the role because my success as a father is contingent upon ongoing and everchanging reinforcements.

Relational Formation Norms

The norms that guide dating, courtship, and mate selection have also changed dramatically and quickly. Major differences exist between children and their parents concerning the behaviors that are expected to dominate adolescence and young adulthood. Dating has been replaced by "going out" and by group events that do not follow the rules that were traditionally associated with dating in the 1950s and 1960s.

Sexual norms have also changed. Although the proportion of adolescents engaging in sexual intercourse has increased somewhat, the changes in the norms associated with this behavior are even more revolutionary. The proportion of adults who believed in total sexual abstinence before marriage dropped from 80% to only 30% between 1963 and 1975.[48] Among adults who responded to the national General Social Surveys, in 1969, 68% believed that premarital sex was wrong, compared with only 39% in 1985. This trend became somewhat more conservative between 1985 and 1987, when 46% reported that they believed premarital sex was wrong. The adults in the latter year were split on the issue: 46% said it was wrong and 48% said it was O.K.[49]

Norms linking pregnancy and marriage have also changed. In the 1960s, youth who became pregnant were expected to get married prior to childbirth. More than one-half of them did. In contrast, by the 1980s more children were being conceived outside of marriage, but less than one-third of these conceptions resulted in the mother's being married by the time of the birth.[50]

Even marital norms have undergone significant transformations. Marriage has become less associated with the confirmation of commitment between partners, and nonmarital cohabitation has become so common that some observers now consider it a stage in the family life cycle—more a choice than a deviation from normal patterns. A 1989 survey found that 31% of American adults consider living together before marriage to be "O.K.," whereas 37% consider it "always wrong." However, age is a major factor in these attitudes. Among those younger than 30, 43% consider living together an acceptable arrangement; only 11% of those older than 60 agree with this position.[51]

These changes suggest a high level of confusion concerning courtship and sexual norms, leaving many avenues for interpretation open to those who are developing relationships or observing these relationships. Without adequate societal guidelines, deviations and confusion concerning what is considered to be acceptable behavior are likely to be considerable.

Relational Maintenance Norms

The ambiguity of relational norms is also reflected in marriage and other adult relationships. These expectations are so confusing that most social scientists have given up on attempting to describe the traditional family life cycle. Researchers who studied a large longitudinal sample of adults (Panel Study of Income Dynamics) were forced to abandon the traditional family-development approach of tracking families over time. They relinquished this strategy because "there were no consistent or acceptable definitions of what constitutes the same family over time."[52]

Today, only a minority of families follows what was once the traditional pattern of getting married, having children, mothers staying at home with the children, children leaving home, and the couple living to old age and death together. Glen Elder cautions that predictable developments in the family are rare because our conception of development is tied to the "reproductive process . . . and is applicable . . . to a restrictive segment of the population that follows the script of a marriage which endures to old age and produces at least one child; variations in family form are excluded."[53]

Nowhere is the ambiguity in family norms more apparent than in the emerging roles of mothers and fathers. The overwhelming majority of adults (78%) believe that couples should have children in order for their marriage to be happy.[54] But parenthood has not only become more voluntary, the role expectations of parents themselves are much less clear. Women, in particular, are less sure about how to incorporate parenting, marriage, and employment into their lives.

Data from recent surveys indicate considerable disagreement over emerging norms affecting the personal and family roles of American women. Only one out of four adults (23%) approves of mothers with preschool children working full time and nearly half (46%) believe that a preschool child will suffer if the mother is employed.[55] These attitudes are in sharp contrast to the reality that more than half of all mothers with preschool children are now in the labor force. Furthermore, 70% of the women under age 30 say they want a family and a career,[56] up from 52% who felt that way in 1964.[57]

Men too are experiencing pressure to change their roles and to accommodate new norms of work, fathering, and being a husband. Men are no longer encouraged to be absent from the home. However, norms for new fathering and homemaking roles are not yet well entrenched.[58] On the one hand, more than one-half of American men (54%) say that the most satisfying accomplishment for a man today is being a father,[59] a situation that has resulted in a noticeable shift toward fathers participating more in children's activities. On the other hand, Frank Furstenburg[60] refers to the development of a "good-dad, bad-dad complex," in which fathers now feel more free to be involved with their children but they also feel more free to leave an unhappy home situation.

Relational Dissolution Norms

As a result of the divorce rate rising for the past several decades and remaining stable at a comparatively high level since the mid-1970s, norms and expectations surrounding divorce also remain relatively unclear. Nearly all couples hope that they will stay married to the same partner. But the acceptance of divorce as an alternative to marital unhappiness has certainly increased. Variations in expectations regarding divorce, however, were expressed by couples participating in the National Survey of Families and Households.[61] When asked whether they approved of unhappy couples divorcing when their youngest child is under five years of age, a portion of the sample was equally divided between those who approved (33%) and those who disapproved of divorce in this situation (33%); the others had mixed feelings. Although we have no trend data on this question, it is very likely that the public tolerance of divorce has increased as the divorce rate has risen.

Frank Furstenberg and Graham Spanier contend that we are experiencing a paradigm shift in family norms in which "conjugal succession" is increasingly being accepted, although not preferred: "Divorce has become so commonplace that it represents, for much of the population, an optional stage in an increasingly variable conjugal career."[62] This paradigm shift, according to Bernard Farber, is largely the result of changes in family status and the lack of clear-cut norms associated with family status. He believes that "the ambiguity of status removes the labels or tags by which stability can be attained. . . . Loss of the distinctive hierarchical character of family and marital statuses increases the vulnerability of the family—and, by extension, all of society—to situational demands for change."[63]

Because most divorced persons remarry, the ambiguity in family norms is carried into new relationships. Even though they are much more common, stepfamily patterns are not yet well defined. Cynthia Fuchs Epstein observes that "new step family ties are not institutionalized and there are no established norms regarding 'proper' behavior in them."[64] Thus each new blended family has to make up its own rules, creating a situation in which all the parties must customize family norms based on uniquely derived rules, as opposed to adopting well-defined social rules. Given this situation, it is little wonder that stepfamily relationships are often strained and that second marriages experience even higher divorce rates than do first marriages.

The Revolution in Family Norms

We are now confronted by a veritable revolution in family norms. While the dominant values undergirding the family have been slowly shifting, norms of family behavior have moved more quickly to take advantage of the freedoms permitted by greater independence and autonomy. The family system that had once been called "the haven" and "respite" from the changes occurring in other organizations, notably business and government, is now even more vulnerable to the status and role confusion in the larger society.

These normative issues have become the new battleground in public debate. What is considered "pro-family" can be interpreted as ultraliberal, ultraconservative, or somewhere in between. Though some family advocates argue about family "values," the real debate generally focuses on norms and expectations of family members, most often parents. Answers to James A. Levine's plaintive question *Who Will Raise the Children?*[65] are not framed in terms of whether children should be taken care of. We all agree that they should. What we disagree about is whether this responsibility, which fairly recently was solely the responsibility of mothers, should now be shared more by fathers and other caregivers. I do not believe that the value associated with children has been diminished that much. What has changed are the expectations regarding the responsibilities for their nurturance.

The norms guiding marriage are increasingly similar to the norms affecting other intimate relationships. John Scanzoni[66] refers to a new family paradigm emerging around norms that include what he calls "sexually bonded close relationships." Among couples without children, he finds the normative patterns of men and women to be very similar and the processes of relational development, maintenance, and disillusion increasingly indistinguishable. Robert Weiss observes that

> marriage is increasingly becoming like co-habitation. The woman may wear a wedding ring, but her name and, of course, her job will be unaffected. . . . For the woman who is a professional or executive, or on her way to becoming one of these, it is no longer possible to use the survey research rule that the social status of a married woman is that of her husband.[67]

As a society we are moving toward relational norms that do not prescribe clear-cut expectations, but in which more latitude for normative flexibility is permitted childless couples, whether married or not. When a third party enters the picture, namely children, some of this flexibility is lost. Many members of our society are still trying to determine how the major indicator of relational transformation, which used to take place with marriage, can now be parenthood. Perhaps the greater attention now being given to child-custody arrangements instead of divorce is evidence of growing societal control over some of the freedom men and women have acquired, especially in the area of parental norms and responsibilities.

AN INTERPRETATION OF FAMILY CHANGE

The fundamental social processes of the family are currently unstable. When these normative changes are coupled with the structural changes occurring in the family and society, we are left with an overall picture of confusion that can be very distressing.

I believe that no clear-cut positive or negative interpretation can be drawn from current trends. It is possible to look at the direction of these changes positively, if one believes that new family patterns are necessary for the new societal conditions within which families find themselves. On the other hand, the disabling aspects of current changes are creating negative outcomes for some groups in our society. If one takes a short-range view, it is easy to be pessimistic.

Clearly, the pessimists are all around us today. In fact, the situation is not that different from the one Clark Vincent described two decades ago:

> Since the earliest writings available, changes occuring in the institution of the family have been used and interpreted to support either an optimistic or pessimistic premise concerning social change, and the pessimists have consistently outnumbered the optimists.[68]

Nevertheless, data on family well-being can be interpreted in very different ways by equally competent scholars. For example, a review of data on American adolescents led Peter Uhlenberg and David Eggebeen[69] to posit a very negative picture of the current situation of American teenagers. However, in a review and extension of the same data, Frank Furstenberg and Gretchen Condran[70] suggest that the situation of American adolescents is not nearly so dire. Similar debates have been held over the consequences of day care for children, the effects of employment of mothers, the causes of declining SAT scores, and so on. After considering these kinds of debates, Pepper Schwartz notes:

> Most commentators dislike the new individualist and utilitarian ethic and blame its emergence on a generation (baby boomers), or on women (for leaving the home and wanting equality), on capitalism (for evaluating relationships according to goods and services distributed), or even psychiatry (for concentrating on the self as opposed to the community). This seems like a lot of tree counting to me when the obvious fact is we are now in a forest.[71]

Most commentators on family decline have too narrow a frame of reference. Whether or not they publicly express their assumptions, they express an underlying nostalgia for an earlier period of imagined family life when women were in the home, men worked outside for good wages, grandparents lived nearby, children went to good schools, marriages lasted for life, and communities were close-knit. These commentators believe that today's families have drifted away from these ideals and that harmful social consequences have resulted. These analysts create what William Goode terms the "classical family of Western nostalgia." Even as some writers deny their nostalgia, they follow Goode's prediction and "write of a period *still* more remote, *their* grandparents' generation, when things were much better."[72]

In his discussions of family decline, David Popenoe notes that the tendency to claim that the current family situation is in decline in comparison with an earlier period has been going on since the beginning of written history. For example, writing a century ago, C. F. Thwing and C. F. B. Thwing interpreted family patterns they observed in the way some family critics do today:

> The last fifty years have changed the marriage relation from a permanent lifelong state to a union existing for the pleasure of the parties. The change . . . is so revolutionary, involving the very foundation of human society, that we must believe it to be the result not of any temporary conditions.[73]

How should we interpret these warnings? Should we ignore earlier dire predictions and pay attention only to recent ones? Has doomsday finally arrived? There are least two possible interpretations.

1. We can assume that the trends being observed are linear and that the family system has been declining (however decline is defined) throughout recorded history. This interpretation assumes that an optimal family pattern once existed and that we have been drifting away from that utopia for centuries. Other than a few radical social evolutionists, such as Marx and Sorokin, this point of view does not have much support.

2. A more likely explanation comes from equilibrium-oriented models of reality. These models posit that stability in systems is the norm and that system change is inherently problematic. Until recently, nearly all sociocultural models were built on this assumption, including the dominant models in history, sociology, anthropology, and psychology. Although the names now attached to these models are relatively new, such as structural-functionalism, cognitive consistency theory, balance theory, and so forth, the premises of stability-equilibrium models have dominated observations of human behavior for centuries.

These models have conditioned observers to be critical of current changes. Following the observation of Goode, "We are all so emotionally involved in our own observations that we are not good observers. Our comments are all too likely to be self-justifications and rationalizations rather than cool attempts to find out how even our own family has operated."[74] Because the family, especially "our family," is so important to us, interpretations of its change can rarely be looked at dispassionately. Our values and fears become intermingled with data, and thus we find equally competent social scientists using the same data to project quite different visions of the future.

Institutional Transition: The Fourth Wave

We are in the early stages of a new "wave" of institutional change, perhaps as significant as the major social reorganizations that have occurred in the past. Three major family system waves have sequentially dominated human history.

The *first wave* was represented by wandering family and communal units in the preagricultural period. In this system, community interests overshadowed family interests because little to no property was controlled by individual families.

The *second family wave* occurred after the domestication of agriculture. Extended families dominated this period because property lines had to be much more clearly differentiated.

The *third wave* emerged after industrialization, and again, a major reorganization of the family took place. Property was no longer as important to family survival, so norms and values were built around independent family units with new, differentiated member roles and responsibilities. This transition into the industrial family, as reviewed by Edward

Shorter, Philippe Ariès, and Robert Bellah and colleagues,[75] resulted in significant family disorganization and in concern about the survivability of the family as an institution.

The *fourth wave* of institutional change is now upon us. The lack of defined family norms and adequate support systems to help us meet some of our basic needs are evidence of this significant transformation. This fourth wave, when it stabilizes, will represent a significant departure from the way in which families are currently viewed or have been viewed in the recent past. I suspect that this new wave will encourage more relationship testing in early adulthood and more coalescence around children in the lives of parents. Divorce rates will probably go down somewhat, in part because formal marriages may not take place until later, but also because the norms and guidelines for forming and maintaining these relationships will be clearer than they are today.

This suggestion that we are at the beginning of a major cultural transformation in relationships is not an isolated one. Many behavioral and social scientists who have attempted to describe marriage and family relationships in nonfunctionalist terms have had to struggle with redefining the concept of family in terms that are not proscribed by static and equilibrium-oriented assumptions. Two decades ago, for example, John Edwards[76] tried to express a process-theory-oriented view of the family in his critique of Charles Hobart's[77] functionalist view of family norms and values. Edwards has continued to refine his thinking and recently stated:

> We desperately need an alternative model of normal development, a model devoid of the present nuclear family bias. . . . It would focus, instead, on the processual nature of youthful development. Crucially, it would delineate the components of well-being and the patterns of "healthy" families, regardless of their structural configurations.[78]

John Scanzoni and his colleagues[79] recently attempted to define the nature of this emerging institution. They replace the functionalist, equilibrium-oriented view of institutions, which is very resistant to change, with a nonfunctionalist process definition of institutions such as the one proposed by Anthony Giddens: "by institutions I mean structured social practices that have a broad spatial and temporal extension . . . and which are followed or acknowledged by the majority of the members of a society."[80]

This new paradigm suggests that institutions represent the accumulations of norms, rules, and roles that reflect contemporary thinking and that they are changed, therefore, by current social processes. This is in contrast with the traditional, equilibrium-oriented paradigm in which institutions are considered outside the perimeter of the contemporary environment and apart from—even resistant to—normative changes that are occurring in the larger society.

If, following this line of thinking, the family is indeed in the midst of a major institutional transformation, then the current level of family instability is temporary. As the attitude surveys earlier reviewed suggest, the hope for a new level of stability lies with the young. The older generations are very concerned about family changes, because they have witnessed significant disruptions in their traditional family roots. Although concerned, the current parent generation is not nearly as anxious about these changes. The young are more hopeful. They see these changes as largely positive, but they worry that the rules and support they need are not there to guide their relationships. As Bellah and his colleagues observe:

> Perhaps most common today, however, is a note of uncertainty, not a desire to turn back to the past but an anxiety about where we seem to be headed. In this view, modernity seems to be a period of enormously rapid change, a transition from something relatively fixed toward something not yet clear. Many might still find applicable Matthew Arnold's assertion that "we are wandering between two worlds, one dead, the other powerless to be born."[81]

Toward Family Adaptation

Many individuals and families are not coping very well with the changes that are occurring in the American family. To take the extreme position that the family is merely adapting is to understate the current level of disequilibrium that many people are experiencing. Many families are currently experiencing severe distress; not enough industry and government supports are available to compensate for many of the services that family members used to provide each other; new roles for husbands, wives, and parents have not yet been well formulated; and potentially valuable informal support networks are not yet well established.

Much of the maladaptation that we currently observe is concentrated in selected pockets of our society. The divorce rates are particularly high among those who marry young and among those who are economically disadvantaged. Family violence is also concentrated in selected ethnic and poor families. Teenage pregnancies are much more common among the economically disadvantaged, and these young women are more likely to rear their children outside of marriage. This is not to say that some families are immune to problems, but it is important to keep in mind that the disabling effects of change are not cutting evenly across society. The majority of first marriages do not end in divorce, the overwhelming majority of families do not experience child or spouse abuse, the majority of teenage girls do not get pregnant, the majority of adolescents do graduate from high school, and the majority of youth and adults consider themselves happy with their lives in this changing world.

Family adaptation is more than a macro process; it is also a micro process in which change is a normal part of relational life. Family "health" is in large part defined as the extent to which families are able to make constructive changes over time. In fact, families that resist making changes in their roles and norms are generally viewed as unhealthy or mal-adapted.[82] In contrast "strong families" are defined today as those who fos-ter cohesion by making ongoing adjustments to the needs of family mem-bers. Therefore, a healthy commitment to marriage, parenthood, and childhood is an unfolding realization of adaptive processes, not a simple expression of continuity and resistance to change.

If the adaptation at the individual family level is normal, why should we expect the opposite at the social level? If resistance to change is con-sidered bad for families, such as the dominating husband not agreeing to let his wife take a job, how can we assume that women entering the labor force in ever-increasing numbers is an indication of family decline?

Cautious Optimism

During the past decade, my writings have drifted somewhat from being quite optimistic to being more cautiously optimistic, a direction some of my colleagues appear to be taking as well.[83] I believe, however, in the potential value of the constructive reorganization of the family sys-tem. Interestingly, I find myself selecting as colleagues in this position persons like David Popenoe[84] and Robert Bellah and his colleagues,[85] because I find considerable hope in their work, even though their inter-pretations of trends are somewhat less optimistic than my own. Yet some of my more pessimistically inclined colleagues claim their positions as well, which probably represents some of the confusion in family social sci-ence today.

The case for cautious optimism can be well supported. The Ameri-can public, particularly youth and young adults, are embracing many of the normative changes that are occurring. Few people, either men or women, agree any longer that "a woman's place is in the home." Most peo-ple agree that women should be given equal opportunity in the job mar-ket. Almost no one expects women or children to stay at home with abu-sive husbands or parents, under the guise that what happens in the home is a "private family matter."

Fears concerning family change remain; in fact, the public is more fearful of change than it ought to be. When more than one-half (59%) of the adults in America in 1988 agreed that "it is not fair to bring a child into the world,"[86] it is either time to fold our academic tents and join those who are lobbying Congress for a return to the family of the 1950s or get out of the way of those who are trying to facilitate policies that will ease the family system into a new era.

IMPLICATIONS FOR POLICY

A new, systematic approach to family policy is needed. The old piecemeal strategies of limited government intervention, weak to uneven business concern, welfare-oriented support systems, and a largely hands-off attitude on the part of schools and churches have contributed more to the problems of family change than to their solution. A new commitment to the value of the family to society must be made, not based on rhetoric or nostalgic visions of the past, but oriented toward the future, with a clearer image of what is happening today and where the family is headed. Daniel Yankelovich says it well:

> . . . for a successful social ethic to take hold, people must form commitments that advance the well-being of society as well as themselves. For this to occur, people must receive clear and distinct signals from the larger society—from political leadership, from mass media, from institutional leadership (business, religion, education, labor, artists and scientists, intellectual community) and from informal interchanges of views with friends and neighbors. These signals should convey the terms of the new giving/getting compact communicating to Americans that we have now entered into a new age, offering new opportunities, tradeoffs, choices and constraints. The signals must permit people to understand how they can link their personal aspirations to the new realities.[87]

What are some of these signals that should be sent? Policies to which we should give priority should meet at least one of two major objectives: (1) to increase the opportunity for families to develop stable relationships between husbands and wives as well as between parents and children; and (2) to reduce the cost of instabilities that may occur because of institutional or family transitions.

Universal Family Benefits

We need a comprehensive set of universally provided benefits that meet basic social and physical requirements for citizens of this society. Just as public education has become a universal benefit provided to all children, we need a safety net of similar programs in areas such as health, housing, and income security. It simply is not fair that a child born in a particular family starts life with enormous social and economic handicaps over which he or she has no choice. If these children are indeed our future, as we often hear, then our future is dim. Not only are they personally disadvantaged, but their frustrations readily create disorganization in their families.

Clearly, the evidence indicates that the two-track system that has evolved in America is not promoting healthy family change. Our current policy of providing low-quality public services to the disadvantaged is helping create ever-greater income inequality. Many of the family norms of the poor are precisely the ones we want to reduce: teenage pregnancies, family violence, single motherhood, and lack of father involvement. The policies of the past have not worked to change this situation. Universal programs that cut across social classes and income groups are better suited to foster opportunity and diminish the class distinctions that are becoming stronger and more prevalent in this society.

Promote Workplace Family Policies

The daily lives of family members are strongly influenced by workplace policies that either encourage or discourage family stability. Industry and government employers have to become full partners in the process of facilitating positive family change.

The initiatives of some industry leaders to develop child-care-related programs and services are to be applauded. But much more needs to be done, including policies that encourage parents to participate in children's activities, promote parental leave, and encourage opportunities for husbands and wives and parents and children to spend time together. We need to discourage policies that require overtime, extended travel, and frequent relocations, except under temporary and necessary conditions. Many business policies and practices are, by default, antifamily. This is not because industry leaders intend to be antifamily, but because they are insensitive to family concerns.

Promote Family and Sex Education among Youth

Many youth are confused about how they can develop family patterns that reflect their underlying belief in strong relationships. Youth do not know how to integrate sexuality and intimacy into relationships. And in the home, the schools, community organizations, and churches, everyone appears to be passing the buck to another, hopefully more capable, system that will do a better job. Unfortunately, no one is doing the job.

How can we expect youth to be sexually responsible and to develop the kinds of intimate relationships that later provide positive marital and parental roles when the models for success are often absent and the information needed is not being disseminated? When adults provide so little guidance, it is no wonder that youth are confused and attempting to make their own way. We need to provide universal sex education and relationship development courses. Much like the values-clarification education that was incorporated into schools during the civil rights era, we need an information revolution in the schools about interpersonal relationships. We have to stop worrying about whether children will be titillated by this information and become more concerned about whether the lack of information will continue to foster confusion in family norms and instability in family relationships.

Require Adequate Child-Support Payments

On one point, most conservative and liberal family policy analysts agree: divorce has become too easy in America today. Some may disagree about whether more thought or time should be required before allowing marital relationships to dissolve, but most everyone is concerned about providing adequate support to children. Children often pay a terrible price for marital dissolution. Although the emotional costs are often repairable and the long-term social consequences of divorce can often be overcome, the economic costs that children sometimes pay because of parental and judicial neglect are inexcusable.

Parents should not be permitted to abdicate their economic responsibility to their families simply because it is inconvenient or because it will cramp their life-style. The needs of children must be taken more seriously by fathers and by the courts. The modest child-support requirements awarded by most courts and the small proportion of fathers who continue to pay child support should not be permitted. The price of having children needs to be enforced. That price should include more awareness of the obligations of fathering and mothering as well as the economic costs of child rearing. Men, women, and children need to know that if the marriage dissolves, the children will continue to receive the best that both parents can provide until the children are economically independent.

Encourage Parent Education

Both fathers and mothers need more and better information on how to integrate parenting into their adult lives. Most men and women still want to be parents, but the normal frustrations of rearing children can decrease perceptions of competence in parents and encourage parents to overuse alternative caregivers, including day care, television, neighbors, and "the street." I agree with Frank Furstenberg, who suggests that traditional parent education has not been effective.[88] Usually, these classes are taught to enhance the self-esteem of already competent men and women.

What we need instead is a steady stream of information directed at current and future parents about parental roles, responsibilities, and costs. This information should be included in schools, neighborhood meetings, workplace seminars, management-training programs, church programs, and the media. Fathers, in particular, need to get the message that their participation in child rearing is valued and that they will be rewarded through better behaved children as well as more successful marital experiences.

Promote Positive Family Values

Finally, we need to recognize that promoting positive family values nationwide is a matter of utmost priority. As the pace of family change has begun to slow, we now have more time to establish priorities and foster the values and norms that are likely to be most conducive to the new family institution that is evolving. We cannot resurrect the family values, norms, and commitments of the past. Instead, leaders at all levels of government and business need to review the underlying family values and behaviors they are promoting in legislation, laws, and policies and to give serious consideration to the consequences, both positive and negative, that these will have on families.

Policies should be evaluated based upon whether they promote the adaptation of families to emerging social and economic conditions in society. Promotion of family values has to start at the top. In businesses in which family policies have been effectively integrated, the leadership initiating such policies has almost always included a key company officer and his or her family. In the military services, where significant advances have been made to promote positive family policies, the leadership for these changes again started at the top.[89] This plea was echoed recently by Peter McDonald, an Australian sociologist:

> In the face of the enormous push toward competition, deregulation, and autonomy, so powerfully reinforced in this area of market forces, we need policies which promote the conviction that men and women are irreducibly social and that we have a strong psychological need for companionship and intimacy. Education for both children and adults must extend beyond the utilitarian to a recognition that we are social beings who have intimate human relationships with others. We need to reiterate the undoubted value of family life; to emphasize the positive rather than rant and rave about the negative.[90]

NOTES

1. John N. Edwards, "Changing Family Structure and Youthful Well-Being," *Journal of Family Issues* 8 (1987), pp. 355–372; Andrew J. Cherlin, ed., *The Changing American Family and Public Policy* (Washington, DC: Urban Institute Press, 1988).

2. Gibson Burrel and Gareth Morgan, *Sociological Paradigms and Organizational Analysis* (Exeter, NH: Heineman Educational Books, 1982).

3. National Commission on Excellence in Education, *Nation at Risk*, Report to the Nation and the Secretary of Education (Washington, DC: U.S. Government Printing Office, April 1983).

4. E.g., *perestroika*.

5. Robert N. Bellah, Richard Madsen, William M. Sullivan, Ann Swidler, and Steven M. Tipton, *Habits of the Heart* (New York: Harper and Row, 1985).

6. Daniel Yankelovich, *New Rules: Searching for Self-Fulfillment in a World Turned Upside Down* (New York: Random House, 1981).

7. Ibid., p. 249.

8. Larry Bumpass and James Sweet, *National Survey of Families and Households* (Madison, WI: University of Wisconsin, 1988).

9. CBS News/The New York Times Poll, *Attitudes toward Marriage*, February 13, 1989.

10. Cherlin, op. cit.

11. George Gallup, "U.S. Women Endorse Jobs, Marriage, and Children," *Gallup Reports* (No. 267, 1987), pp. 24–25.

12. Nicholas Zill and Carolyn C. Rogers, "Recent Trends in the Well-Being of Children in the United States and Their Implications for Public Policy," in Cherlin, op. cit., pp. 31–116.

13. Ibid.

14. Peter McDonald, "Families in the Future: The Pursuit of Personal Autonomy," *Family Matters* 22 (1988), pp. 40–44.

15. Bellah et al., op. cit., p. 142.

16. David Popenoe, *Disturbing the Nest: Family Change and Decline in Modern Societies* (New York: Aldine de Gruyter, 1988), p. 289.

17. Alexis de Tocqueville, *Democracy in America*, trans. George Lawrence, J. P. Mayer, ed. (New York: Doubleday, Archer Books, 1969).

18. Carl Solberg, *Riding High* (New York: Mason and Lipscomb, 1973), p. 259.

19. F. Toennies, *Community and Society*, trans. Charles P. Lomis (Lansing, MI: Michigan State University Press, 1957).

20. Eugene Litwak, "Geographic Mobility and Extended Family Cohesion," *American Sociological Review* 25 (1960), pp. 385–394.

21. William Goode, *World Revolution and Family Patterns* (New York: Free Press, 1963).

22. Marvin Sussman, "The Help Pattern in the Middle-Class Family," *American Sociological Review* 15 (1953), pp. 22–28; Litwak, op. cit.

23. Michael Young and Peter Willmot, *Family and Kinship in East London* (Glencoe, IL: Free Press, 1957).

24. Marvin Sussman, "Relationships of Adult Children with Their Parents in the United States," in Ethel Shanas and Gordon F. Streib, eds., *Social Structure and the Family: Generational Relations* (Englewood Cliffs, NJ: Prentice Hall, 1965).

25. National Opinion Research Center, "General Social Survey," (Chapel Hill, NC: Institute for Research in the Social Sciences, 1988).

26. Bumpass and Sweet, op. cit.

27. McDonald, op. cit., p. 44.

28. Erik Erikson, *Identity, Youth, and Crisis* (New York: Norton, 1968).

29. John Scanzoni, "Families in the 1980s: Time to Refocus Our Thinking," *Journal of Family Issues* 8 (1987), pp. 394–421.

30. David H. Olson, Hamilton I. McCubbin, H. L. Barnes, A. S. Larsen, M. J. Muxen, and M. A. Wilson, *Families: What Makes Them Work* (Beverly Hills, CA: Sage Publications, 1983).

31. CBS News/The New York Times Poll, op. cit.

32. Bumpass and Sweet, op. cit.

33. Daniel Weiss, "100% American," *Good Housekeeping* (No. 207, 1988), p. 120.

34. Peter Brickman, *Commitment, Conflict and Caring* (Englewood Cliffs, NJ: Prentice-Hall, 1987).

35. Maxine Schnall, *Limits: A Search for New Values* (New York: Clarkson N. Potter, 1981).

36. Dennis K. Orthner, *Intimate Relationships: An Introduction to Marriage and the Family* (Reading, MA: Addison-Wesley, 1981).

37. Marie Coleman Nelson, ed., *The Narcissistic Condition* (New York: Human Sciences Press, 1977).

38. Orthner, op. cit.

39. Ashley Montague, *Touching: The Human Significance of Skin* (New York: Columbia University Press, 1971), p. 167.

40. Mavis Hethrington, Martha Cox, and Roger Cox, "Divorced Fathers," *Psychology Today* (April 1977), p. 42.

41. Lewis Harris, *Inside America* (New York: Vintage Books, 1987).

42. Zill and Rogers, op. cit., pp. 31–116.

43. Bumpass and Sweet, op. cit.

44. Yankelovich, op. cit.

45. Joan Aldous, *Family Careers: Developmental Change in Families* (New York: John Wiley, 1978).

46. Gary L. Bowen and Dennis K. Orthner, "Sex Role Congruency and Marital Quality," *Journal of Marriage and the Family* 45 (1983), pp. 223–230; G. Levinger, "Compatibility in Relationships," *Social Science* 71 (1986), pp. 173–177; Olson et al., op. cit.

47. Catherine E. Ross, John Mirowsky, and Joan Huber, "Dividing Work, Sharing Work and In-between: Marriage Patterns and Depression," *American Sociological Review* 48 (1983), pp. 809–23.

48. National Opinion Research Center, *Cumulative Codebook for the 1972–1977 General Social Surveys* (Chicago: University of Chicago Press, 1977).

49. National Opinion Research Center, "General Social Survey," op. cit.

50. Martin O'Connell and Carolyn C. Rogers, "Out-of-Wedlock Births, Premarital Pregnancies and Their Effect on Family Formation and Dissolution," *Family Planning Perspectives* 16 (1984), pp. 157–162.

51. CBS News/The New York Times Poll, op. cit.

52. Gregory Duncan and J. N. Morgan, "The Panel Study of Income Dynamics," in

Glen H. Elder, ed., *Life Course Dynamics* (Ithaca, NY: Cornell University Press, 1985), p. 53.

53. Glen H. Elder, Jr., "Age Differentiation and the Life Course," in E. D. Macklin and R. H. Rubin, eds., *Contemporary Families and Alternative Lifestyles* (Newbury Park, CA: Sage Publications, 1975), p. 178.

54. Harris, op. cit.

55. Bumpass and Sweet, op. cit.

56. Weiss, op. cit.

57. Harris, op. cit.

58. Ralph LaRossa, "Fatherhood and Social Change," *Family Relations* (No. 37, 1988), pp. 451–457.

59. Weiss, op. cit.

60. Frank F. Furstenberg, Jr., and Gretchen A. Condran, "Family Change and Adolescent Well-being: A Reexamination of U.S. Trends," in Cherlin, op. cit., pp. 117–156.

61. Bumpass and Sweet, op. cit.

62. Frank F. Furstenberg, Jr., and Graham G. Spanier, *Recycling the Family: Remarriage after Divorce* (Newbury Park, CA: Sage Publications, 1984), p. 47.

63. Bernard Farber, "The Future of the American Family: A Dialectical Account," *Journal of Family Issues* 8 (1987), p. 432.

64. Cynthia Fuchs Epstein, "Toward a Family Policy: Changes in Mothers' Lives," in Cherlin, op. cit., p. 181.

65. James A. Levine, *Who Will Raise the Children?* (New York: Bantam, 1976).

66. Scanzoni, op. cit.

67. Ibid., p. 465.

68. Clark Vincent, "Familia Spongia: The Adaptive Function," *The Family Coordinator* 21 (1966), p. 31.

69. Peter Uhlenberg and David Eggebeen, "The Declining Well-being of American Adolescents," *The Public Interest* 82 (1986), pp. 25–38.

70. Furstenberg and Condran, op. cit., pp. 117–156.

71. Pepper Schwartz, "The Family as a Changed Institution," *Journal of Family Issues* 8 (1987), p. 456.

72. Goode, op. cit., p. 7.

73. C. F. Thwing and C. F. B. Thwing, *The Family: An Historical and Social Study*

(Boston: Lee and Shepard, 1887).

74. William Goode, *The Contemporary American Family* (Chicago: Quadrangle, 1971), p. 4.

75. Edward Shorter, *The Making of the Modern Family* (New York: Basic Books, 1975); Philippe Ariès, *Centuries of Childhood: A Social History of Family Life* (New York: Vintage Books, 1962); Bellah et al., op. cit.

76. John N. Edwards, "The Future of the Family Revisited," *Journal of Marriage and the Family* 29 (1967), pp. 505–511.

77. Charles W. Hobart, "Commitment, Value Conflict, and the Future of the American Family," *Marriage and Family Living* 25 (1963), pp. 405–412.

78. John N. Edwards, "The Future of the Family Revisited," op. cit.

79. John Scanzoni, K. Polonko, J. Teachman, and Linda Thompson, *The Sexual Bond: Rethinking Families and Close Relationships* (Newbury Park, CA: Sage Publications, 1989).

80. Anthony Giddens, "Agency, Institution, and Time-Space Analysis," in K. Knorr-Cetina and A. V. Cicourel, eds., *Advances in Social Theory and Methodology* (Boston: Routledge and Kegan Paul, 1981), p. 164.

81. Bellah et al., op. cit., pp. 276–277.

82. Olson et al., op. cit.

83. Norval Glenn, "Continuity Versus Change, Sanguineness Versus Concern," *Journal of Family Issues* 8 (1987), pp. 348–354.

84. Popenoe, op. cit.

85. Bellah et al., op. cit.

86. National Opinion Research Center, "General Social Survey," op. cit.

87. Yankelovich, op. cit., pp. 259–260.

88. Frank F. Furstenberg, Jr., "Good Dads-Bad Dads: Two Faces of Fatherhood," in Cherlin, op. cit., pp. 193–218.

89. Bowen and Orthner, op. cit.

90. McDonald, op. cit.

= 7 =

The Family and Civic Life

Jean Bethke Elshtain

D emocracy and the family always exist in tension with one another, as
do capitalism and the family. Moreover, socialism and the family are
not a happy mix. Perhaps this tells us something about the family. In
Spheres of Justice, Michael Walzer criticizes all attempts to restructure
the family, whether from defenders or opponents of the market or the state,
in order to make the family "fit" neatly with some scheme of total justice or
some overarching macroeconomic theory.[1] Such attempts, he argues, are
always problematic, even disastrous. Perhaps a few examples are in order.

PLATO AND HIS CHILDREN

Consider the Plato of *The Republic*. As with all subsequent attempts to
control social reality and to reshape it according to an overarching schema,
Plato must eliminate the family if the ideal city is to come into being. The
ruler–philosophers must take "the dispositions of human beings as though
they were a tablet . . . which, in the first place, they would wipe clean."[2]
Women must be held "in common." If a powerful, all-encompassing bond
between individuals and the state can be achieved, social conflict disap-
pears. Discord melts away. The state resembles a "single person," a fused,
organic entity. Private loyalties and purposes are eliminated.

Plato constructs a rationalist meritocracy that strips away all considerations of sex, race, age, class, family ties, tradition, and history. People are fit
into their appropriate social slots, performing only that function to which
each is suited. Children outside the ruler class can be shunted upward or
downward at the will of the "Guardian," for they are raw material to be
turned into instruments of social "good." A system of eugenics is devised for

---

*Jean Bethke Elshtain is Centennial Professor of Political Science at Vanderbilt University in
Nashville, Tennessee.*

119

the Guardians. Children are removed from their mothers at birth and placed in a child ghetto, tended to by those best suited for the job. No parental loyalties emerge. No child knows who his or her parents are.

What is all this for? What is it a defense against? Plato seeks to eradicate motives for discord. Private homes and sexual attachments, devotion to friends, dedication to individual or group aims and purposes—all of these militate against devotion to the city. Particular ties are a great evil. Only those that bind the individual to the state are good.

Who, today, would try to implement such an ideal, with all its frightening consequences? Totalitarians of all stripes, social engineers of various hues, revolutionaries of several flavors, and a small army of contemporary philosophers. Here are several examples, drawn from feminist politics and philosophy.

Shulamith Firestone's radical feminist "classic," *The Dialectic of Sex*, depicts a world of stark lovelessness in which coercion, manipulation, and crude power roam undifferentially over the landscape. Within the family, the "female sex-class" is dominated by the "male sex-class," and thus the family must be destroyed. In Firestone's scenario, test-tube babies replace biological reproduction. Every aspect of life rests in the beneficent hands of the "new elite of engineers, cybernetricians."[3] The child, no longer "hung up" by authoritarian parents (parents having pretty much melted away), is "free" to bargain for the best deal in contracted households.

Firestone's vision has been attacked as a nightmare by many feminist critics in the past few years because

> it rests on conceptual foundations that have much in common with the presuppositions of researchers and policymakers who would . . . support technological intervention for the sake of the monopoly of power it would make possible. . . . Both see human biology as a limitation to be overcome—for Firestone, because she takes the relations of procreation to be . . . the source of women's oppression; for those who would support "a brave new world," because the diffusion of power among women and families threatens their own power hegemony.[4]

But despite such critiques, the philosophic drumbeat continues: the radical feminist future requires a family-less world. Indeed, Alison M. Jagger, in her widely hailed *Feminist Politics and Human Nature*, even foresees the elimination of gender. She calls for the "ultimate transformation of human nature"—an actual biological reformation of the human species.

> This transformation might even include the capacities for insemination, for lactation and for gestation so that, for instance, one woman could inseminate another, so that men and nonparturitive women could lactate and so that fertilized ova could be transplanted into women's or even into men's bodies. These developments may seem farfetched, but in fact they are already on the technological horizon.[5]

That which is technologically possible is politically and ethically desirable so long as these new means of control are controlled by women, because women are oppressed by "having to be women."[6]

In these examples, we see the animus of philosophers and revolutionaries directed toward the personal lives and ties, especially family ties, of ordinary human beings. Martha Nussbaum, in her remarkable work *The Fragility of Goodness*, offers a wise discussion of why Plato (and, by extension, all later universalizing philosophers) had to destroy the family. Plato's urge to deconstruct is linked to his animus against the poets and tragedians who must be banished from the ideal city. Thus it seems that families, as do tragedians and poets, stir up strong emotions; they rouse pity and fear, excite longing and love. But Plato aspired to "rational self-suffiency." He would make the lives of human beings immune to the messy fragilities of ordinary existence. The ideal of self-sufficiency was mastery: the male citizen was to be imbued with a "mythology of autochthony that persistently, and paradoxically, suppressed the biological role of the female and therefore the family in the continuity of the city."[7] (Consider the irony of late 20th-century feminist philosophers embracing this relentlessly anti-body, anti-female model.) For Plato, moral conflicts suggest irrationalism, which must be "discarded as false." If one cannot be loyal both to families and to the city, loyalty to the family must be bent to serve the city. For Plato and subsequent Platonists of every variety, including Marxists, "Our ordinary humanity is a source of confusion rather than of insight [and] the philosopher alone judges with the right criterion or from the appropriate standpoint."[8] Hence the ascetic plan of *The Republic* aims to purify and to control by depriving human beings of "the nourishment of close ongoing attachments, of the family, of dramatic poetry."[9]

Subsequent universalists take a similar tack. But what drives these attempts to diminish the family for the good of the state? Clearly, it is the suspicion and condemnation of all relationships that are not totally voluntary, rationalistic, and contractual. It is the conviction that the traditional family is the example *par excellence* of imbedded particularity. It is the view that the world will attain the ideal of justice and order only when various proposals to "wipe the slate clean" have been implemented and human beings are no longer constrained and limited by special obligations and inherited (nonvoluntary) duties.

It seems that we must choose. On the one hand, we have visions of total order and rationalistic harmony; on the other, an open, complex, conflicted receptivity to the rich plurality of values that exist in the world of nature and of history. The family contributes to this plurality of values in a way no other social institution can.

PHILOSOPHERS FOR THE FAMILY

In this chapter, I propose a philosophic argument in support of the family in civic life. Furthermore, I sketch a normative vision of the family—mothers, fathers, and children—that is not only *not* at odds with democratic civil society but is in fact, now more than ever, a prerequisite for that society to function. Yet I do not seek to eliminate all tensions, to create some overarching ideal of "The Family" and "The Democratic Order." Rather, I aim to preserve a necessary and fruitful tension between particular and universal commitments, as embodied in the family, without which democratic society cannot flourish.

Consider my basic questions: In what ways is the family issue also a civic issue with public consequences? What is the relationship between democratic theory and the intergenerational family? What ideals of the human person are imbedded in contrasting visions of intimate life? Do we have a stake in sustaining some visions as compared with others? What do families do that no other social institution can? How does current public discourse in the United States undermine family obligations and downgrade the moral vocation of parenting?

In answering these questions, I seek a method of interpretive complexity that is grounded in moral commitments. The philosopher must be interested in the problems created by any way of life and in how human beings deal with those problems. If the political thinker is to avoid being arrogant and lofty, contemptuous of the values and judgments people make, she must philosophize in a way that resembles the complexity and content of our actual beliefs and actions. The only alternative is performing philosophical surgery—cutting and restitching reality—in the hope that actual life may one day be brought into line.

THE DILEMMA OF DEMOCRATIC POLITICS AND THE FAMILY

Democrats are suspicious of traditional authority, from kings and chiefs to popes and lords. And properly so, for democracy requires self-governing citizens rather than obedient subjects. In a democracy, holding authority is a temporary gift, granted only through the consent of the governed.

Democratic authority emerged unevenly over several centuries, as late medieval and early modern cosmologies faltered.[10] Its distinguishing features included the principle that citizens possess inalienable rights. Possession of such rights empowered citizens to offer assent to the governors and the laws, including those procedural guarantees that protected them from the abuses of authority. Equality between and among citizens was assumed. Indeed, the citizen was, by definition, equal to any other citizen. (Not everyone, of course, could be a citizen, but that's another story.) Democratic citizenship required the creation of persons with qualities of mind and spirit necessary for civic participation. Early liberal theorists viewed this creation of citizens as neither simple nor automatic. Many, in fact, insisted upon a structure of education tied to a particular understanding of "the sentiments." This education should usher in a moral autonomy that stresses self-chosen obligations, thereby casting further suspicion upon relations and loyalties deemed unchosen, involuntary, or natural.

Not surprisingly, within such systems of civic authority, the family emerges as a problem. For one does not enter a family through free consent but rather is born into a world unwilled and unchosen by oneself, beginning life as a helpless and dependent infant. Eventually one reaches "the age of consent." But in the meantime one is a child, not a citizen. This situation vexed liberal and democratic theorists, some of whom believed, at least abstractly, that the completion of the democratic ideal required bringing all of social life under the sway of a single principle of democratic authority.

During the 16th and 17th centuries, political thought slowly shifted from a patriarchal to a liberal-contractarian discourse. Patriarchalist discourse in its paradigmatic form—for example, Robert Filmer's *Patriarcha*—concerned itself preeminently with authority, defined as singular, absolute, patriarchal, natural, and political.[11] In Filmer's world there is no differentiation between public and private, family and politics. Indeed, there is no private sphere at all, in the sense of a realm demarcated from political life. Nor is there a separate political sphere, in the sense of a realm diverging from exigencies of the private world. Power, authority, and obedience are fused within God's original grant of dominion to Adam at the Creation. Accordingly, the father has dominion over his wife, his children, and his servants in his own little kingdom. But he, in turn, is subject to the First Father, the lordly King.

In the realm of civil society, countering this patriarchal philosophy proved relatively easy for liberals and democrats. But the issue became trickier when new conceptions of authority seemed to challenge the family. Is a family dominated by patriarchy, however softened in practice, legitimate within the new civic world framed by ideas of consent? If liberals sought to end conditions of perpetual political childhood, were they required to eliminate childhood itself?

Adhering to a strong version of the liberal ideal, "free consent" from birth, was deeply problematic given the nature of human infants.[12] Liberal contractarians were often cautious in carrying their political principles into domestic life. Some contented themselves with contractarianism in politics and economics and with traditionalism in families, not, however, without considerable discursive maneuvering.[13] Filmer's caustic query to his liberal interlocutors concerning whether people sprang up like "so many mushrooms" and his incredulous insistency—"How can a child express consent?"—continued to haunt liberals, in part because they shared with Filmer the presumption that authority must be singular in form if a society is to be coherent and orderly.

John Locke, who was more subtle than many early liberal thinkers, softened his demands for consistency in social practices, arguing instead for the coexistence of diverse authoritative forms. Conjugal society originates through the consent of two adults. But "parental" or "paternal" power within the family (Locke recognizes both but privileges the latter) could not serve as a model for the liberal polity any more than could the norms constituting civil society provide an apposite model for families. Locke strips the father–husband of patriarchal absolutism by denying him sovereignty, which includes the power of life and death. That prerogative is reserved only for democratically legitimized public authority. A father's power is "conjugal . . . not Political" and these two are "perfectly distinct and separate . . . built upon so different Foundations and given to so different Ends."[14]

The child's status is that of "not-yet-adult," hence the child is not part of the consensual civil order. But the education of the child into moral sentiments is vital to that wider order. Locke avoids the seductions of patriarchal authority as an all-encompassing norm. He refuses to launch a mimetic project that mirrors patriarchalism, nor does he demand an overreaching liberal authority principle that turns the family into a political society governed by the same principles that guide liberal public life.

This incongruence between democracy and the family continued to vex post-Lockean thinkers. The position of women, for example, presented philosophical contradictions. For women, having reached the age of consent, could enter freely into a marriage only to find future consent foreclosed. Moreover, because the family itself was perceived as a blemish by those who foresaw the ultimate triumph of rationalism in all spheres of human existence, liberals continued to focus on the relations between the family and politics.

In the 19th century, however, John Stuart Mill, in contrast with Locke, insisted that familial and civic orders be drawn into a tight mesh with one another. For Mill, the family remained a despotic sphere governed by a "law of force" whose "odious source" was rooted in pre-enlightened and barbaric epochs. By revealing the origins of family relations, thus bringing out their "true" character, Mill hoped to demonstrate that the continued subjection of women blunts social progress. He proposed a leap into relations of "perfect equality" between the sexes as the only way to complete the teleology of liberal individualism and equality, to assure the promise of progress.

In his tract *The Subjection of Women*, Mill argued that his contemporaries, male and female alike, were tainted by the atavisms of family life with its illegitimate (because unchosen and prerational) male authority as well as its illegitimate (because manipulative and irrational) female quests for private power.[15] The family would become a school in the virtues of freedom only when parents lived together without power on one side or obedience on the other. Power, for Mill, was repugnant: true liberty must reign in all spheres.

But what about children? Mill's children emerge as rather abstract concerns: blank slates on which parents must encode the lessons of obedience in the aim of authoritatively inculcating the lessons of freedom.

Stripped of undemocratic authority and privilege, the parental union serves as a model of democratic probity.[16]

Mill's paean to liberal individualism can be interestingly contrasted to Alexis de Tocqueville's concrete observations of family life in 19th-century America. He found a society that already exhibited the effects of the extension of democratic norms and the breakdown of patriarchal and Puritan ethics. The fathers of Tocqueville's America were fathers in a different mode: stern but forgiving, strong but flexible. They listened to their children and humored them. They educated them as well as demanded their obedience.

Like the new democratic father, the American political leader did not lord it over his people. Citizens were not required to bend the knee or stand transfixed in awe. Yet the leader was owed respect. If he urged a course of action, his fellow citizens, following democratic consultation and procedure, had a patriotic duty to follow.

Tocqueville's discerning eye perceived changing public and private relationships in liberal, democratic America. Although great care was taken "to trace two clearly distinct lines of action for the two sexes," Tocqueville claimed that women, in their domestic sphere, "nowhere occupied a loftier position of honor and importance."[17] The mother is the chief inculcator of democratic values in her offspring. "No free communities ever existed without morals and, as I observed . . . morals are the work of women."[18]

Although the father was the family's "natural head," his authority was neither absolute nor arbitrary. In contrast with the patriarchal authoritarian family, in which the parent not only has a "natural right" but acquired a "political right" to command his children, a democratic family is one in which the authority of parents is a *natural right* alone.[19] For Tocqueville, in contrast with Mill, this natural authority presents no problem for democratic practices. Indeed, the "right to command" is natural, not political. It is a right of a special and temporary nature: once the child becomes self-governing, the right dissolves. In this way, paternal authority and maternal education reinforce a political order that values flexibility, freedom, and the absence of absolute rule, but requires order and stability.

"Child experts" in Tocqueville's America emphasized kindness and love as the preferred technique of nurturance. Obedience was necessary—to parents, elders, God, "just government and one's conscience"—but the child was no longer constructed as a depraved, sin-ridden, stiff-necked little creature who needed harsh instruction and reproof. Notions of infant depravity faded along with Puritan patriarchalism. The problem of discipline grew more, rather than less, complex. Parents were enjoined to win obedience without corporal punishment or rigid methods, using affection, issuing their commands in gentle voices while insisting quietly on their authority lest contempt and chaos rule in the domestic sphere.

In Tocqueville's image of the "democratic family," children are both ends in themselves and means to the end of a well-ordered society. A widespread moral consensus reigned in the America of that era—a kind of Protestant civic religion. When this consensus began to corrode under the force of rapid social change (and analogues to the American story appear in all modern democracies), certainties surrounding familial life and authority were shaken as well.

Today, no form of authority can be taken for granted. In light of modern challenges to the norms that govern both the familial and civil spheres, a case for the family as a good in itself and as a precondition for democratic society becomes difficult to mount. One can opt for restorationism. Or one can celebrate rationalist hopes that the time is finally ripe to bring society under the sway of wholly voluntarist norms.

If restorationists seek a return to traditional norms, voluntarists seek to nullify the moral significance of all "unchosen" obligations. One might, however, find each of these alternatives to be unrealistic, undesirable, or both. If this is so, the task is to mount a defense of the family within, and for, a world whose members no longer share a single overriding conception of the good life or even repose deep faith in the future of most human institutions. This task is not easy.

There are two possible directions. The first option might be termed the strong case: an unambiguous defense of familial authority in the modern world. By evaluating objections to the strong case, we arrive at the second option, a more ambiguous set of family affirmations. Such qualifications permit us to evaluate whether the strong case remains compelling or, alternatively, whether a softened defense of the family better serves the social goods at stake.[20]

DEMOCRATIC AUTHORITY AND THE FAMILY: THE STRONG CASE

Familial authority, though seemingly at odds with the presumptions of democracy, is nonetheless a prerequisite for the survival of democracy. Family relations could not exist without familial authority. Such relations remain the best way we know to create citizens, that is, adults who offer ethical allegiance to the principles of democratic society. Family authority is the best way to structure the relationships between adults and dependent children who slowly acquire capacities for independence. Modern parental authority, moreover, is shared by the mother and father. Some may take strong exception to this claim, arguing that the family is patriarchal, even today, or that the authority of the mother is *less* decisive than that of the father, or that Mill was right.

Children, however, exhibit little doubt that their mothers are powerful and authoritative, though perhaps not in ways identical to fathers. This ideal of parental equality does not presuppose sameness between the mother and father. Each can be more or less a private or a public person, yet be equal in relation to children.

What makes family authority distinctive is the quality of stewardship: the recognition that parents undertake solemn obligations, under authority that is special, limited, and particular. Parental authority, like all authority, can be abused. But unless it exists, the activity of parenting is itself impossible. Parental authority is essential to democratic political morality, because parents are the primary providers of the moral education required for democratic citizenship.

The *Herzenbildung*—education of the heart—that takes place in families should not, however, be viewed as merely one item in a larger political agenda. To construe it as such is to treat the family merely instrumentally, affirming it only insofar as it can be shown to serve external purposes. Yes, the family helps sustain the democratic order. But it also offers alternatives, even resistance, to many policies that a public order may throw up at any given time.

The loyalties and moral imperatives nurtured in families may often clash with the demands of public authority. For example, a young man may refuse to serve in a war because to do so violates the religious beliefs taught by his mother and father. This, too, is vital for democracy. Democracy emerged as a form of revolt. Keeping alive a potential for revolt, keeping alive the space for particularity, for difference, for pluralism, sustains democracy in the long run. It is no coincidence that all 20th-century totalitarian orders labored to destroy the family as a locus of identity and meaning apart from the state. Totalitarianism strives to govern all of life; to allow for only one public identity; to destroy private life; and most of all, to require that individuals never allow their commitments to specific others—family, friends, comrades—to weaken their commitment to the state. To this idea, which can only be described as evil, the family stands in defiance.

Familial authority simply does not exist in a direct homologous relation to the principles of civil society. To establish an identity between public and private lives would weaken, not strengthen, democratic life. The reason for this is children. They need particular, intense relations with specific beloved others. If a child is confronted prematurely with the "right to choose" or situated too soon inside anonymous institutions that minimize that special contact and trust with parents, that child is much less likely to be "free to choose" later on. To become capable of posing alternatives, a person requires a sure and certain place from which to start. In Mary Midgley's words, "Children . . . have to live *now* in a particular culture; they must take some attitude to the nearest things right away."[21] The family is the social form best suited to provide children with a trusting, determinate sense of "self." Indeed, it is only through identification with concrete others that children can later identify with nonfamilial human beings and come to see themselves as members of a wider community.

Familial authority is inseparable from parental care, protection, and concern. In the absence of such ties, familial feelings would not be displaced throughout a wider social network; they would, instead, be vitiated, perhaps lost altogether. And without the human ties and bonds that the activity of parenting makes possible, a more general sense of "brotherhood" and "sisterhood" simply cannot emerge.

The nature and scope of parental authority changes over time. Children learn that being a child is not a permanent condition. Indeed, the family teaches us that no authority on this earth is omnipotent, unchanging, or absolute. Working through familial authority, as children struggle for identity, requires that they question authority more generally. Examples of authoritarian parents do not disconfirm this ideal case; they do, however, show that familial authority, like any constitutive principle, is subject to abuse. Yet granting particular instances of abuse, familial authority, in both ideal and actual forms, remains uniquely capable of keeping alive that combination of obligation and duty, freedom and dissent, that is the heart of democratic life.

Any further erosion of the ethical life embodied in the family bodes ill for democracy. For example, we can experience the plight of homelessness as a human tragedy only because we cherish an ideal of what it means to have a home. We find it easier to love others if we ourselves have been loved. We learn self-sacrifice and commitment as we learn so many things—in small, manageable steps, starting close to home. Thus, the family, at its best, helps foster a commitment to "do something" about a whole range of social problems. The ideal of family, then, is a launching pad into more universal commitments, a civic *Moralität*. The child who emerges from such a family is more capable of acting in the world as a complex moral being.

To destroy the family would create a general debacle from which we would not soon recover. The replacement for parents and families would not comprise a happy, consensual world of children coequal with adults. It would be a world in which children would become clients of bureaucrats and engineers of all sorts, many of whom would, inevitably, regard children largely as grist for the mill of extrafamilial schemes and ambitions.

DEMOCRATIC AUTHORITY AND THE FAMILY: AMBIGUITIES

The strong case presumes a family that is secure in its authoritative role—a family that serves as the bearer of a clear *telos*. This is spine-stiffening stuff, but it assumes a wide social surrounding that no longer exists. American society ceased long ago to endorse unambiguously the shouldering of family obligations or to locate honor in long-term moral responsibilities. Authoritative norms have fallen under relentless pressures that promote individualistic, mobile, and tentative relations between self and others. Modern life enjoins us to remain as untrammeled as possible in order to attain individual goals and to enjoy our "freedom."

Constraints today are more onerous than they were when it was anticipated that everyone would share them: that is, all women, almost without exception, would become mothers; all men, almost without exception, would become supportive fathers. Young people, finding themselves surrounded by a social ethos that no longer affords clear-cut moral and social support for familial relations, choose in growing numbers to postpone or evade these responsibilities.

In acknowledging these transformations, the case for familial authority is softened but not abandoned. Taking account of shifts in the social ethos does not mean that one succumbs to them as if they comprised a new authoritative norm simply by virtue of their existence. But some alterations are warranted, including articulation of less dauntingly rigorous normative requirements for being a "parent" than are implied by the strong argument. The changes I suggest here are not, I hope, facile reassurances that modern human beings can be both unfettered individualists and encumbered parents in some happy, perfect harmony. Parental authority both constrains and makes possible; it locates mothers and fathers in the world in a way that must be different from that of nonparenting adults. This fact need not lock parents into some dour notion of duty that encourages them to overstate both their power to shape their children and their responsibility for doing so. The modern family is a porous institution, one open to a variety of external influences. Parents are no longer the sole moral guardians. A defense of modern familial authority must take this, too, into account.

Critics might insist that even a softened defense of family authority—indeed, any defense at all—is "arbitrary" in several ways because it privileges procreative heterosexual unions, thereby excluding a variety of other intimate arrangements, whether "nonexclusive," "open" marriages and families, or homosexual unions; because it posits the child as a dependent who requires discipline and restriction, thus shoring up paternalism ostensibly in behalf of children but in reality to deny them their rights; because it limits parental choices by stressing dependability, trust, and loyalty to the exclusion of adventure, unpredictability, and openness; and because it constructs a case for ethical development that is self-confirming in assuming that a set of authoritative norms is essential to personal life.

Perhaps, this critic might go on, behavior modification is a less strenuous and more effective shaper of a child's action. Perhaps children transferred at an early age out of the home and into a group context emerge less burdened by individual conscience and moral autonomy and hence are freer to act creatively without incessant, guilt-ridden ruminations about responsibility and consequence. Perhaps children who learn at an early age to be cynical and not trust adults will become skeptics and better prepared to accept the rapid changes of modernity than are the trusting, emotionally bonded, slowly maturing children of the authoritative family.

Admittedly, a defense of familial authority should recognize that every set of norms contains contingent features, "in the sense that, while they are indispensible to this way of life, there are other forms of living . . . in which this special set would not be necessary."[22] But contingent does not mean arbitrary. In the absence of authoritative rules, the social world would be more rather than less dominated by arbitrary violence, coercion, or crass manipulation.

Take, for example, the incest taboo. It can be construed as wholly arbitrary. A number of radical social critics have described this taboo as both "illegitimate" and "indefensible," contrary to freedom of expression and action. Exposing its arbitrariness, they would liberate children from paternalistic despotism and parents from ancient superstition. Chafing at restrictions of sexual exploration, these antiauthoritarians celebrate total freedom of sexuality.

Their mistake, one might wish to argue, is not their insistence that we recognize the conventional or "arbitrary" features of our social arrangements. It is rather their insistence that such recognition requires elimination of the rules in question. In assuming that some better form of existence might flourish in the absence of authoritative restrictions, the "antis" emerge as naive and dangerous. They would open up social life to more, rather than less, brutalization, including targeting children as acceptable resources for adult sexual manipulation. Yes, acceptance of the incest taboo implicates one in a conventional normative standard. But that standard sustains a social good—protecting children from abuse by the more powerful. We punish abusive parents precisely because we accept the idea that adult power must be limited. Adult power, shorn of the internal moral limits of, for example, the incest taboo, would become more generalized, less accountable, and dangerously unlimited.

A second criticism holds that in defending the family, one privileges a restrictive ideal of intimate relations. More people in America are coming to believe that a society should stay equally open to all alternative arrangements, treating "life-styles" as so many morally identical peas in a pod. To be sure, families coexist with other life-style forms, whether heterosexual and homosexual unions that are by choice or by definition childless, communalists who diminish individual parental authority in favor of the preeminence of the group, and so on. *But the acceptance of plural possibilities does not mean each alternative is equal to every other regarding specific social goods.* No social order has ever existed that did not privilege certain activities and practices as preferable to others. Every social order forges terms of inclusion and exclusion. Ethically responsible challenges may loosen those terms, but they do not negate a normative endorsement of family life. In defining family authority, then, we acknowledge that we are privileging relations of a particular kind in which certain social goods are at stake.

Those excluded by, or who exclude themselves from, these norms should not be denied social space and tolerance. And if that which is at stake were, say, seeking out and exploring those creations of self that enhance an aesthetic construction of life and sensibility, the romantic bohemian or rebel might well get higher marks than the Smith family of Fremont, Nebraska. But regarding what families do, those explorations are not at stake.

Accordingly, we should be cautious about going too far in the direction of a wholly untrammeled pluralism of intimate relations. It is possible to become so vapid that we no longer distinguish between the moral weightiness of, say, polishing one's Porsche and sitting up all night with a sick child. The intergenerational family creates irreplaceable and invaluable social goods by nurturing recognition of human frailty, mortality, and finitude and by inculcating moral limits and constraints. A revamped defense of family authority, then, takes account of challenges to its normalizing features. It also opens it to ambiguities and paradox. But the essential defense remains.

Neatness Isn't Everything

What about the worries of liberal thinkers historically about the family's anomalous position within a civic world governed by contractarian and voluntarist norms? It seems to me, finally, that those worries are misplaced. Ironically, what such analysts fear is what I here endorse: a form of familial authority that does not mesh perfectly with democratic principles. That form, I contend, remains vital to the sustaining of a diverse and morally decent culture. This paradox is one of many that social life throws up and that civic philosophers would be well advised to recognize and to nourish. For the discordance embodied in this uneasy coexistence of familial and democratic authority sustains the struggles over identity, purpose, and meaning that form the very stuff of democratic life. To resolve this untidiness, we could simply declare a set of unitary authoritative norms. Or we could simply eliminate all norms as arbitrary and oppressive. But to do either is to jeopardize the social goods that democratic and familial authority—paradoxical in relation to one another—promise to citizens and their children.

NOTES

1. Michael Walzer, *Spheres of Justice* (New York: Basic Books, 1983).

2. Plato, *The Republic*, Book 6, Bloom translation (New York: Basic Books, 1968), pp. 500c–501b.

3. Shulamith Firestone, *The Dialectic of Sex* (New York: Bantam Books, 1972).

4. Anne Donchin, "The Future of Mothering: Reproductive Technology and Feminist Theory," *Hypatia* 2 (No. 2, Fall 1986), p. 130.

5. Alison Jagger, *Feminist Politics and Human Nature* (Totowa, NJ: Rowman and Allanhead, 1983), p. 132.

6. Ibid., p. 132.

7. Martha Nussbaum, *The Fragility of Goodness* (Cambridge, England: Cambridge University Press, 1960), p. 40.

8. Ibid., pp. 135, 141.

9. Ibid., p. 214.

10. This is not to say that all features of these ontologies are, in principle, no longer available to us. Many people continue to structure their lives primarily in and through such ontologies of faith, but not, I would argue, without conflict.

11. See Robert Filmer, *Patriarcha and Other Political Works*, Peter Laslett, ed. (Oxford: Basil Blackwell, 1949).

12. Here, as elsewhere, Hobbes is an anomalous thinker, fusing absolutism with consent in all spheres, including the family, and accepting coerced "choice" as legitimate.

13. See Mary Lyndon Shanley, "Marriage Contract and Social Contract in Seventeenth-Century English Political Thought," in Jean Bethke Elshtain, ed., *The Family in Political Thought* (Amherst, MA: University of Massachusetts Press, 1982), pp. 80–95.

14. John Locke, *Two Treatises of Government*, Peter Laslett, ed. (New York: New American Library, 1965), p. 357.

15. John Stuart Mill, *The Subjection of Women* (Greenwich, CT: Fawcett, 1970).

16. Not even Mill took the argument for consent to its *reductio ad absurdum*, as has been done in some recent versions of "children's liberation." See Richard W. Krouse, "Patriarchal Liberalism and Beyond: From John Stuart Mill to Harriet Taylor," in Elshtain, ed., op. cit., pp. 145–172.

17. Alexis de Tocqueville, *Democracy in America*, vol. 2, Phillips Bradley, ed. (New York: Vintage Books, 1945), p. 223.

18. Ibid., p. 209. There is an echo of Rousseau in this.

19. Ibid., pp. 203–204.

20. William E. Connolly, "Modern Authority and Ambiguity," *Politics and Ambiguity* (Madison, WI: University of Wisconsin Press, 1987), pp. 127–142. Connolly argues that ambiguity is necessary to a defense of authority in modernity.

21. Mary Midgley, *Beast and Man: The Roots of Human Nature* (Ithaca, NY: Cornell University Press, 1978), p. 291.

22. Connolly, op. cit., p. 138.

=8=

A Christian View
Of the Family

Gilbert Meilaender

I n his engagingly titled book, *What's Wrong with the World*, G. K. Chesterton argued that his fellow citizens could not repair the defects of the family because they had no ideal at which to aim. Neither the Tory (Gudge) nor the Socialist (Hudge) viewed the family as sacred or had an image of what the family at its best might be.

> The Tory says he wants to preserve family life in Cindertown; the Social-ist very reasonably points out to him that in Cindertown at present there isn't any family life to preserve. But Hudge, the Socialist, in his turn, is highly vague and mysterious about whether he would preserve the family life if there were any; or whether he will try to restore it where it has dis-appeared. . . . The Tory sometimes talks as if he wanted to tighten the domestic bonds that do not exist; the Socialist as if he wanted to loosen the bonds that do not bind anybody. The question we all want to ask of both of them is the original ideal question, "Do you want to keep the family at all?"[1]

The result of such confusion, Chesterton thought, was that in his own day "the cultured class is shrieking to be let out of the decent home, just as the working class is shouting to be let into it."[2]

In such circumstances one needed an ideal—a point from which to begin and on the basis of which to think about the world. Chesterton began "with a little girl's hair."

> That I know is a good thing at any rate. Whatever else is evil, the pride of a good mother in the beauty of her daughter is good. It is one of those adamantine tendernesses which are the touchstones of every age and race. If other things are against it, other things must go down. . . . With the red hair of one she-urchin in the gutter I will set fire to all modern civilization. Because a girl should have long hair, she should have clean

---

Gilbert Meilaender is Professor of Religion at Oberlin College in Oberlin, Ohio.

hair; because she should have clean hair, she should not have an unclean home; because she should not have an unclean home, she should have a free and leisured mother; because she should have a free mother, she should not have an usurious landlord; because there should not be an usurious landlord, there should be a redistribution of property; because there should be a redistribution of property, there shall be a revolution. That little urchin with the gold-red hair, whom I have just watched toddling past my house, she shall not be lopped and lamed and altered; her hair shall not be cut short like a convict's; no, all the kingdoms of the earth shall be hacked about and mutilated to suit her. She is the human and sacred image; all around her the social fabric shall sway and split and fall; the pillars of society shall be shaken, and the roofs of ages come rushing down; and not one hair of her head shall be harmed.[3]

I am not myself capable of such a peroration, but I confess to more than a little sympathy for Chesterton's approach. I did not actually think about him, however, until I had made my way through several recent documents on the family issued by Protestant bodies in this country.

Well-meaning they surely are, as well as sincerely troubled by human need. But, feeling it necessary to "affirm" every person in whatever state he or she may be, the authors of these documents find it difficult to set before us any clear ideal at which we ought to aim. To articulate such an ideal might seem too much like condemning those who do not meet it. Because there are blended families, group families, and single-parent families—all of them constituted by people whose needs the churches aim to serve—one may become increasingly reluctant to affirm an ideal. That, at any rate, seems to me a reasonable—and charitable—explanation of our current circumstances.

A very recent study illustrates this point. Still in draft form and entitled *Living in Covenant with God and One Another*, it was prepared for the World Council of Churches.[4] It makes a virtue of our necessities: "Families take many forms. We tend to idealize the family form we know. Yet no single structure captures the heart of the family."[5] It should be no surprise to discover that the document has almost nothing to say about the relation of parents and children. Rather, its attention is focused on certain moral quandaries or on those who find themselves in troubling situations. Thus, after a section on "healthy sexuality" (devoted chiefly to exploration of false dualisms), the document treats divorce and remarriage, domestic violence, homosexuality, singleness, abortion, and AIDS. The closest it comes to a discussion of what the family ought to be is in a discussion of single life. We are told that the Bible is a "family-oriented book"—which means that ancient Hebrew society was organized in a patriarchal clan structure and that lines of descent and rules of family obligation were emphasized. Jesus, however, though aware of the importance of family love, reinterpreted the meaning of the family. Thus, for example, in Mark 3, Jesus is told that his mother and brothers are waiting to see him. But looking at the crowd standing around him, he replies:

"Here are my mother and my brothers! Whoever does the will of God is my brother, and sister, and mother."[6] The document comments:

> Jesus, it seems, was saying that what is most important is not the family form or structure, though these are necessary for society, but the quality of love, trust, caring and so on that are products of our basic love of God. He was redefining family, not in terms of the need of society for stable families, but of persons to be members of a community that seeks to serve God."[7]

One might wish to argue with this interpretation. For example, we might rethink any characterization of ancient Hebrew society and reevaluate the uniqueness of what Jesus says when we remember that the call of Yahweh to the patriarch Abraham was already a call *away* from family: "Go from your country and your kindred and your father's house to the land that I will show you."[8] To be sure, the hard sayings of Jesus about the family are important. But they are far more than just a reinterpretation of the family and they are certainly not simply a claim that all that counts morally is the "quality" of a relationship. They may call upon us to transcend the family, but we must first know and value the thing we are transcending if our action is to have religious significance.

> The sight of a Christian rebuking his mother, though tragic, may be edifying; but only if we are quite sure that he has been a good son and that, in his rebuke, spiritual zeal is triumphing, not without agony, over strong natural affection. The moment there is reason to suspect that he enjoys rebuking her—that he believes himself to be rising above the natural level while he is still, in reality, grovelling below it in the unnatural—the spectacle becomes merely disgusting. The hard sayings of the Lord are wholesome to those only who find them hard.[9]

We need to be persuaded that, in disavowing any ideal of what the family ought to be, we are rising above, not simply falling below, the natural realm.

Living in Covenant with God and One Another appears to be a representative document. Like most recent statements from Protestant church bodies, it attests to the seriousness with which such Christians still take the marital bond, which continues to be understood as the most appropriate context for sexual relations. In addition, one can find many statements from Protestant churches about certain problems or quandaries that may impinge upon the family, such as abortion, gender role conflicts, and homosexuality.

But what is said about the family itself? On this topic, we find chiefly an affirmation of diversity. One will not find this emphasis articulated more simply and straightforwardly than in the statement on "family life priority" adopted by the United Church of Christ in 1981. It calls for the identification and development of resources "which will enable all families to be ministered to creatively and all persons, regardless of their family patterns, to be affirmed and supported in the life of the Church."[10] Behind such statements lies an emphasis articulated already in 1978 by G. William Sheek, then Director of Family Ministries and Human Sexuality of the National Council of Churches. He suggested that the "quality" rather than the "structure" of relationships should define the family.[11] And he did so in the belief that this is the New Testament vision: a family "built around the quality of relationships shared by the members of God's kingdom rather than blood ties."[12] Similarly, the 1980 *Book of Resolutions* of the United Methodist Church says:

> Marriage and family patterns have always had historical and cultural features that vary under changing circumstances. Basic to any family form is commitment to one another's care and welfare. Responsible family relationships may be expressed in a variety of ways. . . . The church is concerned about the well-being of all persons in all family forms.[13]

This is, of course, not the only thing the churches have had to say. But their chief wisdom about the family seems to lie in this simple statement: "The family appears in many forms in different times and places."[14]

Yet this *leitmotif* may say both too much and too little about the family. It may seem radical, but it turns out to be rather bland. We say *too little* about the family because we find ourselves unable to articulate what it should be at its best. We say *too much* because we do not take with full seriousness the way in which the family—even at its best—is not just reinterpreted but transcended in the kingdom of God. When our focus is only on "quality of relationship" versus "structure," the family tends to become chiefly a locus of self-fulfillment for singular individuals. Thus, for example, a "Family Life Statement" prepared in 1980 by the American Lutheran Church's Division for Life and Mission in the Congregation suggested:

> Families need to clarify the role and function of each individual on the basis of that person's uniqueness. . . . Role expectations, since they contribute to the structure of relationships, must be taken seriously. These roles, however, should never become more important than the persons involved.[15]

A more helpful example of a recent church statement is the *Evangelical Catechism*.[16] A translation and adaptation of the United Evangelical Lutheran Church of Germany's *Evangelischer Gemeindekatechismus*, this volume was prepared under the auspices of the American Lutheran Church. The chapter on "Parents and Children," perhaps because it is aimed at catechetical use, seeks to provide some guidance. Even here, however, there is a certain reluctance to speak normatively. For example:

> It is no longer possible to assume that a child lives with two parents, a father who works outside the home and a mother who works at home. This idealized picture of family life was never completely accurate, but today it is just one style of family life among many others. Today children are brought up in a variety of settings, with a variety of adult models and types of care.[17]

As a descriptive statement, this is no doubt unexceptionable. But, again, a desire to help everyone, whatever his or her family circumstances, makes it more difficult to provide one particular sort of help: it is harder to depict what a family at its best ought to be.

And if we are not careful, such an approach can fail to capture what the family ought to be and often has been. Thus, for example, the *Evangelical Catechism* notes that we have learned a good bit about the importance of nurture in a child's early years, "and we understand how important parents—adult persons who care for children—are."[18] That formulation, applicable to personnel at day-care centers and babysitters, is certainly inadequate to describe what is meant by a parent. That the adults working at day-care centers may sometimes provide more nurture for children than do their parents is a description of our problem, not a reason to redefine those adults as parents.

In short, in a culture quite uncertain about the meaning of parenthood, a church eager to serve and affirm the lives of countless different men and women is able to say relatively little about the structure of the parent–child bond. It is reduced to speaking about the quality of relationships. That, at least, is my hunch about the reason for the relative paucity of material about the family coming from the churches and the character of what material there is.

What to do in such circumstances? We might take heart from the comments Karl Barth made upon the publication of the first volume of his *Church Dogmatics*. Recognizing the disarray of the church, he wondered how it was possible to speak on its behalf. Nevertheless, he wrote, "[b]ecause I think anyone would wait in vain till the day of judgment for an Evangelical Church that took itself seriously, unless in all humility he was willing to risk being such a Church in his own place and as well as he knew how,"[19] he took up the task. In that spirit, we will consider some of the pressure points at which the church might articulate its vision of the bond between parents and children.

THE KINGDOM AND THE FAMILY

First, however, a point must be made that was only faintly adumbrated in the World Council of Churches statement's suggestion that Jesus had redefined the family: the fellowship of the kingdom of God, though it may be spoken of as a family, is neither generated nor sustained through biological transmission of life or by the love given and received in the history of our families. The kingdom is not a continuation, or even a reinterpretation, of the family as we know it; rather, it is a new creation.

I have not forgotten the day when, as a graduate student at Princeton, I sat in that university's Firestone Library talking with a fellow graduate student who happened to be a Benedictine monk. In the course of our conversation I uttered some platitude about the family being the fundamental unit of society. To this he responded—with the immediacy of what had become for him a natural response—"Oh, I don't know. After all, Jesus said, 'Whoever loves father or mother more than me is not worthy of me.' " And he had a point. We have already cited Jesus' words in Mark 3:35 that "whoever does the will of God is my brother, and sister, and mother." A similar lesson is found in the well-known story of the boy Jesus, left behind by his parents in the temple, recounted in the gospel of Luke. His parents, fearful that he is lost, eventually find him in the temple, "sitting among the teachers, listening to them and asking them questions." His mother expresses her anxiety, a very natural parental concern, and Jesus' answer must have seemed a harsh response. He asks: "How is it that you sought me? Did you not know that I must be in my Father's house?"[20]

Thus Jesus is proclaimed as the revelation of a God who is not dependent on the natural orders of this world to achieve his ends. To those who have confidence in such natural orders John the Baptist says: "Do not presume to say to yourselves, 'We have Abraham as our father'; for I tell you, God is able from these stones to raise up children to Abraham."[21] And why not? This is the God who had set his hand upon Jacob rather than Esau, the firstborn son of Isaac. It is such a God whose presence Jesus announces and embodies.

> To another he said, "Follow me." But he said, "Lord, let me first go and bury my father." But he said to him, "Leave the dead to bury their own dead; but as for you, go and proclaim the kingdom of God." Another said, "I will follow you, Lord; but first let me say farewell to those at home." Jesus said to him, "No one who puts his hand to the plow and looks back is fit for the kingdom of God."[22]

The prophet Micah had characterized the evils of his time in part through family imagery as a time when

> the son treats the father with contempt,
> the daughter rises up against her mother,
> the daughter-in-law against her mother-in-law;
> a man's enemies are the men of his own house.[23]

But this very picture becomes for Jesus the possible and, in some instances, necessary result of his preaching of the kingdom.

> Do not think that I have come to bring peace on earth; I have not come to bring peace, but a sword. For I have come to set a man against his father, and a daughter against her mother, and a daughter-in-law against her mother-in-law; and a man's foes will be those of his own household. He who loves father or mother more than me is not worthy of me; and he who loves son or daughter more than me is not worthy of me.[24]

In the face of this recurrent theme of the Gospels, we would do well to be careful in our praise of the family. As Karl Barth put it, we "must not blind ourselves to [the fact] that the kingdom of God has come from heaven to earth, that it has taken solid shape amongst us, and that it has foreshadowed the end of all human history and therefore of the child–parent relationship."[25] Barth adds, rightly, that we cannot deduce from this any general rule about how all Christians must live. But we also cannot deny that even here and now some may be called away from the family by God. For some it may mean that "there is an orphaned state required for the sake of the kingdom of heaven, in which a man who like all others is the child of his parents must symbolise with his being and action the present but hidden creation which is not a mere prolongation of the old, but the new creation in relation to which the old has already passed away."[26]

This is, therefore, the first word that must be spoken: of discontinuity between the kingdom of God and any earthly order, even one as significant as the family. But two more things must also be said. First, as was quoted above: "The hard sayings of the Lord are wholesome to those only who find them hard." If the world is the good creation of God, then such discontinuity must be experienced first as painful and troubling.

Second, through and beyond the painful experience of discontinuity between the earthly family and the call of God may also come some sense of continuity. Even Barth cannot keep from saying that the discontinuity "is not a question of the destruction but of the radical renewal of the child–parent relationship."[27] He notes that the very last verse of the Old Testament looks forward to a time "before the great and terrible day of the Lord" when God "will turn the hearts of fathers to their children and the hearts of children to their fathers."[28] And, in fact, we are hard pressed to find better imagery with which to describe the promised kingdom— imagery for which there is dominical warrant. Jesus, whose call may draw one out of the orbit of the family, yet describes the promise of the coming kingdom precisely in familial terms.

> Truly, I say to you, there is no one who has left house or brothers or sisters or mother or father or children or lands, for my sake and for the gospel, who will not receive a hundredfold now in this time, houses and brothers and sisters and mothers and children and lands, with persecutions, and in the age to come eternal life.[29]

What such a transformed familial community will be like one can scarcely say. To be sure, the life of the church in this age gives only the barest of hints. But it is significant that in reaching for images to describe the hoped-for king-dom we are driven to see—beyond the death of all earthly communities at the cross and the experienced discontinuity the cross brings—a certain conti-nuity between the promised new life and the very best that we have known and experienced here and now. But, of course, this presumes that we can and should be able to say something about the structure of this "very best" in order that we may know how great is the worth of the bond we may have to give up in answer to Jesus' call and in order to find words to describe, however haltingly, the community of promise.

BIOLOGICAL COMMUNITY

When we think about the bond of parents and children, we must speak first of the family as a biological community. Through this bond we are embedded in the world of nature, are marked by lines of kinship and descent, and are—from birth—individuals within communities.

Like the other animals, humans "bring forth . . . according to their kinds" and, in more peculiarly human fashion, pass on to children their image and likeness.[30] Our personhood is marked by that inheritance as we incarnate the union of the man and the woman who are our parents. They are not simply reproducing themselves. In reaching out to each other, they forge a community between two who are different and separate. When from their oneness they create a new human being, that act testifies to the truth that love for one other than the self—even, and especially biologically, within the sexual differentiation—is a love that does not seek simply to see its own face in the loved one. This love is creative of community. And the bond formed between parents and children does in fact bind; with it come obligations. Parents have, whether they want it or not, the honor and responsibility to stand before their children as God's representatives. And children have that most puzzling of duties: to show gratitude for a bond in which they find themselves without in any way having chosen it. In what seems to be merely a biological fact, we find moral significance embedded. The psalmist writes that children are "a heritage from the Lord."[31] The child as a gift of God is a sign of hope, of God's continued affirmation of his creation. Still more, the presence of the child indicates that the parents, as co-creators with God, have shared something of the mystery of divine love: their love-giving has proved to be life-giving. That such complete giving of the self should, in fact, give new life is the deepest mystery of God's being and is hinted at, as if in analogy, in the birth of a child.

We are, of course, free in many ways to transcend our embeddedness in nature, but we ought also to respect the embodied character of human life. As parents of children and children of parents, we are marked by the biological communities in which we find ourselves. We are not just free spirits, free to make of ourselves what we will. There is, in part at least, a "givenness" to our existence that limits us. Part of the task of a faithful life is to learn to receive that givenness with thanksgiving and to be trustworthy in the duties it lays upon us.

If this is in part the meaning of the bond of parents and children, we should be clear about one important truth. This bond may very often make us deeply happy; indeed, it may have the capacity to bring some of the greatest joys into human life. But though it often fulfills us, it does not exist simply for the sake of our fulfillment. Parents are not reproducing themselves; they are giving birth to an other human being, equal to them in dignity and bound to them in ties of kinship, but not created for their satisfaction. To desire a child of "one's own" is understandable, but such language should be used only with great caution. Biological parenthood does not confer possession of children, nor should it lead us to hope for a "perfect" child. Rather, it calls us to the historical tasks of rearing, nurturing, and civilizing our children so that the next generation may achieve its own relative independence. Self-giving, not self-fulfillment, lies at the heart of the parents' vocation. If such self-giving should prove to be deeply satisfying, we have reason to be thankful. But such a symmetrically satisfying result is not guaranteed, and to seek it is not the best way to prepare for parenthood. To give birth is a venture that should always be carried out in hope and in faith that the creator will continue to speak his "yes" upon the creation.

HISTORICAL COMMUNITY

If we wish to think properly of the family as a biological community, we must think of it also as a historical community. In love a man and a woman turn from themselves toward each other. They might be forever content to turn toward each other, and to turn out from themselves no more than that. But in the child, their union, as a union, quite naturally turns outward. They are not permitted to think of themselves as individuals who come together simply for their own fulfillment. In the child they are given a task. Their union plays its role in a larger history and it becomes part of their vocation to contribute to the ongoing life of a people. Certainly both Jews and Christians have commonly understood the bond of parents and children in this way.

> I will utter dark sayings from of old,
> things that we have heard and known,
> that our fathers have told us.
> We will not hide them from their children,
> but tell to the coming generation
> the glorious deeds of the LORD, and his might,
> and the wonders which he has wrought.
> He established a testimony in Jacob,
> and appointed a law in Israel,
> which he commanded our fathers
> to teach to their children;
> that the next generation might know them,
> the children yet unborn,
> and arise to tell them to their children,
> so that they should set their hope in God.[32]

In many ways this is the most fundamental task of parents: transmission of a way of life. When the son of the ancient Israelite asked, "What does this mean?" his father told again the story of the mighty acts of God, the story of their common life as a people. When a woman of Israel appeals to the biological bond and cries out to Jesus, "Blessed is the womb that bore you, and the breasts that you sucked," he responds: "Blessed rather are those who hear the word of God and keep it."[33] He points to a further bond that ought to be built upon the basis of biological community but which, in any case, is finally more crucial: initiation into a way of life. The apostle writes that fathers should not provoke their children to anger, but should "bring them up in the *paideia* and instruction of the Lord."[34] That task of *paideia*, of nurture and inculcation of a way of life, is the calling of parents.[35]

Of course, these biblical passages refer to the transmission of a religious tradition: the story of God's care for his people. But we need not deny that they also point more generally to something fundamental. Parenthood is not just biological begetting. It is also history—a vocation to nurture the next generation, to initiate it into the human inheritance of knowledge and obligation. If today many feel that the family is "in crisis," that may be in large part because parents have little commitment to or sense of a story to pass on.

But passing on a story is what binds the generations together, and it is something quite different from the shared association of those concerned above all else about their respective career trajectories. It is also quite different from an understanding of parental nurture aimed principally at "enriching" the lives of individual children. In a family that understands itself as a historical community sharing a way of life not its alone, it seems appropriate that some should make sacrifices for the sake of others and that all should make heavy claims upon one another.[36] Understood in this way, a family is something quite different from a political community, and the language of "rights"—which has served us well in the political sphere—is peculiarly unable to capture the texture of family life. Perhaps the most common use of the language of parental rights is to protect the possessive claims of those whose history of abuse or neglect as parents has largely undermined their claim to the title. But the language of "children's rights" is not likely to serve us much better. Surely at times the state must intervene in the life of families in order to protect children, but it is more likely to be effective in acting against manifest evils than in positively restructuring families. For the state is a community of quite a different kind, and it simply has "no mode of entry" into the give-and-take of genuine family life. "Creatures so close to each other as husband and wife, or a mother and children, have powers of making each other happy or miserable with which no public coercion can deal."[37]

In the family understood as a historical community, we ought not shy away from thinking in terms of roles played by parents—even while we acknowledge and respect the truth that each set of parents will accomplish this in a way peculiarly theirs. Consider the fact that a mother is biologically equipped to nourish her newborn infant. In our historical freedom we are able to transcend that natural fact, and we certainly need not let it determine our understanding of what motherhood means. But we should also not ignore it, as if our embodied condition carried no personal significance. No doubt many different ways exist to find and live out such significance, but we ought to seek them and not simply seek freedom to be whatever we wish.

Perhaps this sense of motherhood as both nature and history can be conveyed by suggesting that a mother, though not "in her place," should seek to "be place" for her children. For she is that—the womb from which they come, the place to which they remain connected even as they gradually work out their separateness.[38] The role of mother is so firmly grounded in biology that it can come to seem only necessity and not at all free opportunity, all biologically given and no freely developing history. Hence, in thinking about it we are probably not wrong to emphasize our historical freedom. The opposite is true of a father's role. Lacking so obvious a biological attachment to the child, a father may too easily think himself free of that role or may be uncertain of what it means that he should be a father. Perhaps, however, the image of father as judge—one who ought to aim at fairness even when mediating between his children and the world outside the family—has some value. If it should be true, as Carol Gilligan has argued, that men are drawn toward a morality of abstract justice and women toward a morality of connected webs of caring and that neither of these taken by itself constitutes the whole of the moral realm, then mother and father together—but in different ways—may inculcate and transmit moral value and commitment.[39] Just as history brings freedom from rigid role definitions, it may also give us the freedom to think seriously again about what it means to be not simply a parent, but a mother or father in particular.

As noted earlier, the idea of the family as a biological community points us in the direction of self-giving love. The same is true when we envision the family as a historical community. Here, even more clearly and starkly, the risk and venture of parenthood come into view. Parents commit themselves to initiating their children into the human inheritance and, more particularly, into the stories that depict their way of life. In so doing they shape, mold, and civilize their children. But there are no guarantees that the final "product" of this process will be what the parents anticipated. Parents know this, of course, and are therefore understandably anxious about their children's future. Even if such anxiety is often understandable, it still constitutes a great temptation—the temptation to try to be the guarantor of our children's future, to protect them from all disappointment and suffering. And yet, to do that would be to deny their freedom to be an other like us, equal to us in dignity. This means that parents must seek more than their own satisfaction in rearing their children. They must give of themselves in faith and hope, recognizing that they are no more than co-creators and that they cannot shape the future.

A WORD THE CHURCHES MIGHT SUPPLY

Imagine yourself in social conversation with a stranger, conversation in which you are identifying yourself. You depict yourself in terms of your role as mother or father. The question eventually follows, as surely as night follows day, "And what do you do for yourself?" At that point, unless you do not wish to be taken seriously, you espouse commitment to a career.

If the twofold characterization of the family made in this chapter—as biological and historical community—is accurate, we ought not be surprised to discover that today we are radically confused when trying to think about the family. For ours is a world that insistently raises the question, "What do you do for yourself?" And, in the words of Gabriel Marcel, a family "is not created or maintained as an entity without the exercise of a fundamental generosity."[40] To put it bluntly, in the family, we largely find ourselves by giving ourselves to our functions. We lose our life—that grasping need to "be someone"—and then learn to see ourselves in a larger context of meaning. To give birth and to nourish and sustain that new life are acts of self-spending that can only be compared with a gift. They imply a certain fundamental generosity, a willingness to expend one's energies and one's person in nourishing and sustaining the next generation. And it may not be easy to decide why or how that should be done if we are too busy pondering what we should do for ourselves.

If the family ought to be the sort of community that demands a great deal of us, why might we want or need it? Why undertake the effort it involves? A social and theological case can be made for commitment to the family, and we can begin with the lesser and move toward the greater. Renewal of the species and rearing of the next generation might, of course, take place apart from anything remotely resembling the family. That is a very old idea. Plato had Socrates propose it when constructing the ideal city in the *Republic*. He suggests that by making kinship universal we could eliminate the divisive passions that ordinary family preference involves. In today's setting we could establish a universal system of day-care centers to which children were given at birth and in which everyone had a hand in the care of all children—and in this way begin to approximate Socrates' proposal. If, however, the family is the sort of community I have described, doing this would make war on the elements written very deeply into our nature. And no doubt Aristotle had something like that in mind when he suggested that Socrates' proposal would do more than combat divisive passion; it might also dilute a sense of concern and responsibility for those who come after us.[41]

We can expand a little upon that claim. A parent, after all, is not simply a public functionary charged with looking after a certain number of children. The special attachment that characterizes the parent–child bond serves, at its best, as a kind of guarantee of love—almost an analogue to divine grace. (That it does not always work this way indicates only that it is

144

no more than an analogue and that quite often we are not at our best.) The child is loved unconditionally, *for no particular reason.* I love my children not because they are especially talented or qualified in one way or another, but simply because they have been given to me and placed into my care. And only such love, founded on no particular quality or attribute, can offer something approaching unconditional acceptance.

If I love my son because he plays the piano well, or my daughter because she executes the pick-and-roll with precision, if that is the ground of my special attachment, then it is subject to change. There can be little certainty that my commitment will endure; for it is likely that others will play both piano and basketball better. But when, by contrast, parental love is grounded in the facts of biological and historical bonding, the child lives in a setting that offers the kind of acceptance human beings need to become capable of adult commitment—a setting in which individuals who are separate but connected can grow and flourish. Thus, Michael Walzer has perceptively commented that

> [o]ne might . . . liberate women from childbirth as well as parents from child care, by cloning the next generation . . . or by purchasing babies from underdeveloped countries. This is not the redistribution but the abolition of parental love, and I suspect that it would quickly produce a race of men and women incapable even of the commitment required for an affair.[42]

At least this much can be said about the social purpose of the family among our earthly communities.

But from a Christian perspective our commitment to the family cannot and ought not be grounded simply in its importance for our common life. However treasured and significant, this remains only penultimate. The family is also something more than a basic social unit. It is a sphere in which God is at work on us, shaping and molding us, that we may become people who genuinely wish to share his life of love. The overarching interpretive rubric within which to understand the spheres of human life—here, in particular, the family—is Augustine's statement that the servants of God "have no reason to regret even this life of time, for in it they are schooled for eternity."[43] In biblical terms we might cite 1 John 4:20: "[H]e who does not love his brother whom he has seen, cannot love God whom he has not seen." The family is a school of virtue in which God sets before us, day after day, one person or a few persons whom we are to love. This is the *paideia* of the heavenly Father at work upon both children and parents, building upon the love that comes naturally to us in our families, but transforming it also into the image of his own love. Here he begins to turn us into people who have learned to love and who will want to live with him in a community of love.

Such straightforward religious talk may, of course, seem alien to the common life of our society, and no doubt it is to some degree. Yet, it may be precisely the language for which we are searching. We tend to make of the family both too much and too little. Too much is made of it, as parents seek to reproduce themselves in their children, feverishly seek children "of their own," and try as much as possible to protect those children from all experience of suffering and sacrifice. In doing this we ask of the family—which remains, after all, only a penultimate sphere of life—more than it can give and we place upon it expectations that must inevitably be disappointed. Too little is made of the family, in that we can so seldom discover in the family anything more than an arena for our personal fulfillment, in that we fail to see it as a community that ought to transmit a way of life. What we really need is language that can affirm the importance of the family as biological and historical community without depriving that bond of a still greater *telos*, of a larger aim and meaning. Perhaps we would do well to learn from Augustine to think of the family as a school of virtue, or from 1 John of the family as a sphere in which we learn the meaning of commitment to a few and begin to learn the steps of the greater dance of love. And surely, if Christian churches have any distinctive insight to offer, any picture to paint of what the family might be, it is this.

The Trinitarian shape of Christian faith affirms that God is love. From eternity the Father begets the Son—that is, offers his life, all that he is and has, to the Son. Such self-giving begets a Son eternally willing to receive life with joy and humility, and to offer that life back to the One who gives it. The self-giving of the Father evokes a like response from the Son; it gives rise to a mutuality in love, the bond of love uniting Father and Son, which is the Spirit. As a school of virtue for both parents and children, the family exists to draw us into the love of this God.

Husbands and wives learn that in giving themselves fully to each other they forge a mutual bond of love that can be fruitful and creative. Mothers and fathers learn that in struggling with the demands of nurturing their children they develop a love that seeks the good of those children, not simply the good that parents alone can bestow. Parents learn that, in setting aside their own craving for fulfillment and giving themselves over to their parental functions, they can, in fact, become someone—a someone who has a history that individuates. Children learn to flourish in a context in which they are loved unconditionally and are encouraged to think of themselves as dependent, as grateful recipients of a gift to which they have no rightful claim. To be sure, at their best our families may only approach this ideal, and no doubt they often fall very short of it. But perhaps they come closer than we think more often than we think. Perhaps what they need is a word the churches might supply: a word that interprets the bond of parents and children in this light and gives to us all a renewed sense of what it means to live within a family.

NOTES

1. G. K. Chesterton, *Collected Works IV* (San Francisco: Ignatius Press, 1987), p. 212.

2. Ibid., p. 65.

3. Ibid., pp. 217f.

4. Robyn Smith, *Living in Covenant with God and One Another*, Draft of a Study on Sexuality and Human Relations requested by the Sixth Assembly of the World Council of Churches (Geneva, Switzerland: Family Education Office, World Council of Churches).

5. Ibid., p. 18.

6. Mark 3:34–35.

7. Smith, op. cit., pp. 32f.

8. Genesis 12:1.

9. C. S. Lewis, *God in the Dock* (Grand Rapids, MI: Eerdmans, 1970), p. 191.

10. "The Family Life Priority," wording adopted by General Synods 13 and 15 (1981 and 1983) of the United Church of Christ.

11. G. William Sheek, "Families: Diversity and Public Policy," Unpublished paper delivered to the Open Session on Families, Board for Homeland Ministries—United Church of Christ (November 4, 1978), p. 2.

12. Ibid.

13. Quoted in *A Compilation of Protestant Denominational Statements on Families and Sexuality* (New York: National Council of Churches, 1982), p. 1.

14. Lutheran Church in America, "Statement on Sex, Marriage and Family" (1970). Quoted in *A Compilation of Protestant Denominational Statements on Families and Sexuality*, p. 2.

15. "Family Life Statement," prepared by the Division for Life and Mission in the Congregation, The American Lutheran Church (The American Lutheran Church: Minneapolis, MN, 1980).

16. *Evangelical Catechism: Christian Faith in the World Today* (Minneapolis, MN: Augsburg Publishing House, 1982).

17. Ibid., pp. 305f.

18. Ibid., p. 306.

19. Karl Barth, *Church Dogmatics*, Vol. I, Part 1 (Edinburgh: T. & T. Clark, 1936), pp. xii–xiii.

20. Luke 2:41–51.

21. Matthew 3:9.

22. Luke 9:59–62.

23. Micah 7:6.

24. Matthew 10:34–37.

25. Karl Barth, op. cit., Vol. III, Part 4, p. 260. My discussion in the several preceding paragraphs is greatly indebted to Barth.

26. Ibid., p. 261.

27. Ibid., p. 264.

28. Malachi 4:6.

29. Mark 10:29–30.

30. Genesis 1:24; 5:3.

31. Psalm 127:3.

32. Psalm 78:2–7.

33. Luke 11:27–28.

34. Ephesians 6:4.

35. Karl Barth, op. cit., Vol. III, Part 4, pp. 281f.

36. Stanley Hauerwas, *A Community of Character* (Notre Dame and London: University of Notre Dame Press, 1981), pp. 160f.

37. G. K. Chesterton, op. cit., p. 68.

38. Robert Farrar Capon, *Bed and Board* (New York: Simon and Schuster, 1965), p. 62.

39. Carol Gilligan, *In a Different Voice: Psychological Theory and Women's Development* (Cambridge and London: Harvard University Press, 1982), p. 165.

40. Gabriel Marcel, *Homo Viator: Introduction to a Metaphysic of Hope* (New York: Harper Torchbooks, 1962), p. 87.

41. Aristotle, *Politics*, II:iii, p. 1261b. Cf., A. W. Price, *Love and Friendship in Plato and Aristotle* (Oxford: Clarendon Press, 1989), p. 188.

42. Michael Walzer, *Spheres of Justice* (New York: Basic Books, 1983), pp. 238f.

43. Augustine, *City of God*, I, 29.

=9=
The Jewish Family
In American Culture

Steven Bayme

W hat do Jewish families do? This question can be divided into two parts. First, how do Jewish history and philosophy influence family functioning in the Jewish community? And second, what is the impact of contemporary American culture upon the Jewish family? Because these are large questions, let us begin at the beginning: with the Jewish story of creation. The Book of Genesis teaches that "it is not good that man live alone."[1] Moreover, the first commandments to man are to "be fruitful and multiply" and to build society.[2] The earliest family history recorded in Genesis describes conflict, culminating in the murder of Abel by his brother Cain. Genesis concludes with the reconciliation of Joseph and his brothers: a divided family becomes whole again. Thus the overall theme of the Book of Genesis is that of building family—a necessary prerequisite to the later theme, found in the Book of Exodus, of building nationhood.

JEWISH FAMILY FUNCTIONS

What are the purposes of the family? First, as Genesis indicates, families overcome loneliness. Second, the first injunction to and imperative for families is that of procreation. The act of procreation affirms the covenant between God and man. Rabbinic tradition offers to men and women the opportunity, through procreation of the species, to become partners with God in the ongoing act of creation. Third, family creates the social bonds and building blocks of community. Finally, the family serves to transmit Jewish heritage—to pass on a way of life—and therefore functions as a bulwark against assimilation.

Steven Bayme is the Director of the Jewish Communal Affairs Department and the William Petschek National Jewish Family Center at the American Jewish Committee in New York City.

In Jewish thought, therefore, family and community closely inter-twine. The health of one depends upon the health of the other. This model of social thinking in many ways runs counter to the Enlightenment model of individualism, which emphasizes self-fulfillment and individual opportunity. Jewish tradition envisions self-fulfillment as possible and desirable, but through the family in the context of the community.

Throughout the turbulence of Jewish historical experience, the Jew-ish family has functioned as an island of stability and a normative anchor. In the modern Jewish experience, however, the encounter with modern culture and the value system of the Western Enlightenment has attenuat-ed this close connection between family and community.

In this light, it is easy to identify the characteristics of successful mar-riages among Jews. First, marriage was considered a universal norm, some-thing that virtually everyone experienced at one time or another. More-over, marriage provided an arena for sexuality, which Jewish thinkers always regarded with positive attitudes and saw as a vital aspect of success-ful marital partnerships. Third, marriage ensured companionship— an anti-dote to the lonely and existential condition of humanity. Fourth, marriage served the purposes of procreation. A union that produced fewer than two children was considered unsuccessful. Finally, marriage served as the vehi-cle for the transmission of Jewish tradition and identity and as the key to Jewish continuity.

These assumptions were facilitated historically by the presence of the extended family—aunts, uncles, grandparents, cousins, and other rela-tives. However, the extended family has been undermined by the modern experience in which mobility, professionalism, and individual entre-preneurship have become dominant norms among Jews.

Family life, to be sure, held both responsibilities and opportunities for individual growth. Family life taught relationship to others, responsi-bility, and the opportunity to become partners with the Almighty in the continuing act of creation. Moreover, family responsibilities meant tran-scending personal desires and self-centeredness.

The implication of this tradition for contemporary family life is clear: to understand family as an antidote to the reluctance, now pervasive in our culture, to make commitments beyond the self. Perhaps the best example of this concept of family lies in the Jewish theme of fathering. Historically, the Jewish father was teacher and nurturer. Being a father was central to the identity of the Jewish male. The responsibilities of father-hood, according to the ancient rabbis, were a balance of practical and spir-itual roles: training children for an occupation, transmitting Jewish tradi-tion, and teaching the skills of survival, such as swimming.[3]

Thus the Jewish family serves as the principal mediating institution between the individual and the community. The family enables children to grow into responsible community members. By strengthening families, the community strengthens itself.

The Jewish concept of fatherhood is part of an overall emphasis on the development of children. One of the best-known myths of Jewish family life is that adulthood begins with the bar mitzvah. Yet historically, in contrast with this myth, Jewish teenagers were never considered to be adults. They were instead regarded as adolescents who were often irresponsible and who experienced strong but unfulfilled sexual desires.[4] For the Jews, children were regarded as children. The responsibility of adults was to ensure their healthy development.[5]

What does that say about the bar mitzvah, an often misunderstood and much-maligned rite of passage? The bar mitzvah signifies approaching the edge of adulthood, the beginning of taking responsibility legally for one's actions. In our era, when many are reluctant to assume responsibility for their actions, this rite of passage can be a powerful reminder that we begin to become legally responsible for things that we do.

THE JEWISH FAMILY IN AMERICA TODAY

What is the relevance of these historical and philosophical themes? Contemporary Jewish families exhibit considerable continuity with earlier models. Divorce, singles, the presence of women in the workplace, and the use of surrogate child care are constant features of Jewish history and are by no means new in the modern context.

The crucial point of comparison springs from the ethos of modernity, which emphasizes individualism and shatters community control over private life. For example, Jews in the Middle Ages required the permission of the community to marry. Today one would never dream of communal regulation of marriage between individuals. However, the close relationship between family and community may still suggest relevant principles for public policy, especially policies that empower parents to exercise their functions. Considerable precedent for such public-policy measures already lies within Jewish tradition, which promotes special care for the single parent, who is regarded as vulnerable, makes provisions for child care when parents work, and fosters public-education initiatives to encourage family life.

To be sure, Jewish families today are in flux and in transition. Indeed, current trends raise the question of whether we can continue to expect Jewish families to fulfill their traditional functions. For example, today we ask of Jewish schools not only to transmit the knowledge and cultural literacy of Judaism but also to transmit Jewish identity and consciousness. Yet research demonstrates that without the involvement of families, Jewish schools can achieve very little. In other words, the trends of modernity will necessitate changes both in family functioning and in how society relates to families. However, the Jewish historical experience remains relevant, both in highlighting the core role of the family in society and also in suggesting the rich interdependence between building healthy families and building healthy societies.

How do Jewish families look today? Demographically, Jews continue to want marriage and to have small families. In 1982, 75% of Jewish college students expressed their desire to marry. Only 3% had ruled it out. More than 90% of American Jews marry at some point in their lives.[6]

What has changed is a delay in the age of marriage. In the 1960s, 45% of Jews ages 18 through 24 had been married. By 1970 only 25% of this age group had been married.[7] This delay is consistent with patterns for educated, upper-middle-class Americans generally. Thus today, only two-thirds of adult Jews are currently married, creating prolonged periods of singlehood.

This fact raises policy issues for the Jewish community. Jewish communal affiliation tends to correlate closely with being married and having children. Prolonged periods of singlehood and voluntary childlessness, therefore, may create unbreakable patterns of nonaffiliation with the Jewish community. Moreover, prolonged periods of singlehood and voluntary childlessness may result in decreased fertility, owing to increases in sterility after age 30 as well as to heavy investment in high-powered careers that may not be conducive to having children.

The issue of small Jewish families is thus important for the Jewish community. Currently Jews have a birthrate of 1.7 children per family, a rate that is usually described as negative population growth. In this respect, American Jews are perhaps the best example of what Ben Wattenberg has called "the birth dearth."[8]

Jews have special reasons for concern about low fertility. First, numbers are significant simply in terms of the cultural vitality of American Jewry. A critical mass of Jews is necessary in order to develop a cultural elite. Parental status is closely correlated to participation in the Jewish community. When Jews do not have children, they are unlikely to affiliate with organized Jewish life. Second, the political influence of Jews is in large measure a function of their heavy concentration in politically significant regions and states. Third, a critical mass of Jews is necessary to ensure the institutional health and vitality of the Jewish community. For instance, Jewish schools cannot survive if there is a dearth of Jewish pupils. Finally, on a metaphysical level, population decline symbolizes a loss of verve, energy, and vitality. Population decline has been associated with societies in decadence. For Jews, particularly, one generation after the Holocaust, further numerical losses could undermine their sense of themselves as a creative and energetic people.

The "Divorce Deficit"

A distinguishing feature of Jewish families is the Jewish divorce deficit. Currently, Jews divorce only half as frequently as do Protestants. Moroever, Jews divorce only two-thirds as frequently as do Catholics, despite the strong religious proscriptions against divorce in Catholicism, which are nonexistent in Judaism.[9]

More interestingly, among Jews affiliated with synagogal movements—Orthodoxy, Conservatism, and Reform—the chances of marriage ending in divorce are approximately one in eight. Among Jews who are unaffiliated with the Jewish community, the chances of divorce rise to one in three. Significantly, among affiliated Jews, Orthodox Jews divorce the least and Reform Jews divorce most frequently.[10] To be sure, rates of divorce are higher among young couples than among older Jewish couples, indicating that as the younger generation ages, the rates of Jewish divorce may rise and perhaps even approximate national American patterns.

However, these data on Jewish divorce suggest a strong relationship between Jewish religious commitment and strong marriages. The experience of Jews suggests that, literally, the family that prays together stays together. In large measure, this is true because of the family context of Judaism as a faith. The rituals of Judaism are family oriented; thus the ties to Jewish tradition also cement family ties. The most vivid illustration of this is the *shabbat*, or Sabbath, dinner—a moment of time set aside for quality family conversation, removed from the day-to-day struggles and travails of the world. Furthermore, Jews tend to value marital success as central to personal self-worth and self-respect. They define themselves as successful when they enjoy happy marriages. Conversely, they suffer loss of self-esteem when marriages fail. This identification of self-esteem with marital success is, of course, a basic factor in marital stability and success today in the wider society as well.[11]

To be sure, divorce causes significant dislocations for Jews, as it does for all other families. In the wake of divorce, the single Jewish parent is very vulnerable for two main reasons. First, the economic downturn for women and children that frequently accompanies divorce raises significant barriers to participation in Jewish communal activities. Similarly, the psychological consequences of divorce, in particular the devastating impact upon children, exacerbate the vulnerability of the single-parent home. Research in this area has indicated, however, that ties to Jewish tradition and involvement in communal activities can serve as a stabilizing factor in a single-parent home, reminding children that, even in a turbulent world, enduring values remain.[12]

Intermarriage

Another distinctive feature of contemporary Jewish life is the increase of intermarriage. Intermarriage has occurred in virtually every society in which Jews seek to accommodate themselves to the wider cultural surroundings. However, by historical standards, intermarriage remained quite low in America until the 1960s. By the 1970s, however, intermarriage had reached approximately 30%—that is, almost one of every three Jews was marrying someone not born in the Jewish faith. Although this rate varies regionally and in terms of the population size of the particular Jewish community, the overall rate remains approximately 30–35%.

This high rate is troubling to the Jewish community in terms of future identity and continuity. Intermarried couples tend to participate minimally in Jewish communal activities. Without the conversion of the non-Jewish spouse to Judaism, one may hold little hope for future Jewish continuity in the second, or much less the third, generation. Although some have argued that intermarriage will increase the Jewish population by conversion to Judaism, little evidence for this idea exists. Indeed, as intermarriage has become a more legitimate option in American society, the rate of conversion to Judaism has actually declined. This concern must be placed within a context of endogamous Jewish marriages remaining the norm—most Jews continue to marry other Jews. Yet certainly the growing rate and legitimacy of intermarriage in recent years have caused much concern among Jewish communal leaders.[13]

Employed Mothers

The popular stereotype of Jewish women is that they are highly edu-cated and therefore likely to pursue full-time careers. Yet the facts in this regard are quite mixed. Jewish mothers of preschoolers are, in fact, more likely to stay at home than to work full time. Those who have school-age children are more likely to be employed. Part-time employment has been especially popular among Jewish women as a means of maintaining both family and career. The statistics are revealing: the Rochester Jewish com-munity reports that only 25% of married Jewish women with preschool children work full time and 33% work part time. The other 42% are stay-at-home mothers. In Milwaukee, approximately 55% work either full or part time. In Cleveland, by contrast, 50% of married Jewish women with children younger than five hold full-time jobs.[14]

These variations suggest that it is necessary for us to pay careful attention to the actual, on-the-ground attitudes about family and work that are evident in our society. The realities are complex and pluralistic. Yet our public rhetoric tends to be one-dimensional. Especially in political discourse, these trends are usually presented in highly ideological, simpli-fied terms. David Blankenhorn has argued, for example, that the notion of the rapidly vanishing stay-at-home mother—frequently repeated in the media and in legislative hearings—is simply a misconception (see chapter 1, page 13). More than one-third of all mothers with preschoolers stay at home. Of those who work, a differentiation must be made between those employed full time and those working part time. Evidence in the Jewish community corroborates Blankenhorn's argument. No single model pre-dominates among Jewish families.

Further evidence, however, indicates that Jewish parents value "independence training" for their children. In this respect, the stereotype of the overprotective Jewish mother must be revised. In Pittsburgh, where half of Jewish mothers of preschool children opt to stay out of the work force, 83% nevertheless send their children to day care or early childhood

programs. This fact illustrates the value that Jews place upon early socialization experiences for their children.[15]

In general, this portrait of the Jewish family describes a changing social
institution with a diversity of forms. We have in recent years witnessed the
growth of alternative family structures—particularly singles, childless families, intermarried couples, and single-parent homes. At the same time, with
all of the concern to accommodate alternative family forms, we ought not
ignore the continuing vitality and strength of the traditional family structure
in the minds and hearts of contemporary American Jews.

CONTEMPORARY CULTURE AND JEWISH FAMILIES: STEREOTYPES AND REALITIES

Given this picture of Jewish families in America today, does America's contemporary cultural climate permit Jewish families to fulfill their
historic functions? One way to approach this issue is to explore today's cultural myths and stereotypes of the Jewish family.

One myth, for example, concerns the stability of the Jewish family.
Jewish families are commonly perceived as being warm and tightly knit,
with a strong sense of what it means to be a family. To some extent the
stereotype is a matter of nostalgia and to some extent a matter of pride. It
also reflects contemporary anxiety about whether current families are
meeting previous standards.

Certainly many aspects of modern culture inhibit the effective functioning of Jewish families. Consider several examples:

● Historically, the role of the Jewish father was that of nurturer, teacher,
and provider. Yet the current economic and cultural ethos surrounding the
Jewish father celebrates the successful male as a workaholic, a high-powered professional who devotes day and night to career success. That image
of the Jewish father as a successful professional—over and above what
used to be called a good family man—devalues the historical functions of
the father as teacher and nurturer.[16]

● Similarly, the often-cited stereotype of the Jewish mother—overpossessive,
overprotective, constantly worried about her children, and uninterested in
sex—serves culturally to devalue and delegitimize the historical functions of
marriage: companionship, overcoming loneliness, and sexual fulfillment.
Strong Jewish families exhibit these characteristics; for these Jews, their
marriages are emblems of self-esteem and self-fulfillment. Yet the widespread
image of the Jewish mother as Sophie Portnoy or of the young Jewish woman
as the "Jewish American Princess" undermines the expectation that marriage
to a Jewish woman will be personally fulfilling and will also provide appropriate companionship and partnership in building society.[17]

● Third, contemporary culture often portrays raising children as a costly
affair. Projections that raising a child will cost $180,000 over 18 years can

be frightening for young couples. In that respect, the reproductive function of families is affected directly by a contemporary culture that seems to place a low premium on bringing people into the world or, to use the language of Jewish values, to be partners in creating life.

● Fourth, contemporary culture legitimates intermarriage through widespread dissemination of portraits of successful and happily intermarried couples. Historically, Jews avoided intermarriage for two reasons: an ideological commitment to marry other Jews and the perception that intermarriage could not work. The widespread dissemination of successful intermarriage role models in television programs, such as *Thirtysomething*, *LA Law*, and Jackie Mason's *Chicken Soup*, individually and together nurture a climate in which intermarriage appears to be a valid option. In contrast, no program on television today features a married Jewish couple. This fact is especially disturbing because, as noted earlier, most Jews—in life, if not on TV—continue to marry endogamously. To be sure, one ought not condemn television for portraying significant aspects of reality, and intermarriage is one of them. What must be questioned, however, is to what extent the cultural climate that legitimizes intermarriage runs counter to the messages of Jewish communal leadership exhorting Jews to build Jewish families by marrying other Jews.

● Similarly, the public debate over day care, in which Jews have been vocal advocates for wider availability of day-care facilities and settings, may not, in fact, have created alternatives that meet the needs of contemporary Jewish families. The day-care debate has focused primarily on the need for full-time child care. Yet, as noted earlier, that form of day care fails to meet the current needs of most Jewish families, who have different choices regarding the balance of work and family. Many mothers have opted for part-time employment; others have chosen temporarily to stay out of the work force. Well-intentioned social policy that fosters only the broader availability of full-time day care may, therefore, run counter to the needs and desires of many Jewish families. Many of these families would profit best from the availability of part-time day care. Others would be better served by policies that support mothers or fathers who choose to stay at home with their preschool children.

POLICY STRATEGIES FOR THE FUTURE

How should our society target social policy initiatives to help today's families? Many policy advocates are rightly concerned with assisting at-risk and dysfunctional families. For instance, in the debate over parental notification laws concerning abortion for minors, many argue persuasively that it would be harmful to require parental notification when so many dysfunctional families—to put it bluntly, so many bad parents with vulnerable children—would be affected by such laws. In purely legal terms, that is a fair argument.

Yet when we consider the cultural climate, the core question changes. If we adopt policies primarily to assist dysfunctional families, what is the impact of those policies on functional families? If we oppose parental notification, for example, what message do we send to millions of teenagers from functional families? The answer is obvious: we tell them that their sexual and reproductive behavior is none of their parents' business. Is this the right message? Is this the "story" of family life that we wish to see written in our laws and institutions?

This argument extends to many other areas. Many analysts today, for example, urge a redefinition of the term "family." The goal is to accommodate the needs and rights of cohabiting couples, gays, and lesbians. Certainly, social policy should seek to meet the needs of these alternative family constellations. Yet if we go very far down this path, we unavoidably send a message to our children that all living arrangements are equally valid and equally desirable. We say to them that social norms are by definition invalid. Family values are a matter of personal taste. Moral decisions are questions of private preference. Again, do we really believe this message? Do we believe that such a message will help families to fulfill the expectations that society has placed upon them? If we do not believe this message—and it's hard to see how we could—then surely we must reconsider the currently fashionable idea of "redefining" the family.

What is our strategy for the future? First, we should build upon the fact that Jews continue to value family as the most prized and cherished component of their personal lives. That fact is highly consonant with the overall picture of Americans, who place family among their most enduring values, and it provides a building block on which we might foster a cultural climate that emphasizes what is good about being a family. In this respect, the educational strategies suggested by David Popenoe—who recommends that we vigorously assert the values of the family at the cultural level—are very appropriate.[18] We ought not underestimate the importance of such an educational and ideological strategy.

Within the Jewish community, modern Orthodox Jews have created communal norms of families with three children and low divorce rates. These features should not be understood as functions of their religious beliefs *per se*—restrictions on divorce are nonexistent in Judaism and restrictions on birth control are minimal. On the contrary, modern Orthodox Jews are willing to be influenced by modern culture. Rather, their norms signify the importance of communal culture: a peer community that values family and thereby strengthens marriage.[19] In sum, the experience of the American Orthodox Jew suggests that the public sphere can influence private behavior through the creation of a climate that advances communal ideals and norms.

Additionally, in targeting social policy to assist dsyfunctional families or to accommodate alternative life-styles, we need to distinguish more clearly between respect for personal choices and support of public norms.

Concern for civil liberties and freedom of choice requires certain policy directions. In pursuing these directions, our strategy ought to be vigorous enforcement of the rights of individuals to lead their own lives. Yet this respect must be coupled with strong statements of the ideal family norms and models that society values. Toleration must not be confused with endorsement. What is permitted is not identical to what is encouraged; recognizing what exists is not the same as stating what ought to be.

In several specific areas, Jewish tradition can enlighten general thought concerning the family. Jewish teaching concerning the responsibilities of fatherhood can add greatly to the image of the family we are trying to construct in America. This idea means building upon the theme of the family as the most cherished of institutions and as critical to our sense of self-esteem.

Finally, changes in the work climate would enable parents to be both employees and parents. We require greater availability of part-time employment opportunities, flexible hours, and accessible high-quality child care. These practical strategies, however, must be placed in the context of ideology and values. In the debate on family policy, we must simultaneously articulate family values. We should be advancing a public climate that underscores the centrality of family to societal well-being as well as the responsibility of society to help parents to be parents.

Francine Klagsbrun has put this best in her book *Married People*.[20] She argues that removal of the stigma surrounding divorce in recent years has been progressive in the sense that divorce may be the necessary solution to a failed marriage. But we should be replacing that stigma with a bias in favor of marriage. In other words, in place of negative stereotypes about divorce, we require realistic and positive images of what makes marriages work. We need to foster a sense of commitment as the key to successful marriage. We should be presenting positive role models of successful and happy marriages in the media and in the overall culture. We greatly need, in sum, a cultural climate that reflects both the joys of family and the real sacrifices required for effective family functioning. This vibrant cultural ethos in support of family life should be the main goal of our educational and cultural strategies.

NOTES

1. Genesis 2:18.

2. Genesis 1:28.

3. Chaim Waxman, "The Jewish Father: Past and Present," in Harry Brod, ed., *A Mensch among Men* (Freedom, California: Crossing Press, 1988), pp. 60–61.

4. This historical Jewish emphasis on the development of children may be the strongest refutation of the historical scholarship of Edward Shorter and Philippe Ariès, who tend to view children in premodern society as "little adults."

5. See David Kraemer, ed., *The Jewish Family: Metaphor and Memory* (New York: Oxford, 1989), chaps. 4–5.

6. Steven Bayme, "Family Policy: Current Debates and Challenges," in *Spotlight on the Family: Public Policy and Private Responsibility* (New York: The American Jewish Committee, 1988), p. 2.

7. Samuel Heilman, *The Jewish Family Today: An Overview* (New York: Memorial Foundation for Jewish Culture, 1984), pp. 9–12.

8. Ben Wattenberg, *The Birth Dearth* (New York: Pharos Books, 1987), pp. 113–114.

9. Steven M. Cohen, *American Modernity and Jewish Identity* (New York: Tavistock Publications, 1983), pp. 120–122.

10. J. Brodbar-Nemzer, "Divorce and the Jewish Community: The Impact of Jewish Commitment," *Journal of Jewish Communal Service* 61 (No. 2, Winter 1984), pp. 152–153.

11. J. Brodbar-Nemzer, "Marital Relationships and Self-Esteem: How Jewish Families Are Different," *Journal of Marriage and the Family* 48 (No. 1, February 1986), pp. 90–96.

12. Thomas Cottle, *Divorce and the Jewish Child* (New York: American Jewish Committee, 1981), pp. 22–27; Natalie Friedman, *The Divorced Parent and the Jewish Community* (New York: American Jewish Committee, 1985), pp. 52–54.

13. Uziel Schmelz and Sergio DellaPergola, "Basic Trends in American Jewish Demography," in Steven Bayme, ed., *Facing the Future: Essays on Contemporary Jewish Life* (New York: American Jewish Committee, 1989), pp. 87–94; Egon Mayer, *Love and Tradition: Marriage Between Jews and Christians* (New York: Plenum Press, 1985), chaps. 8–9.

14. Sylvia Fishman, "The Changing American Jewish Family in the '80s," *Contemporary Jewry* 9 (No. 2, Fall 1988), pp. 15–18.

15. Ibid., p. 14.

16. Nina Beth Cardin, "Fatherhood and the Jewish Family," *Newsletter*, William Petschek National Jewish Family Center, 2 (No. 3, July 1982), pp. 2–3.

17. Zena Blau, "The Strategy of the Jewish Mother," in Marshall Sklare, ed., *The Jew in American Society* (New York: Behrman Books, 1974), pp. 179–180.

18. David Popenoe, *Disturbing the Nest* (New York: Aldine de Gruyter, 1988), chaps. 12–14.

19. Francine Klagsbrun, *Married People* (New York: Bantam Books, 1985), pp. 87–88, 311–312; Steven Bayme, "Marriage and Divorce: Cultural Climate and Policy Directions," *American Family* 10 (No. 7, September 1987), pp. 1–2.

20. Klagsbrun, op. cit.

═10═
Individualism
In Family Law
Bruce C. Hafen

T he extreme individualism now reflected in American family law is a
trend that, put simply, is harmful to the family as a social institution. To explore this idea, this chapter discusses autonomy as a constitutional concept and evaluates the recent shift from "familistic"
to "contractual" attitudes toward family relationships.

THE DECLINE OF COMMUNITY

A natural tension has always existed between individual and community interests. Traditionally, the family has mediated between those two
interests as a legal and political entity that protected the autonomous
development of personal values and preferences, even as it also taught the
value of belonging to a larger social order.

Yet we are witnessing a gradual decline in the legal and social significance of community interests. As Robert Nisbet put it, we can see Western history as "the decline of community."[1] As part of this process, the
family's role as a legal institution has declined. According to Sir Henry
Maine, "The movement of the progressive societies has . . . been distinguished by the gradual dissolution of family dependency and the growth of
individual obligation in its place. . . . The [legal and social] unit of an
ancient society was the Family, of a modern society the Individual."[2]

Despite this historical current and a gradual narrowing of the economic functions performed by families during the past century, American
laws and judicial decisions continued until well past 1950 to reason from
the premises of our fairly stable 19th-century family law inheritance. Even
though 19th-century American society and legal institutions favored indi-

Bruce C. Hafen is Provost and Professor of Law at Brigham Young University in Provo, Utah.

vidual interests, the family premises of that era took for granted that the family's institutional character represented an ideal model.

However, the individual-rights movements of the 1960s and 1970s launched a forceful attack upon both the family's institutional authority and the cultural norms on which that authority was based. This development was not primarily the result of conscious and documented dissatisfaction with existing patterns in family law; rather, the family was only one of many institutions whose authoritarian and role-oriented traditions were subjected to the searching scrutiny of a general social and political movement that viewed the family's "vital role in authoritarianism" as "entirely repugnant to the free soul in our age."[3]

Reflecting on this recent history, family law scholar Carl Schneider observes that American family law has been "twice transformed"—once in the 19th century and again since 1960. Schneider sees two themes in the recent transformation: a "diminution of the law's discourse in moral terms about the relations between family members, and the transfer of many moral decisions from the law to the people the law once regulated."[4]

Our once idealistic attitudes toward marital commitments, spousal support obligations, and sexual behavior outside marriage have been replaced by a more realistic ethic that is far less judgmental and demanding. Courts are now less likely to rely on moralistic language or moral judgments in the entire range of domestic relations issues, from divorce to child custody or child neglect.

In addition, family law now reflects less confidence in the value of marriage- and kinship-based models of family form, in part because of increased sensitivity to those who have felt the social disapproval of not fitting ideal patterns. In fact, the legal system is generally less confident of its once normative postures, even in the context of criminal law. As Francis Allen wrote regarding the decline of the rehabilitative ideal in the criminal justice system:

> It is not only the institutions of criminal justice that have [recently] suffered significant losses of confidence. All the institutions traditionally relied on for socializing the young and directing human behavior to the achievement of social purposes have . . . sustained massive losses of confidence and corresponding erosions of morale. Scrutiny of contemporary attitudes toward the family, the schools, and what may inexactly be described as therapy, reveals deep-seated skepticism about the capacity of traditional institutions to achieve beneficial direction to human behavior and aspirations.[5]

This development reflects more than simply reduced attention to moral standards as such. It also reflects a new level of concern with the increasing heterogeneity of American society. As Mary Ann Glendon has noted, the reluctance of courts and legislatures to impose values other than tolerance, equality, and individual liberty reflects a "posture of legal neutrality" that has been welcomed by judges and legislators who are "otherwise hard put to justify preferring the values of one sector of the population to those of another."[6]

But whatever its causes, our declining confidence in ideal family forms seems more the result of recent general trends in modern law than it is the result of conscious policy choices that balance the costs and benefits of traditional models in family law. For this reason, as Glendon notes, many "normative legal propositions" in family law "have tended to be phased out" in recent years, "even when they are quite widely shared."[7]

Perhaps the most significant of the new trends is the emphasis on individual liberties. This emphasis has been taken further by the American system than by any other legal system in the world. For example, one recent comparative study of abortion and divorce laws in developed Western countries found that, despite many shared assumptions with other countries, the American approach has become so individualistic that it is losing its balance by severing the connections between personal values and social values. European legal systems, by comparison,

> have imagined the human person as a free, self-determining individual, but also as a being defined in part through his relations with others. The individual is envisioned, more than in our [American] legal system, as situated within family and community; rights are viewed as inseparable from corresponding responsibilities; and . . . [p]ersonal values are regarded as higher than social values, but as rooted in them.[8]

This observation is, of course, subject to some qualifications. Despite the pervasive and growing influence of individualistic tendencies, American family law has in some ways remained surprisingly resistant to the pressures of cultural fragmentation. The Supreme Court has not yet extended the concept of constitutional privacy to include sex between unmarried adults. Even though the Court now protects certain personal decisions regarding the prevention and termination of pregnancy outside marriage, and even though it protects parent–child relationships outside marriage, it does not give preferred constitutional status to the relationship between unmarried partners. In addition, the state laws that define the term "family" have remained relatively stable. The rights of children and spouses under inheritance, tax, and wrongful death laws are confined to relationships based on marriage and/or kinship. Even the famous Lee Marvin "palimony" case in California (1976) was based on a contract theory, because the California Supreme Court did not equate cohabitation with marriage and viewed the state's family law code as inapplicable. In addition, in spite of constitutional challenges, no state has yet legalized homosexual marriage.

THE FAMILY AND "PERSONAL AUTONOMY"

Nonetheless, individualistic legal concepts have come to play an influential role in the way courts and legislatures approach family relationships. Consider, as an example, the concept of personal autonomy as an emerging value in legal analysis. Today's preoccupation with autonomy is vividly reflected in constitutional law cases and literature, which have increasingly overlapped with and influenced family law. Nowhere is the emphasis on individual interests more pronounced than in constitutional law, largely because the potent political theory of the American Constitution begins with natural individual rights as its major premise. Still, it is easy for the contemporary mind to forget that the concepts embodied in the Bill of Rights were originally intended to define the political relationship between individual citizens and the state—not the domestic and personal relationships among the citizens themselves.

The U.S. Supreme Court has, over the past generation, dealt in constitutional terms with so many family-related issues that we have witnessed what some scholars call "the constitutionalization of family law." In the process, the Supreme Court has often wandered in uncharted territory, frequently finding itself in analytical thickets that confuse more than clarify our understanding of the relationship between individual and community interests. This confusion, in turn, both reflects and amplifies the ambivalence of the surrounding culture about that same relationship.

The Hardwick Case

To illustrate the autonomy concept, consider the Supreme Court's response to the 1986 case of *Bowers v. Hardwick*. In this case, a policeman in Georgia entered a dwelling looking for Michael Hardwick, who was wanted for questioning regarding some minor offense. Someone in the dwelling pointed toward a bedroom door. The policeman entered the bedroom, where he found Mr. Hardwick engaged in homosexual relations with another man. The state conducted a preliminary hearing against Mr. Hardwick on the charge of violating Georgia's sodomy law, but decided to drop the charge rather than taking it to a grand jury. Mr. Hardwick then himself brought suit in federal court to challenge the constitutionality of the law. The court of appeals for the Eleventh Circuit eventually held that the state statute was unconstitutional on the ground that it violated Mr. Hardwick's fundamental rights of privacy and intimate association.

In a controversial and highly publicized 1986 decision, the Supreme Court reversed the Eleventh Circuit decision by a vote of five to four, holding that the constitutional right of privacy does not guarantee the right to engage in homosexual sodomy.[9] Justice Byron White's majority opinion acknowledged that although no right of privacy is mentioned in the text of the Constitution, the Court's prior decisions have established a constitutional right of privacy. However, wrote White, these prior cases were limited to circumstances involving the family, marriage, and procreation; the rule of those cases does not extend to all forms of "private sexual conduct between consenting adults."[10] Justice White expressed concern about the risks of subjective judicial lawmaking when a new substantive right is identified outside the express limits of the constitutional text. He noted that the "Court comes nearest to illegitimacy when it deals with judge-made constitutional law having little or no cognizable roots in the language or design of the Constitution."[11]

In stating the appropriate constitutional test for determining when courts should recognize a right that is not enumerated in the text of the Constitution, such as privacy, the Court quoted earlier cases establishing such extraordinary protections only for personal liberties that are "implicit in the concept of ordered liberty" or "deeply rooted in this Nation's history and tradition."[12] Justice White found that homosexual conduct did not fall within these categories.

The Court did not directly address the question of whether the recognized area of constitutional protection would extend to the sexual privacy of heterosexual unmarried adults. That issue could well become a major point of focus before some future Supreme Court. The question would then be whether the Court's treatment of Hardwick was based primarily on his sexual orientation, his status as a single person, or both.

Justice Harry Blackmun wrote a vigorous dissent that spoke for four of the justices. He argued that Hardwick's right to express his own sexuality and to choose his own form of intimate association is protected by "the most comprehensive of rights and the right most valued by civilized men," namely "the right to be let alone."[13] The dissent asserted that the right of privacy protects one's intimate, personal decisions, especially if those decisions involve conduct in one's own home.

Justice Blackmun views individual autonomy as a core constitutional right: "We protect those rights not because they contribute . . . to the general public welfare, but because they form so central a part of an individual's life."[14] Accordingly, the right to marry and have children is protected not because of society's interest in childbearing or "a preference for stereotypical households," but instead because "individuals define themselves in a significant way through their intimate sexual relationships with others."[15]

His dissent rejects the idea that social values may be determined by a long-established consensus: "The fact that [homosexual acts] 'for hundreds of years, if not thousands, have been uniformly condemned as immoral'" is not "a sufficient reason to permit a State to ban them today." Indeed, he wrote, the ultimate test of a constitutional freedom is whether it protects the personal "right to differ as to things that touch the heart of the existing order."[16]

Having thus given personal autonomy a preeminent position, the dissent shifted the burden to the state to show a truly compelling interest that would justify intrusions on so fundamental a freedom. None of the state's arguments about public morality or social interests rose to the demanding level of the dissent's test. The dissenters found, furthermore, that the case involved "no real interference with the rights of others."[17]

This autonomy theory clearly reflects the dominant view of the literature in contemporary legal journals. Indeed, one of today's best-known constitutional scholars, Laurence Tribe of Harvard Law School, wrote the brief and argued the case for Michael Hardwick. In addition, the dissenting opinion is significant because it evidently came close to being the plurality opinion. The *Washington Post* reported shortly after this case was handed down that Justice Lewis Powell had originally voted to overturn the sodomy statute because it permitted what he thought was a cruel and unusual punishment; however, Justice Powell changed his mind for undisclosed reasons and eventually voted to uphold the statute.[18]

Prior to *Hardwick*, most state and lower federal courts had not reached definitive decisions on sexual privacy issues. However, the highest courts of two influential states, New York and Pennsylvania, had in 1980 upheld rights of nonmarital sexual privacy among consenting adults. The New York case protected the right to seek "sexual gratification" in "private settings" that included vehicles parked on city streets in the early morning hours.[19] The Pennsylvania case gave constitutional protection to sex acts performed in a public lounge between dancing performers and lounge patrons, holding that a law prohibiting deviate sex acts between unmarried persons discriminated against them on the basis of their marital status.[20]

Court decisions of this kind have a very different effect from legislative decisions that remove statutory penalties or otherwise "decriminalize" sexual conduct. If a *legislature* removes criminal penalties against, say, fornication, this action will protect unmarried cohabitants from prosecution for sexual acts. But it will not give their relationship the same constitutional status as marriage. Thus, decriminalization of fornication laws would not give unmarried couples such marriage-related legal rights as tax preferences, inheritance rights, or marital property interests. In addition, the state would have an easier time imposing regulations that regard unmarried cohabitation as potentially harmful, even if it is not criminal. For example, even after repealing its criminal laws against fornication, a state could, upon a reasonable showing of potential harm, constitutionally prevent a child-custody placement with a cohabiting parent. Or it could decide that a pregnant but unmarried elementary-school teacher sets a bad example for impressionable students.

In contrast, if a *court* finds that a state's fornication or sodomy laws violate a constitutional right of privacy and autonomy, sexual conduct between unmarried people would be not just legally *permitted*, but constitutionally *protected*. As a result, the state's interest in protecting traditional sexual morality in a variety of noncriminal ways would be suspect; its regulation in custody placements or its standards affecting the personal lives of schoolteachers would invade constitutional rights.

For instance, after the New York Court of Appeals in 1980 struck down that state's antisodomy law on constitutional privacy grounds, a lower New York court permitted one adult homosexual to adopt another adult homosexual. This decision in effect created a "family" relationship, even though homosexual marriage is not permitted in the state of New York. The lower court noted that prior New York case law would have barred such adoptions as violating public policy, but the adoption court found that the Court of Appeals' sexual freedom opinion disposed of the public policy issue.[21] Similarly, developing its earlier precedent, the New York Court of Appeals in 1989 held that the term "family" should not be construed so narrowly that it justifies the eviction of a homosexual companion from a rent-controlled apartment following his lover's AIDS-related death.[22]

In short, judicial use of personal autonomy theory has a far deeper social impact than does legislative action to decriminalize sexual conduct. If the Supreme Court should overrule *Hardwick*, or if it should uphold a right of sexual privacy between unmarried heterosexual adults, we would probably see a ripple effect in the public consciousness. Those who favor Michael Hardwick's position before the Supreme Court understand this distinction between judicial and legislative action. They are not concerned primarily with protecting Hardwick against criminal prosecution. No prosecution was actually pending. Rather, they see the judicial process as the ideal forum in which to urge the courts to assume bolder leadership in altering the public consciousness. They believe that the Supreme Court is—and should be—at the cutting edge in creating a new cultural consensus. At times, the Court is on that edge. Whether it should be is a different matter.

Should society's core moral values, which shape our ideas about family relationships, be codified through majoritarian electoral and legislative processes? Or should they emerge from judicial deference to the claims of political minorities? Those who favor the autonomy theory of the *Hardwick* dissent argue that traditional moral values violate the civil liberties of minorities precisely because "traditional moral values" are inherently majoritarian. In their view, personal autonomy must become a central constitutional value, making it impossible for any majoritarian policy or process to limit the individual choices of individuals in the absence of serious and demonstrable harm.

This personal autonomy argument requires society to carry the burden of justifying traditional standards. It asserts that the right of individuals to choose "deviant" behavior is at the heart of the Constitution. Given this reasoning, it is clear why today's trend toward personal autonomy as a source of constitutional protection carries such dramatic—and unsettling—implications for family law, and also, therefore, for the family as a social institution in America.

Yet the autonomy-based approach of the *Hardwick* dissent is now well supported in recent legal theory. The older influence of natural law, which dominated legal thinking from Aristotle to Aquinas to Locke, has been in obvious decline for many years. It has been strongly challenged by legal positivism, legal realism, and most recently, by the critical legal studies movement. However, during the last quarter century a new view called neo-natural law has emerged in the work of such legal philosophers as Ronald Dworkin and John Rawls.[23]

Neo-naturalism

Neo-natural law holds that some moral absolutes exist, a position that distinguishes this view from the relativism of most prior 20th-century legal theory. But what is the beginning premise for reasoning about moral absolutes? The answer is the primacy of individual autonomy. In particular, this school of thought emphasizes the autonomy of the least advantaged, those whose autonomy rights have been most abused by traditional laws and established orders.

Under this model, the framework for legal and moral meaning does not originate from any larger set of surrounding social principles. Instead, the universe must find its meaning by reference to individual interests. Thus Dworkin assumes that individual rights rather than legal rules should dictate judicial decisions in close cases. In the same vein, Rawls argues that individual dignity does not derive from maximizing the social good and it should be assigned an independent status. Moreover, inequalities should be arranged not according to the greatest good for the greatest number, but according to the greatest benefit of the least advantaged.[24]

This extreme version of autonomous privacy not only reverses the historic relationship between the individual and her traditional sources of meaning, but reverses our way of thinking about constitutional relationships as well.

The Constitutional "Right to Privacy"

Consider how autonomy-based legal theories found their way into constitutional law. The Supreme Court first mentioned a constitutional right of privacy in 1965 in the case of *Griswold v. Connecticut*, which held unconstitutional a state law that prohibited the use of contraceptives by married couples. The best-known opinion from that case, although it did not speak for the majority, was the plurality opinion of Justice William O. Douglas.[25]

Douglas acknowledged that the Court should not recognize constitutional rights that are not part of the constitutional text. He recalled the heavy criticism directed at the court in the 1930s when the justices had wandered from a base fixed in the founders' language. He then proceeded to locate the constitutional right of privacy within several provisions of the Bill of Rights.

Other justices took a very different approach. Although they agreed that the state could not constitutionally regulate contraceptive use by married couples, they feared that Douglas's theory was an invitation for judges to roam freely, breaking new constitutional ground wherever their fancy took them. They preferred to ground the concept of marital liberty in what came close to a natural law approach, recognizing that a few obviously cherished personal rights were so well established and so universally accepted in our traditions and our social consciousness that our collective sense of justice required their recognition. Such cases included the right of persons accused of crimes to be protected by the safeguards of a fair hearing or the right of parents to direct the upbringing of their children.

The strength of this alternative approach was its insistence on the *universal recognition* of the protected interest—that is, an interest characterized by a long tradition and widespread acceptance. Evidence of universality gives external validation to the right in question. It ensures that a constitutional right would never represent merely the subjective or contemporary opinions of a few judges.

These two clashing approaches to nontextual constitutional rights in the area of personal privacy next surfaced in 1971, when the Court extended the right to obtain contraceptives to unmarried persons. In 1973, *Roe v. Wade*, which relied expressly on the right of privacy to protect a woman's right to obtain an abortion, further extended the debate.

Roe v. Wade

Our ongoing and passionate national debate about the legality of abortion marks *Roe* as among the most controversial cases the Court has ever decided. But quite apart from the rightness or wrongness of the Court's result on the merits of abortion, Justice Blackmun's analysis in this case created hopeless confusion. Unfortunately, as a justification for recognizing a right not enumerated in the Constitutition, Justice Blackmun indiscriminately mixed the concept of community tradition with the contradictory concept of personal autonomy.

Alternatively, the Supreme Court's privacy cases can be understood as flowing from the preferred position of kinship and family life in our constitutional heritage. Under that view, these cases do not create a right of personal autonomy. Rather, they seek to protect the traditional institutions of kinship and marriage because of the universally recognized importance of family life for the continuity of democratic society. Indeed, the majority opinion in the *Hardwick* case is consistent with this interpretation.

Yet in *Hardwick*, the dissent's personal-autonomy view came very close to prevailing. It has already gained widespread acceptance among the legal scholars and lower-court judges from whose ranks future Supreme Court justices will come. In addition, as the current Supreme Court has become less willing to expand the Court's earlier notions of privacy, a number of state supreme courts—as suggested by the New York and Pennsylvania cases—may well continue to develop their own theories of autonomy and privacy in the name of state constitutional rights.

The autonomy approach reverses a longstanding assumption, namely, that those challenging the status quo must bear the burden of proof. More generally, autonomy as a core constitutional value alters our analytical assumptions by 180 degrees. Obviously, traditional social values at times require alteration, as in the case of racial discrimination. But in the area of core social values and moral norms—those "habits of the heart," as Tocqueville called them—a constitutional preference for personal autonomy creates a deeply troubling dilemma. Such a preference could alter our entire approach to the crucial question of whether society may sustain any normative values at all (especially in cases in which it is impossible to prove in the short run whether a particular practice is in fact harmful).

John Stuart Mill argued more than a century ago that society has the right to regulate personal conduct only to prevent harm to others.[26] The Supreme Court has not yet accepted this general proposition, although it has flirted with doing so. But this proposition begs a fundamental question. What happens when we do not know whether a given behavior is socially harmful? Who should bear the risk of harm? The majority in *Hardwick* would place that risk on the individual, whereas autonomy theory would place it on society. In the context of the family, the first approach puts the burden of proof on the individual and the second puts the burden on the family as an institution.

Consider the core moral values that sustain our culture. Is it possible to prove conclusively that abandoning those values will cause individual or social harm? In many cases, the answer is no. For example, available research is inconclusive on the question of whether nonviolent pornography is personally or socially harmful. It may be harmful, but we can't yet prove that—if only, perhaps, because we lack adequate empirical methods. Just as we may not be certain whether we have irreparably harmed the ozone layer of the atmosphere, we may not be able to prove that sexual permissiveness can destroy a society, until it is too late. But because of the gravity of the risks at stake in such questions, we have previously assumed that we should make cautious choices and resolve our empirical doubts in ways that protect society's interest in its own cultural continuity.

This historical preference for social stability, moreover, sustains the conditions that nurture individual liberty in the long run. But the new moralistic passion for personal autonomy as a first principle could change all that. If I were to illustrate my point by drawing a cartoon, I would show a bloody and tattered lawyer standing in rags before a judge whose desk and chambers are a pile of rubble. Holding up a few shreds of paper, the lawyer would say, "*Now* I think I can show, your Honor, that those practices were harmful to society."

Family Ties, Contractual Ties

Another key trend toward individualism in family law is the shift from "familistic" to "contractual" expectations in family relationships. This analysis draws on the work of sociologist Pitirim Sorokin, who distinguishes among three types of personal relationships: familistic, contractual, and compulsory.[27]

In familistic relationships, shared commitments and mutual attachments transcend individual self-interest. These relationships are rooted in *unlimited* personal commitment—not merely to another person, but to the good of the relationship and to the family entity as a larger order. Because of the unlimited nature of such commitments, detailed lists of rights and duties can neither describe nor prescribe a familistic relationship. Familistic ties can require considerable personal sacrifice. Yet experience demonstrates that familism can also engender a productive, even liberating, sense of personal fulfillment and belonging. As "familistic" implies, the ideal prototype for this social system is a harmonious family life, even though, obviously, not all, or even most, families live consistently at this level.

Contractual relationships, by contrast, combine solidaristic and antagonistic elements. By definition, these relationships are *always limited* in both scope and intensity. Parties enter a contractual relationship primarily because of self-interest. They weigh their commitment to the relationship, calculating the return of profit, pleasure, or service. Thus, the defined sphere of solidarity is "coldly legalistic" to the point of being "a lawyer's paradise," and the parties may "feel quite virtuous . . . if they conform to the legal rule," even if their conduct is otherwise unethical or unfair.[28] Neither party may assume that the other acts in constant good faith because, reflecting free-market assumptions, both parties are expected to interpret the limits of their commitment according to self-interest.

The third type, compulsory relationships, are exclusively antagonistic: master and slave, conqueror and captive. The dominant parties in these relationships frequently develop ideologies that justify their coercion on the grounds that the parties are "fundamentally different in nature," such as "pure" and "impure" races. Sorokin observes that compulsory interaction may at times appear "pseudo-familistic" or "pseudo-contractual" when the coercing party wishes to legitimize a false claim that he or she is motivated by benevolence, or that the subordinate party is acting voluntarily.

Western history reflects a steady increase in the proportion of relationships that are best described as contractual. This development has unfolded in two ways. One is a liberating strand: increasing numbers have been freed from the oppression of compulsory relationships in favor of contractual interaction. The other strand is more morally ambiguous: familistic relationships are becoming increasingly fewer, as families and other institutions that were traditionally quasi-familistic have become more contractual. This shift from familistic to contractual interaction has long been under way, but in recent years has greatly accelerated its pace.

Robert Bellah and his colleagues in *Habits of the Heart*, for example, document the new ethos of marriage in our society, which is shifting away from familistic and toward contractual attitudes. Contemporary men and women frequently, perhaps typically, now enter marriage with contractual assumptions of self-interest. They view marriage with a self-focused "therapeutic attitude [that] denies all forms of obligation and commitment in relationships."[29] In the legal context, Carl Schneider has similarly observed that family members today tend to think of themselves "as a collection of individuals united temporarily for their mutual convenience and armed with rights against each other."[30]

The Supreme Court's cases of the past generation reflect this shift. The political rights doctrines it has employed are inherently oriented toward self-interested contractualism. For this reason, new constitutional concepts are both a cause and an effect of the movement away from familistic norms. For example, when the Court recognized the right of unmarried persons to obtain contraceptives, Justice William Brennan stated: "The marital couple is not an independent entity with a mind and heart of its own, but an association of two individuals each with a separate intellectual and emotional makeup."[31] The Court reasoned from similar assumptions in concluding that the father of an unborn child may not veto the mother's decision to have an abortion and that parents may not veto their unmarried minor daughter's abortion decision.[32]

The reform of American divorce laws during the 1960s and 1970s reflects this same shift. Divorce was clearly available prior to the reform era. But marriage laws were based on the familistic assumption that marriage is an unlimited, life-long commitment. Divorce was obtainable, but only upon proof of grievous fault, such as adultery or desertion. These prior laws also reflected certain assumptions about families with young children. They favored maternal child custody and duty-oriented paternal alimony and child support following divorce. But as family life in our society changed, the reality of divorce became increasingly separated from idealistic legal expectations. Indeed, the frustration of state legislators with the hypocrisy of the old laws was itself a major impetus for reform.[33]

The revised laws shifted the focus of divorce proceedings away from evidence of fault and toward evidence of actual marital breakdown. Theoretically, the new laws imposed on judges the duty to grant a divorce only upon real proof that the marriage could not be salvaged. However, such findings are routinely and superficially arrived at in today's family courts. In virtually all states now, if both parties to a marriage wish to terminate it, regardless of their reasons and regardless of the potential for the continuity of their relationship, they may do so. And a number of states now allow unilateral termination. The extreme individualism of American law has thus "taken the idea of individual freedom to terminate a marriage" further than the law of any Western nation.[34]

The divorce reform movement originally intended, among other goals, to foster equal treatment of the sexes in divorce cases. However, the shift away from gender-based presumptions—which had earlier favored paternal support obligations, maternal custody, and alimony—now appears to have reduced, not increased, gender equality in the economic effects of divorce. Commonly, women now bargain away their claims to equitable financial settlements in exchange for child-custody rights, which they continue to seek much more often than do their husbands.[35] Empirical evidence regarding the long-term effects of these reforms is not yet complete. Yet a few legal scholars are already sensing that such individualistic and contractual approaches are producing "a body of family law that protects only the autonomous self," thereby failing "to nurture the relationships between individuals that constitute families."[36]

THE WANING OF BELONGING

Individualistic themes of autonomy and contractualism also apply to legal trends related to children. The traditional doctrine of minority legal status, for example, sought to protect children against their own immaturity. Contractualist assumptions did not apply to children. They were thought to lack the capacity needed to enter into voluntary and binding contracts. In many ways, our social and legal institutions treated children as the preferred beneficiaries of a familistic paternalism, as suggested by our traditional commitments to public education, juvenile courts, and legal protections against parental neglect.

In recent years, however, some social scientists and lawyers began to see children not in familistic terms, but in "compulsory" terms. Like minorities or women, children became one more class of victims of unfair discrimination. As Judge Patricia Wald wrote, for instance, "the child's subjugated status [is] rooted in the same benevolent despotism that kings, husbands, and slave masters claimed as their moral right."[37]

The children's-rights movement in the late 1960s and early 1970s extended certain forms of constitutional rights to children in such areas as public schools, juvenile courts, contraception, and abortion.[38] The Supreme Court also found that the concept of illegitimacy violated the Constitution's equal-protection clause. Moreover, a national child-abuse awareness movement stimulated greater alarm over child abuse by parents and other adult caretakers.

Yet the children's-liberation movement fell far short of eliminating the general concept of minority status, even though some children's-rights advocates had urged that ultimate result. For example, the Supreme Court has recently narrowed the concept of free-expression rights for children in public schools[39] and has stressed children's lack of legal capacity in refusing to extend the death penalty to certain underage juveniles.

At the same time, the children's-rights movement has clearly altered public consciousness regarding familistic paternalism in behalf of children. Recent research on the background and effects of major child-advocacy cases suggests that discretionary paternalism—which had previously characterized most child-related institutions—has today been replaced by an adult-style due-process model. However, this same research casts doubt on whether due process approaches actually reduce harmful state intervention. It also suggests that such approaches may deprive children of needed guidance by, in effect, abandoning them to their procedural rights.[40]

In a subtle but pervasive sense, adults and children now seem increasingly liberated from one another, heading toward a kind of contractual egalitarianism. Not long ago, a contemporary cartoon showed a man and woman standing with two smiling children in front of a neighbor's door, which the neighbor had just opened. The man said to the neighbor, "Hi! We're your new neighbors! I'm Jack Jones, this is my wife, Mary Smith, and these are our kids, Jason Brown and Beth Townsend." Even a common "familistic" name is abandoned on the grounds of psychologic claustrophobia.

Some authors begin their interpretation of our cultural history with the assumption that our social and legal institutions were established by men for the purpose of protecting their power over women and children. This view considers the traditional American family not in familistic or contractual terms, but as an example of compulsory interaction. Such a view would make the current trend toward contractual interaction in family life seem progressive.

If one accepts the premise that deeply rooted beliefs in gender inequality pervade our culture, and if one essentially regards the familistic model as an unrealistic myth, one can see the husband–wife and parent–child relationship as a compulsory one. The male oppressor implicitly believes "that the parties are fundamentally different in nature" (male and female, adult and child) and deceitfully employs pseudo-familistic terminology to justify his continuing domination.[41] This deceit would, of course, consciously overromanticize the domestic realm, marriage, and motherhood and it would stress the natural dependency of children. With this picture in mind, one can logically conclude that shifting to a contractual vision of marriage and family life is not a backward step away from relationships of enduring and genuine commitment; rather, it is a forward step from centuries of oppression toward legally assured protection.

However, a major question that lingers in this hypothesis is whether those who believe the hypothesis simply claim that the familistic model never has and never could actually exist, or whether they would reject it even if it can and does exist. If that model is nothing but a Machiavellian myth, our future attempts at reform should not aspire beyond contractual family ties. Otherwise, perpetuation of the myth would allow continuation of unfair oppression. But if it is not a myth, excluding the familistic model from our aspirations discourages the potential source of our most transcendent relationships.[42]

When Laurence Tribe applies the principles of contractualism and autonomy to children, he expects future legal developments to lead to a liberation of "the child—and the adult—from the shackles of such intermediate groups as [the] family."[43] Some of this emancipation has already begun to occur. Historically, children's lack of capacity has made them seem ineligible to interact fully at adult levels. But television's mass appeal erases distinctions between adults and children.[44] The sexual revolution and marital instability have made children increasingly seem to be equal partners, and at times equal victims, with their parents. These trends foster the illusion that children have the capacity for unrestricted adult experience.[45] The fragmentation of our cultural morality, combined with individual-rights concepts in public schools, now nourishes the idea that children are "capable of choosing their own morality as long as they do not commit crimes."[46]

One major difficulty with this idea is that it creates a conflict of interest for adults. To liberate children is also to liberate adults. To liberate adults is to distance them from their familistic sense of unlimited commitment to their children. As that happens, "a motif of absence—moral, emotional, and physical—plays through the lives of many children now. It may be an absence of authority and limits, or of emotional commitment. [Whatever it is,] there appears to be a new form of [adult] neglect: absence."[47] As we free ourselves from the confining bondage of familistic commitment in favor of more limited contractual ties, we are altering our sense of belonging. Indeed, ours is the age of the waning of belonging.

NOTES

1. Robert Nisbet, *The Quest for Community* (New York: Oxford University Press, 1953), p. 75.

2. Henry Maine, *Ancient Law* (London: J. Murray, 1870), p. 163.

3. Paul Adams, "The Infant, the Family and Society," *Children's Rights* 51 (No. 52, 1971), p. 90.

4. Carl Schneider, "Moral Discourse and the Transformation of American Family Law," *Michigan Law Review* 83 (1985), pp. 1807–1808.

5. Francis Allen, *The Decline of the Rehabilitative Ideal* (New Haven, CT: Yale University Press, 1981), pp. 19–20.

6. Mary Ann Glendon, *The Transformation of Family Law* (forthcoming, Chicago: University of Chicago Press), manuscript p. 498.

7. Ibid.

8. Mary Ann Glendon, *Abortion and Divorce in Western Law* (Cambridge, MA: Harvard University Press, 1987), p. 133.

9. *Bowers v. Hardwick*, 106 S. Ct. 2841 (1986).

10. Ibid. The 50 or so cases of which Justice White spoke involve illegitimacy, unwed fathers, foster parents, the right to marry, children's rights, contraception, and abor-

tion. I have elsewhere summarized these cases in an attempt to provide a rationale for the distinction Justice White drew between, on the one hand, interests arising from marriage and kinship and, on the other, interests arising from sexual expression unrelated to marriage and kinship. See Bruce C. Hafen, "The Constitutional Status of Marriage, Kinship, and Sexual Privacy—Balancing the Individual and Social Interests," *Michigan Law Review* 81 (1983), pp. 463–574.

11. *Bowers v. Hardwick*, op. cit.

12. Ibid.

13. Ibid. (dissenting opinion).

14. Ibid. (dissenting opinion).

15. Ibid. (dissenting opinion).

16. Ibid. (dissenting opinion).

17. Ibid. (dissenting opinion).

18. *Washington Post*, July 13, 1986, p. A1.

19. *People v. Onofre*, 415 N.E.2d 936 (1980).

20. *Commonwealth v. Bonadio*, 415 A.2d 47 (1980).

21. In *re: Adoption of Adult Anonymous*, 435 N.Y.S.2d 527 (1981).

22. *Braschi v. Stahl Associates*, 554 N.Y.S.2d 784 (July 6, 1989).

23. Edgar Bodenheimer, *Jurisprudence*, 2d ed. (Cambridge, MA: Harvard University Press, 1982).

24. Ibid., p. 157.

25. *Griswold v. Connecticut*, 381 U.S. 479 (1965).

26. John Stuart Mill, *On Liberty* (London: R. McCallum, 1946), chapter 1.

27. Pitirim Sorokin, *Society, Culture, and Personality: Their Structure and Dynamics*, 2d ed. (New York: Cooper Square Publishers, 1962), pp. 99–108. For further development of this theme, see Bruce C. Hafen, "The Family as an Entity," *University of California–Davis Law Review* 22 (1989), pp. 865–916.

28. Sorokin, op. cit., p. 105.

29. Robert N. Bellah, Richard Madsen, William M. Sullivan, Ann Swidler, and Steven M. Tipton, *Habits of the Heart* (Berkeley, CA: University of California Press, 1985), p. 85.

30. Schneider, op. cit., p. 1859.

31. *Eisenstadt v. Baird*, 405 U.S. 438 (1972).

32. *Planned Parenthood v. Danforth*, 428 U.S. 52 (1976).

33. Herbert Jacob, *A Silent Revolution: Routine Policy Making and the Transformation of Divorce Law in the United States* (Chicago: University of Chicago Press, 1988).

34. Glendon, *Abortion and Divorce in Western Law*, op. cit., p. 78.

35. Lenore Weitzman, *The Divorce Revolution* (New York: Free Press, 1985).

36. Martha E. G. Minow, "'Forming Underneath Everything that Grows': Toward a History of Family Law," *Wisconsin Law Review* (1985), p. 894.

37. Patricia Wald, "Making Sense Out of the Rights of Youth," *Human Rights* 4 (1974), pp. 13, 15.

38. For some discussion of the children's rights movement in these contexts, see Bruce C. Hafen, "Developing Student Expression through Institutional Authority: Public Schools as Mediating Structures," *Ohio State Law Journal* 48 (1987), pp. 663–731; "Children's Liberation and the New Egalitarianism: Some Reservations about Abandoning Youth to Their 'Rights,'" *Brigham Young University Law Review* (1976), pp. 605–658.

39. Bruce C. Hafen, "Hazelwood School District and the Role of First Amendment Institutions," *Duke Law Journal* (1988), pp. 685–705.

40. Bruce C. Hafen, "Exploring Test Cases in Child Advocacy," *Harvard Law Review* 100 (1986), pp. 435–449.

41. Cf. Sorokin, op. cit.

42. The author has presented this argument in Hafen, "The Family as an Entity," op. cit., p. 901.

43. Laurence Tribe, *American Constitutional Law* (Mineola, NY: Foundation Press, 1978), section 988.

44. Neil Postman, *The Disappearance of Childhood* (New York: Delacorte Press, 1982), pp. 79–80.

45. Marie Winn, *Children without Childhood* (New York: Pantheon Books, 1983).

46. Gerald Grant, *The Character of Education and the Education of Character*, (Washington, DC: U.S. Department of Education, 1982), p. 146.

47. *Time*, August 8, 1988, p. 32.

Chapter concerning Mass media & family values.

=11=
The Loss of Moral Turf: Mass Media and Family Values

Lynette Friedrich Cofer &
Robin Smith Jacobvitz

How do the visual media portray families and children? From their infancy, technological developments in the visual media excited the public and held out the promise of great educational contributions. Yet, also from the beginning, these media fueled controversy. Would sensational content violate family and community values? How could a democratic society regulate commercial interests in order both to harness their potential and reign in their powerful social influences? How could parents and communities compete with the attractions of motion pictures and television for the time and energies of young people?

In analyzing these issues historically, several key themes emerge: the inability of local communities to turn profit-oriented media industries away from sensationalism, often focusing on youth, that features distorted portrayals of family life; the inability of social scientists and policymakers to achieve the long-cherished goal of tapping the educational potential of movies and television; the inability of our society to offer young people opportunities that challenge them to recognize not only their rights, but also the responsibilities of citizenship and parenthood; and finally, the inability of our society to preserve and expand free-press ideals.

THE PROGRESSIVE ERA MEETS THE MOTION PICTURE

The advent of motion pictures in the first part of this century coincided with a great array of social movements concerned with bettering the lives of children. It was a time of widespread social concern, as foreign immigration and the movement of the American population from farm to

Lynette Friedrich Cofer is Professor of Psychology and Robin Smith Jacobvitz is Assistant Professor of Psychology at the University of New Mexico in Albuquerque. The authors wish gratefully to acknowledge the contributions of Charles N. Cofer to this essay.

city threatened to undo established patterns of family and community life. Social bonds seemed to be weakening. Fears emerged about the supposed physical and moral degeneracy of Americans.[1] John Dewey's vision of the school responded to these fears. Schools were to bind together the disparate members of a democracy in a common weal. The child—the future citizen—was to be "saturated with the spirit of service" and provided with the "instruments of effective self-direction."[2]

At the same time, motion pictures became a popular form of entertainment for children and young people. Concern over their content grew among social workers, educators, and religious leaders.[3] One prominent early commentator was Jane Addams, director of Hull House. In *The Spirit of Youth and the City Streets*, published in 1909, she described the motion picture theater as a "'veritable house of dreams,' infinitely more real than the noisy streets and the crowded factories."[4] She also noted the influence of films on young persons' moral development:

> While many young people go to the theatre if only to see represented, and to hear discussed, the themes which seem to them so tragically important, there is no doubt that what they hear there, flimsy and poor as it often is, easily becomes their actual moral guide.[5]

What is seen in the theater becomes "the sole topic of conversation" among young people, "forming the ground pattern of their social life."[6] She refers to the theater as a "huge factory of sentiment"—not only a place of amusement, but a place of culture, where people learn how to think, act, and feel. "Seldom, however, do we associate the theatre with our plans for civic righteousness, although it has become so important a factor in city life."[7] Addams also pointed out that motion pictures might become a substitute for active social participation, removing youth from the life of the community.

Movies thus dramatically symbolized diminishing local control over moral norms as a factor in American society. Reluctance to relinquish this control motivated many individuals and groups to agitate against the medium's growing influence. Regulatory ordinances, mostly concerned with content, sprang up in cities across the country. At the same time, many progressive educational and religious leaders celebrated the educational potential of a medium that could cut across class boundaries and bring democratic art to the populace.

The release of *Birth of a Nation* in 1915 laid to rest the notion that film was mere entertainment. The power and artistic genius of W. D. Griffith's account of the Reconstruction period dealt with a social issue of national importance—the role of the Negro in American society. The film, based on the racially provocative novels of Thomas Dixon,[8] conveyed the idea that Negroes, once freed from slavery, regressed toward a natural state of bestiality, epitomized in the rape of white women. The retrogression argument was combined with an appeal for national white unity and the view of the Reconstruction era as "the Tragic Era" in which the activities of the Ku Klux Klan were justified and glorified.[9] The arch-villain, Stoneman, is a thinly veiled but much distorted portrayal of Thaddeus Stevens, the principal author of the 14th amendment. One still shot features a quotation from President Woodrow Wilson: "It is like writing history with Lightning. And my only regret is that it is all so terribly true."[10]

The newly formed National Association for the Advancement of Colored People protested. Censorship battles ensued. Terry Ramsaye credited at least part of the film's huge profits to the controversy: "The roaring denunciations from the high places sent the whole public to the theatre to see what the row was about. It has been estimated that more than $15,000,000 has been spent in box office admissions."[11] The child welfare advocates, academics, women's clubs, clergy, and boards of local and state censors saw an industry that was capable of far more cultural and social influence than they had imagined. The powers of the new medium were not lost on the U.S. government, which used film effectively as war propaganda in subsequent years.[12]

A second seminal event in 1915 was the U.S. Supreme Court decision in *Mutual Film Corporation v. Ohio*. In a unanimous decision, the Court dismissed the company's complaint against Ohio's prior-censorship law: "It cannot be put out of view that the exhibition of moving pictures is business pure and simple, originated and conducted for profit, like other spectacles, not to be regarded . . . as part of the press or organs or public opinion."[13] The company's films, therefore, were not protected by the First Amendment.

The consequences of this decision were profound: local and state boards of censors could operate without fear of Constitutional challenges. It is important to note, however, another side of censorship history: The National Board of Censorship (founded in 1909), later to become the National Board of Review (in 1915), was formed at the request of the industry itself in order to fend off public pressures. The philosophy was that films should be previewed by voluntary representatives, who would make suggestions to the industry about offensive materials and about "better films."

Although the possibility of more far-reaching federal censorship remained an industry concern, this fear failed to stem the tide of ever more sensational films. Lewis Jacobs notes:

> In keeping with this new-found realistic outlook went a loss of respect for spiritual values and increased regard for material ones. The philosophy of self-aggrandizement, the regard for elegant clothes and polished manners, the veneration of the successful businessman and wealth and the fashion of high pressure salesmanship—all of which were to become dominant in films of the post war period—now began receiving favorable attention on the screen.[14]

Theda Bara—the vamp—made about 40 films, including such titles as *Eternal Sin*, *Purgatory*, and *She-Devil*. Crime films and white slavery films flourished.

MOTION PICTURES IN THE 1920S AND 1930S

By the 1920s moviegoing had become a regular feature of Ameri-can life. In 1923 there were 15,000 motion picture theaters; admission fees reached $520 million. Businesses were quick to seize on the motion picture's ability to cause changes in dress, fashion, hairstyles, and home decoration.[15] The industry increased the production of films involving sex and crime, despite the efforts of censorship boards and in defiance of their own self-censorship codes. Many felt that this new medium was altering family and community life in ways they could not control. Robert and Helen Lynd's classic study, *Middletown*, chronicles this widely held belief:

> The kinds of vicarious living brought to Middletown by these (society) films may be inferred from such titles and press releases as: "Alimony—brilliant men, beautiful jazz babies, champagne baths, mid-night revels, petting parties in the purple dawn, all ending in one terrific smashing climax that makes you gasp" . . . or "Flaming Youth: . . . red kisses, pleasure-mad daughters, sensation-craving mothers, by an author who didn't dare sign his name; the truth bold, naked, sensational."[16]

Other titles included *Married Flirts, The Daring Years, Sinners in Silk, Women Who Give* and so forth.[17] They continue:

> The judge of the juvenile courts lists the movies as one of the "big four" causes of local juvenile delinquency, believing that the disregard of group mores by the young is definitely related to the witnessing week after week of fictitious behavior sequences that habitually link the taking of long chances and the happy ending. While the community attempts to safe-guard its schools from commercially intent private hands, this powerful new educational instrument, which has taken Middletown unawares, remains in the hands of a group of men—an ex-peanut-stand proprietor, an ex-bicycle racer and race promoter . . . and so on—whose primary concern is making money.[18]

The Lynds also document the fragmentation of family and commu-nity life that movies seemed to encourage. Children were attending movies with other children, not their parents. Leisure time became an individual or small-group affair, running counter to the tradition of clubs and other community-based leisure-time pursuits.[19]

Social Scientists Enter the Debate: The Payne Fund Studies

Within this social context, major funding was obtained from the Payne Fund by a distinguished set of social scientists to carry out research on motion pictures between 1929 and 1933. The 12 studies fell into groups. One focused on motion-picture content and on children's attendance at commercial movie theaters. The second sought to measure the effect of motion pictures upon children. The research reflected an interdisciplinary approach, and many of their findings remain relevant to contemporary concerns.

In 1930, approximately 11 million children younger than 14—and a total of about 28 million minors—attended motion pictures each week. After age eight, both boys and girls reported going most frequently with their friends rather than with family members. Particularly frequent attendees were children with histories of delinquency and poor school performance.

Some 500 feature films were analyzed for content. The three major themes of 1930 were love, crime, and sex. Nearly 80% of films showed alcohol consumption; 72% of all leading men smoked, as did 30% of leading women. Settings and plots depicted lurid love, luxurious life-styles, and magical endings.[20]

The effects of films were, of course, far more difficult to assess. Yet a range of techniques—from physiological measurements to questionnaires, diary accounts, and interviews—established that children remembered a great deal from movie plots. Adolescent males showed more physiological responsiveness to romantic scenes than did younger children. Incorrect information, if shown in the movies, was largely accepted as true by children. Social attitudes, including racial prejudices, could be affected. For example, the attitudes of white children who had no experience with Negroes were negatively affected by viewing *Birth of a Nation*. Moreover, those attitudes persisted over time.[21]

Autobiographical and interview studies of adolescents elicited accounts of how young people used motion picture content in the scheme of their own lives. Many adolescents consciously imitated make-up, hair-dos, mannerisms, love-making techniques, and in some cases even criminal behavior from films.[22] Indeed, some of the most highly debated of all of the Payne Studies findings were questionnaire data from criminals and delinquents indicating that some of them were affected by sex and crime pictures. Crime techniques and criminal patterns of behavior, the easy money and luxury, the bravado and daring of successful heroes, the sexual prowess of attractive people—all these themes stimulated the imagination and aroused ambitions. One report suggested that movies appeared especially to influence "children reared in socially disorganized areas," with an influence "proportionate to the weakness of the family, school, church, and neighborhood."[23]

The summary volume concluded that although reports from delinquents were not totally reliable, "the fact still remains that enough of them can quote chapter and verse to show that crime and sex pictures are at least an aggravating influence in their conduct."[24] The volume ended with a recommendation that the film industry establish a "children's department" to produce higher-quality movies for young people:

> This research organization is clearly indicated. It does not appear that such experimentation would be expensive. The simple obligation rests upon those producers who love children to find a way of making the motion picture a beautiful, fascinating, and kindly servant of childhood.[25]

Foreshadowing future social science interactions with the television industry, a battle was waged over two exaggerated accounts of the Payne

Fund research. One side smoothed over all the cautionary notes and over-simplified results into an attack on the film industry. Industry, in turn, financed a rebuttal, and a debate over methodology raged that reached even the floor of the U.S. Senate.[26] The unfortunate long-term result was the discrediting of fine studies by people who never read them. The immediate result was a more widespread belief that reigning motion picture content was not in the best interests of children or family life. The researchers' dream—to bring about a new quality of motion pictures for children—was not realized.

The Legion of Decency and Industry Self-Censorship

By 1932 nearly 40 national religious and educational organizations were calling for greater federal regulation of the motion picture industry. The most direct pressure came from the Catholic Legion of Decency, joined by many Protestant and Jewish groups. More than 20 million citizens pledged to abide by the movie ratings established by the Legion of Decency. In addition, in the midst of the Great Depression, the movie industry felt particularly vulnerable to economic threats. The Legion succeeded in forcing the industry to strengthen its commitment to the Production Code of self-censorship.[27]

Marked changes in motion picture content soon followed. Explicit depictions of violence and sex, as well as profanity and racial slurs, were forbidden; portrayals of women also changed. Long-established formats, featuring women as victims and vamps, gave way to comedies with bright and breezy career girls.

Margaret Thorp contends that 1938–1939 stands out as the finest year in U.S. movie history.[28] Movies that year were filled with portrayals of America's pioneer past and realistic portrayals of families—for example, *Mother Carey's Chickens* and *Daughters Courageous*. The Hardy Family series, extremely popular from 1936 to 1946, showed the wise Judge Hardy helping his son through adolescent crises. There were the brilliant films of Frank Capra—*Mr. Deeds Goes to Town*, *It Happened One Night*, *You Can't Take It with You*, and others. Musicals and dance flourished. Given the quality of these works, it is difficult to support the view that self-censorship, albeit forced, led to creative decline or box office failures.

THE DEMISE OF CONTROL, TELEVISION, AND ADOLESCENT EXPLOITATION

The demise of self-censorship in the 1950s was rooted, in part, in a series of Supreme Court decisions that ruled, in contrast with the 1915 opinion, that film is a form of constitutionally protected speech.[29] But perhaps a more direct influence was economic pressure from two sources: foreign films and, more important, the new medium of television. By 1957 movie attendance had dropped more than 50%, and, of those attending,

72% were younger than 30.[30] In this newly deregulated and increasingly competetive environment, several trends—alarming from the perspective of the family as a social institution—became increasingly evident.

Thomas Doherty, in his book *Teenagers & Teenpics: The Juvenilization of American Movies in the 1950's*, chronicles the development of "exploitation pictures" geared to teenagers. Subject matter had to be not only sensational but timely, thus attracting the free publicity that surrounds current news events.[31] And to a degree unthinkable only a decade earlier, the '50s exploitation pictures favored the bizarre, the licentious, and the sensational. The staples of this low-budget fare featured souped-up cars, switchblades, fights, and tight-sweatered teenage girls. The classics of this genre include *The Wild Ones, Blackboard Jungle, Crime in the Streets, The Rebel Breed, Teenage Crime Wave*, and others of a similar ilk. Frequently, in what has been termed "Warner Brothers environmentalism," societal failure, rather than individual choice, is blamed for youthful criminality and deviance.

Other business enterprises also discovered the new, lucrative teenager market. R. J. Reynolds sponsored *Camel's Rock-'n'-Roll Dance Party*, Lucky Strike sponsored *Your Hit Parade*, and General Motors launched a new automobile engine "to create the image of a 'hot car.'" Cosmetics, grooming, and clothing also discovered teenagers. By 1959, the teen market was worth about $10 billion.[32]

Culturally, these events fostered a subcultural identity for teenagers at odds with the values of the wider society and drove wedges between the generations. Teenagers were portrayed as irresponsible, impulsive, and driven by sensation. Parents were removed from the sphere of teenagers' autonomy. Mainstream family pictures no longer made it at the box office. For example, *Andy Hardy Comes Home* (1958) was a financial flop. One Iowa theater owner, remembering the mobs that appeared for every Hardy movie a generation earlier, commented sadly on the empty house:

> The "pee-pul" seem either to have become so sophisticated by the intellectual processes of quiz programs, or so convinced by the propaganda that delinquency has taken over both our theater screens and our society, that they can no longer adjust to the simplicities of family life in its idyllic state. If life isn't infested with abnormalities, phobias, and manias, it seems to have lost its appeal on screen.[33]

Indeed, audience research shows that those very families who formerly watched Andy Hardy in the theater were now at home with their newly purchased television sets, watching what we now call the programs of "The Golden Era." Adults had largely abandoned movie theaters to teenagers. Instead, they were watching *Father Knows Best, Ozzie and Harriet, The Donna Reed Show, The Life of Riley*, and *I Love Lucy*, among other popular programs.

Here, on television, were hardworking parents raising their children, helping them to solve problems, protecting them from experiences for which they were not prepared, and participating in community life. Children had, by later standards, wonderful choices: *Kukla, Fran and Ollie, The Mickey Mouse Club, Mr. Wizard, Captain Kangaroo,* and others. In 1951, 27 hours per week of children's programming were broadcast by the networks on weekdays between 6:00 and 8:00 P.M.[34]

By 1960, eight of every ten American homes had at least one television set, which was turned on for an average of five hours each day.[35] The programming of the "Golden Era" had been developed with one goal in mind—to sell television sets. Because network executives believed that the presence of children's programs would serve as a stimulus to sales, programming for children reached 37 hours per week in 1956.[36] But by the 1960s programming for children had been demoted to time slots that were least attractive to adults, particularly Saturday morning. Low-cost animation, including violent cartoons, replaced productions using live actors. Children, moreover, were increasingly targeted as a market for advertising.[37]

Popular family television programs in the 1960s included *The Untouchables, Mission Impossible,* and *The Man from UNCLE*—each far more violent than any TV fare in the past—as well as *The Lawrence Welk Show, The Beverly Hillbillies,* and *The Dick Van Dyke Show.* And by 1964 the National Association for Better Radio and Television reported that the amount of television time devoted to crime drama showed a 20% increase over 1958 and a 90% increase over 1952. More than two-thirds of the violence shown in 1964 appeared before 9:00 P.M.—that is, before children's bedtimes.[38]

THE 1970S: ATTEMPTS AT REFORM

The main legal basis for federal regulation of television is the Communications Act of 1934, which established that the airwaves belong to the public. The Federal Communications Commission (FCC) is the agency charged with granting and revoking broadcast licenses in a manner that serves the "public interest, convenience, and necessity" and also insures that the government does not "interfere with the right of free speech."[39] In 1960, children's programs were identified as one of 14 program types usually necessary in order for broadcasters to meet their public-interest obligation. Hence the industry was given notice that its offerings to children were to be monitored. Moreover, the increasing attention given to the relation of media violence to societal violence held out the threat of further efforts to enforce public accountability.

Beginning with the Kefauver Committee on Juvenile Delinquency in 1954, social scientists played an important role in the debate over television's impact on children and family life. One early warning was issued by Paul Lazarsfeld: research, because it could never definitively prove causality, could become an "alibi" for inaction. "Let us just wait until we have enough research and then we will do something."[40] Nevertheless, Lazarsfeld himself, as well as industry executives, continued the cry for more and better research.[41]

In the Dodd Hearings in 1961, the Senate Subcommittee on Juvenile Delinquency in 1964, and the National Commission on the Causes and Prevention of Violence in 1968, the issue of the relationship of television violence and societal violence was debated vigorously. Social science research became elevated to an ever more central role in that debate, the major controversy of which concerned proof of direct causality.

Responsible researchers were obliged to acknowledge the limits of their paradigms. The common ground on which academicians and broadcast industry representatives could meet was the need for further research. Yet in its final report, The National Commission on the Causes and Prevention of Violence rejected industry charges of inconclusive research. The commission insisted that the industry "stop asserting 'not proven' to charges of adverse effects from pervasive violence on television when they should instead be accepting the burden of proof that such programs are not harmful to the public interest."[42]

In addition, broadcasters were enjoined to abandon cartoon violence, to reduce violence in dramatic programs, and to cooperate with social scientists in conducting further research. Other recommendations included greater funding for the Corporation for Public Broadcasting and an evaluation of the effectiveness of the then-new movie rating system.[43] Ironically, but not surprisingly, only one of these recommendations—more studies—became a reality.

In 1969, Senator John Pastore, Chairman of the Senate Subcommittee on Communications, sought to investigate further the link between media violence and aggressive behavior in children. He requested a study from the U.S. Surgeon General, administered through the National Institute of Mental Health. The result: 23 studies, papers, and literature reviews, which filled five volumes of technical reports.

According to these studies, the networks had not reduced levels of televised violence, despite years of controversy and many promises. Approximately 80% of network dramatic programs contained violence. Cartoons aimed at children still had the highest frequency of violence. Virtually all families had television sets; many had two. Despite wide variations among children, it was clear that television was occupying a large amount of time in children's lives. Children from lower socioeconomic strata watched more television and more violent television than did those from more affluent homes. Black children watched more than white children did, even with social class controlled.

Well-controlled laboratory studies, building on earlier research, showed that viewing violent television led to aggressive behavior on the part of both children and adolescents. Researchers found no support for the "catharsis" thesis that viewing images of aggression "drained off" aggressive impulses. Field studies of young children and adolescent boys demonstrated deteriorations in self-control and increases in interpersonal aggression— particularly for more aggressive children—after viewing televised violence.

Correlational studies involving thousands of subjects across widely differing levels of age, socioeconomic status, and ethnic backgrounds yielded consistently modest but positive correlations between viewing naturally occurring violence on television and aggressive behavior.

The longitudinal studies supported the hypothesis that this relationship persists over time. They also supported a bidirectional model of causality: television violence influences aggression, and aggressive predispositions influence the preference for television violence. The major question about correlational studies was the possibility that some other variable contributes to the association between viewing and aggression. Despite exhaustive examination of such factors as parental warmth or punitiveness, social class, parental aggression, and so forth, no variables emerged in these studies that could account for the relation between viewing and aggression.

In short, all of these different research efforts—laboratory, field, and correlational studies with different methods and measures—revealed a convergent pattern of positive association between the viewing of television violence and aggressive attitudes and behaviors. This evidence was quite persuasive to most social scientists.[44]

At the hearings following publication of the Surgeon General's report on television violence, industry representatives again promised that each major network would enforce self-regulation, reduce violence, and increase programming quality. Indeed, Joseph T. Klapper of CBS agreed with Senator Pastore that "much violence on television . . . was unnecessary."[45] Prospects for reform seemed promising, with support offered by the American Medical Association (AMA) and the Parent–Teacher Association (PTA). Yet when all the shouting was over, despite some temporary changes, network programming was not affected.

By the mid-1970s, public protest about program content was directed not only at the networks themselves but also at the sponsors. Threats of product boycotts were included in thousands of protest letters received monthly by the FCC in 1975. A newly formed organization, Morality in Media, presented a 100,000-name petition calling for FCC hearings throughout the United States on television sex and violence. The National Citizens Committee for Broadcasting (NCCB), headed by former FCC Commissioner Nicolas Johnson, began a monitoring system to identify the companies that paid for violent programming. Although the NCCB did not mention boycotts, they offered their monitoring results to advertisers. The AMA gave financial support to the NCCB; the PTA funded a plan that included grass-roots monitoring of television, public hearings, license challenges, and boycotts. The Interfaith Center on Corporate Responsibility revealed a campaign to use stockholder resolutions against the company sponsors of violence identified by the NCCB.[46]

The 1977 season showed a decrease in violence. Many groups believed that success, finally, was at hand. Others detected an increase in sexual content even as violence decreased. This led to another round of protests launched by the National Federation for Decency (NFD). By early 1981, the NFD combined forces with the Moral Majority to form the Coalition for Better Television.

Despite threats of a large-scale boycott, no lasting reforms were wrought by these advocacy movements. As soon as the immediate pressures lessened and advertisers became less vulnerable, violent and sexual content again began to rise.[47] In her recent book *Target: Prime Time*, Kathryn Montgomery examines how networks and advertisers have been able to ward off the repeated volleys of well-organized and broadly based protest groups.

> After 1977, there were mechanisms in place for more carefully routinized surveillance of the programming in which their commercialized messages appeared. The content policies, and the screening companies that carried them out, were able to respond quickly to the winds of pressure and to flag sensitive content. . . . These [mechanisms] would . . . help networks handle violent content as they had learned and were continuing to learn to handle other kinds of sensitive program material.[48]

Deregulation

By the mid-1970s, in response to public-interest groups, including Action for Children's Television, the FCC took a new, more aggressive approach to regulating programs. In 1974, the FCC declared that each broadcaster was required to make a "meaningful effort" to provide programming for preschool and school-aged children. Such programs were to air during both weekday and weekend periods when children were most likely to watch. Restrictions were placed on the amount of advertising during children's programs, and host-selling—using program characters to promote products—was prohibited.[49]

But by 1978, little had changed. When it was demonstrated that the amount of educational and informational children's programming had not increased, television proceedings were held, and new studies reaffirmed network noncompliance. As a result, a Notice of Proposed Rulemaking was issued in 1980 that would have required each broadcaster to provide a minimum of 7.5 hours per week of age-specific programming for children.[50]

The Marketplace Approach

Yet before further action could be taken, a major political change occurred. Ronald Reagan was elected President, and he appointed Mark Fowler as FCC chairman. Fowler advocated less regulation and more reliance on marketplace competition, suggesting that the public would ensure adequate service by supporting only those broadcasters who delivered programming the audience desires. His stance concerning the needs of children is revealed in his widely quoted assertion:

When there is a decline in children's programming in over-the-air television, the reason is no mystery. . . . Other programs may be more profitable
or more popular. I don't think that the FCC should second guess those
judgments.[51]

In 1984, the FCC removed virtually all guidelines on general program content, including those limiting the amount of advertising. Noting
the new alternatives in programming—including videos, cable, and public
broadcasting—the FCC suggested that such alternatives could relieve
individual stations of responsibility for programs for children.

Critics responded that these policies would penalize many lower-
income children, who are particularly heavy users of television for information and education as well as entertainment.[52] A rapid decrease
occurred in the amount of children's educational programming by commercial network affiliates and independent stations between 1981 and
1983. Today these broadcasters do not provide any educational children's
programs. Moreover, higher-income families, who can afford VCRs,
videocassette rentals, and cable subscriptions, have turned to these alternatives for their children's entertainment and education.[53] Dale Kunkel's
analogy captures the flaw in FCC logic:

it could be argued that the city of Anaheim, California, need no longer
provide public parks because Disneyland is available nearby. Since children's needs for open space and recreation can be met by this alternative,
the public interest would no longer require that parks be maintained. Of
course the fundamental flaw here is that Disneyland charges a price for
admission that not all can afford. Disneyland cannot meet their needs
nearly as well as a public park.[54]

However, at this time, greater regulation of the broadcast media is
far from a certainty. For example, President Bush has indicated that he
would veto a bill that would restore the Fairness Doctrine.[55]

In the wake of deregulation, unbridled commercialism in children's
programming has increased shockingly, including the advent of programs
created solely to merchandise toys.[56] On the other hand, even during the
years of government regulation, adolescents were never considered a group
deserving of special programming or protection from advertising.

DEREGULATED PORTRAYALS OF
YOUTH AND FAMILY LIFE

This history of conflict between the public interest and profit making—of the relentless encroachment of mass media onto the moral turf of
family and community—sets the stage for the current furor over television, MTV, films, and last, but by no means least, television news.

Prime-Time Families

By the late 1980s prime-time television's portrayal of the family had
changed markedly, though not according to the contours of diversity and

complexity that early cable seemed to promise. Cable, home video, and the expansion of independent stations decreased the proportion of prime-time audiences held by the networks: from 90% in 1981 to 68% in 1989.[57]

Although cable created some alternative programming, the same economic forces that controlled network broadcasting also shaped the development of cable, especially as a small number of major corporations bought cable systems throughout the country. Additionally, because the cable industry is not licensed by the government, it has no legal requirement to serve the public interest.

During this period, all three major networks were purchased by giant corporations, which in turn imposed cutbacks in the networks' standards and practices departments. In an era of deregulation, there was little to lose by reducing these departments. Moreover, regarding public protest, a new "cooperative" strategy emerged: advocacy groups, including academicians, became consultants to the networks and producers. This technique led to established routines for handling controversies, thus transforming these groups from a disruptive force into a "feedback system."[58] "The networks may remain willing to 'dialogue' with advocacy groups, as part of their continuing strategy for deflecting pressure. But without effective political leverage, groups are unlikely to have their demands and concerns taken seriously."[59]

The networks must now play a furious "game" in which almost anything that promises to increase ratings, hence profits, is tried, then dropped if it does not deliver. Brandon Tartikoff, president of NBC, describes the attitude at General Electric, the owner of NBC: "They just know that there's this oil well gushing, spilling off $500 million into buckets. And they just gather up the buckets."[60] The quality of programs is, to put it charitably, not the main issue.

All three networks now routinely capitalize on sensational press stories for free publicity to promote what are euphemistically called "fact-based dramas"—a technique that is identical to the one used by the movie industry in the 1950s. Special prime-time "mini-series" dramatize the headlines, ranging from *The Oliver North Story* and *The Preppie Murder Case* to the televised portrayal of "real" crimes and emergencies, as seen in programs such as *Unsolved Mysteries* and *911*. The underlying trend is ominous: the intentional blurring of fact with fiction—of news with entertainment, of reality with fantasy—to such a degree that it may soon become meaningless or futile to attempt to make these traditional distinctions at all in describing television content.

In 1982, Neil Postman, in his provocative book *The Disappearance of Childhood*, charged that television had undermined the concept of childhood by abolishing differences between adults and children in dress, games, language, and sexuality.[61] What is broadcast for adults is broadcast to children, thus depriving parents of the opportunity to provide knowledge appropriate for the child's developmental level. Children not only see commercials for all products, but are also used as the sellers of many products.

In both programs and commercials, meaningful portrayals of work are rare, although celebrations of consumerist affluence are typical. Television children are precociously world-wise, capable of engaging in free and foul exchanges with parents and adults on any topic. Portrayals of parents as protectors and nurturers of traditional values are lost in scripts that present children as backdrops for wisecracks and foils for quickly resolved conflicts between individual adult interests.

Roseanne, one of the two most popular current programs, illustrates Postman's concerns. On the premiere episode of the 1989 series, one of the daughters refers to her sister as a "nymphomaniac" and receives an equally salacious label in return, all in the presence of the parents, who don't seem to mind. The children thrive on exchanging sarcasm and vulgarities with each other and with their parents to keep the laughs rolling.

Some critics have compared *Roseanne* with Jackie Gleason's classic show from the 1950s, *The Honeymooners*, a blue-collar comedy. But remember, Ralph and Alice Kramden had no children. Their humor and hostility formed an equal exchange among adults. Placing children within such a scenario, further laced with sexual innuendo and vulgar language, distorts and undermines the traditional distinction between the needs of children and the responsibilities of adults.

Sexual Content in Movies and Television

References to and depictions of sexual activity on television have increased dramatically in the past decade. In soap operas popular with adolescents, rates of sexual contact have increased 21% since comparable data were gathered in 1982, and 103% since 1980.[62]

Many of the prime-time movies shown on television today would not have passed network censors even a few years ago. In movie theaters, the trend is similar. And clearly, children and young people are watching such movies and programs. Greenberg and his colleagues found that more than half of the 15- and 16-year-olds surveyed in three cities in Michigan had seen at least half of the most popular R-rated films of 1982–1984, either in movie theaters or on videocassettes.[63]

A comparison of movies in 1959, 1969, and 1979 revealed that although movie sex has become more far more explicit, the underlying themes remain constant. Sex is the province of the young. It is intended more to initiate male–female social interaction—a kind of ice-breaker—than it is to express affection in long-standing relationships. Precautions against pregnancy or disease are never discussed.[64]

At the same time, in the real world, both male and female adolescents are initiating sexual intercourse earlier than ever before. In 1971, only one of every seven 15-year-old girls had had intercourse. By 1986, the ratio was one in four. One in ten gets pregnant each year, and one in seven teenagers currently has a sexually transmitted disease.[65]

Portrayals of Violent Sexuality

Increasingly, modern media products combine sex and violence and, in so doing, become ever more frightening and demeaning to both sexes. The so-called slasher films—in which young women are raped and gruesomely mutilated and murdered—typify this genre. Increasingly, heterosexual behavior is associated with violence or displays of power.[66] The content of music videos, watched primarily by adolescents, has been described as more sexist, pornographic, and violent than is most other television fare.[67] Meanwhile, in the real world, one national survey concluded that about one-fourth of college women in the United States have been raped or sexually assaulted since they were 14 years old.[68]

"Real" Portrayals of TV Sex and Violence: The Rise of the Talk Show

Another particularly toxic fruit of modern deregulation is the so-called TV talk show. Aired weekday mornings and afternoons, these shows are hosted by Oprah Winfrey, Phil Donahue, Geraldo Rivera, Sally Jessie Raphael, and others. Throughout the day "kickers" offer titillating previews of upcoming topics. These shows, like their movie predecessors, ostensibly deal with "real" problems from sensational newspaper stories. But what are these real problems?

A recent student survey found that the two most frequent topics presented by Geraldo, for example, were crime and sex. Just a few examples: "Gang Rape," "Kids Who Kill," "Teenage Sex Offenders," "Teens Trade Sex for Dope," "Children Who Kill Their Children," "Satanic Breeders: Babies for Sacrifice." Phil Donahue, who presents a facade of social concern, explored topics such as "First Time Sex," "Women Who Seduce Teenage Boys," "Brothers and Sisters in Love," and "When Dad Has a Sex Change." In the summer, all children can watch such shows; during the school year, many of these programs are there for after-school viewing. It is time to speak plainly about these programs. If, for some reason, a new federal law required television networks to do everything possible to cheapen the social value of the medium, to violate our society's traditional understanding of childhood, and to inflict gratuitous harm on the family as a social institution, the networks could do no better than simply continuing to beam these programs each day into millions of American homes.

Contrasts with Other Countries

Much more than in any earlier era, adolescents today have great access to, and control over, television viewing. Most mothers of teenagers work outside the home at least part time. Nationally, nearly 70% of mothers of school-age children work outside the home either part time or full time.[69] One Michigan study found that two-thirds of all adolescents possess their own television sets.[70] Recent studies indicate that mothers' work outside the home indirectly affects the amount of time adolescents spend watching television by reducing the likelihood that mothers will impose restrictions. Moreover, the father's absence from the home is also associated with more time spent with media, irre-spective of whether or not formal restrictions are imposed.[71] As a result, television offers our children increasingly frightening and distorted views of a violent, hedonistic, sex-crazed world at a time when many parents are simply not at home.

Embarrassingly, many other countries consider the after-school time slot to be special and important—a sort of prime time for children and ado-lescents. For example, in Britain, an excellent program, *Newsround*, has been broadcast for 17 years in this time slot, with a viewership of approximately 25% of British children. In Australia, all commercially licensed stations are required to broadcast an hour of children's programming each weekday after-noon. Japan has two public channels that provide programs each day in the time slots that are appropriate to child and adolescent viewing.[72]

We find it unconscionable that in the United States no similar pro-tection is provided to young people. If the network sponsors cannot be dis-suaded from funding socially irresponsible sensationalism, they should at least be required to place these offensive programs in late-night time slots that will effectively reduce the number of child viewers. If we are at all concerned about the remorseless crowding out of family values by the mar-ketplace, then this very mild form of government regulation is a minimal, but essential, first step.

FREE-PRESS IDEALS AND CURRENT FARE

Newpapers in the Corporate Era

Finally, we must consider the news, the free press that is the lifeblood of an informed citizenry. First, consider developments in the print media. They are highly concentrated and becoming more so. In 1920 700 cities had competing daily newspapers. In 1986, though the country's population had more than doubled, there were only a dozen.[73]

The huge resources of press conglomerates have not been used to improve news coverage: news makes up less of the paper than it did in the early 1950s.[74] While there has been an increase in the number of pages from 31 in 1940 to 61 in 1980, this increase represents mostly ad pages. Most of the added editorial pages consist not of hard news but instead occupy a gray area between news and ads, called "fluff" in the trade. Fluff is sought by advertisers to create a buying mood.

Hard news—contemporary events and commentary—in 1940 was four pages of a 31-page paper, or 13%. In 1980, it was five of 66 pages, or

7.5%.[75] Between 1971 and 1977, the nonadvertising content of daily papers changed in important ways: less coverage of local and state government, national government, education, labor and national wage rates, and minorities issues; more space devoted to puzzles and horoscopes, comics, nonlocal human interest and life-style articles, business, finance, and crime.[76]

The growing reality is that newspaper chains lose editorial autonomy to profit-minded central offices. The resulting reliance on fluff and on simple, noncontroversial news may be compatible with free-market economics, but it is not compatible with a free marketplace of ideas.

Television News and Public Accountability

With the rise of VCRs, cable television, and other competitive pressures, television news is rapidly turning into entertainment, designed primarily to attract the largest number of consumers. The Fairness Doctrine was created to foster diversity in news. It required individual broadcast stations to devote time to controversial issues and to air varied opposing views. The old FCC sought to induce vertical diversity—that is, variety within each individual station's programming. But deregulation has had a devastating effect on news quality.[77]

In 1981, the television networks each owned five stations in leading markets, giving them direct access to 33% of the homes in the country. They also owned book and magazine publishers, record companies, and movie theaters. These investment portfolios suggest that television corporations use their large profits not to enhance news quality, but instead to branch out into other media pursuits. Nor do ratings competitions produce diversity in program offerings. Since the introduction of television, the types of shows have declined and repetition and imitation have increased.

In the late 1980s each network eliminated many positions from news divisions. One survey, comparing 1986 to 1975, shows a 37% decrease in domestic news coverage and a 50% increase in human interest stories.[78] Although journalists of stature such as Fred Friendly have decried the trend toward "docudramas" and so-called "recreations," reliance on marketplace competition is sure to feed this sad trend, just as it has fed all sensational trends. Not surprisingly, in national news, families and adolescents only appear in crimes or disasters. During the three-week period when the minimum wage was being discussed by Congress, no young persons were shown on network television addressing this issue that directly affects them. The only portrayal of youth was the extensive coverage given to the gang rape of an investment banker in New York City.[79]

Ben H. Bagdikian provides some insights into the situation:

> Today the advertiser is sovereign in newspapers, broadcasting and magazines. It is not sovereign in the sense that the advertiser necessarily dictates the nonadvertising content explicitly, though that may be a significant practical effect. The advertiser is sovereign by the simple businesslike

decision to place its ads in the newspaper, broadcast station, or magazine that reaches the most affluent consumers in the most precisely targeted way and with content that most maximizes the selling power of
the ads. The form and content of contemporary American newpapers,
magazines and broadcasting are, of course, a combination of what the
advertiser wants and what the audience wants. But with each passing
year, newspapers and broadcasting have put more weight on what
makes for effective advertising than on inherent community interest
and need.[80]

Advertising, Show Business, and TV Journalism

Bill Moyers, in the PBS series "The Public Mind," explores the thesis
that our society's willingness to face reality has been deeply affected by the
"triumph of visual images as the grammar of times." He examines the ways
in which quick images, borrowed from advertising, conveying pleasant
moods and surroundings, have come to replace thoughtful statements by
opinion leaders, political candidates, officials, and analysts.

In Ronald Reagan's 1980 campaign, 70% of his network time was
devoted to 30-second commercials. Another 25% consisted of five-second
commercials. Only 5% consisted of longer messages.[81] The techniques of
the "photo opportunity," devoid of content, were carried over into his
Presidency and also into his successor's.

A whole generation of voters, therefore, has simply not encountered
serious content in election campaigns. The ubiquitous pressure for higher
ratings and profits results in pleasant pictures and the conception of the
evening news as one more "show" in prime-time entertainment. Walter
Lippmann's idea of the news as a "picture of reality on which the citizen
can act" has no place in the show.

WHAT IS TO BE DONE?

Three brief propositions summarize our view of the relationship
between the mass media and family values:

● The history of the mass media in our society is, in large part, the history
of the encroachment of profit-seeking entertainment corporations onto
the moral turf of families and communities.
● This successful invasion of moral turf inflicts serious harm on the family
as social institution.
● As the mass media's power to influence family life has become stronger
and stronger, the family's power to influence the mass media has become
weaker and weaker.

At only one point in our history, during the Great Depression, was
there a moral coalition of sufficient magnitude to alter, even temporarily,
the course of sensation for profit. Since deregulation, we have seen a

renewed power—at times, it seems, a renewed pride—in the ability of the marketplace to displace or override family values. The current situation, in which entertainment and the cherished "free press" are owned by a smaller and smaller number of corporate giants, requires nothing less than disaster relief. We offer the following proposals:

1. *Provide activities to nurture family values and civic virtue.*

Jane Addams's fears of a commercial invention replacing the richness of family and community life have been realized to a degree unimaginable only 40 years ago. For many families, television is the center around which life turns. We must understand not only what people are watching, but also what people are not doing because they are watching. Moreover, parental absence—a major family trend of our time—is related to laxity of parental control over both television content and also amount of children's viewing.

Since the mid-1970s, the erosion of state requirements for physical education in public schools and the diversion of funds at the high school level to elite athletic programs have meant a decline in children's physical fitness. More than 75% of youth are excluded from participation on athletic teams. Elementary-school children in inner-city schools have suffered most from the budget cuts.[82] Our media-directed vision has focused on adult, professional levels of athletic competition, and we have been blind to the needs of children.

In the context of the mass media, those children who do not participate in athletics are, not surprisingly, the same children who are at risk because of their television viewing. For many of these children, the parks and streets are unsafe for after-school play. Parents and other adults use television as a babysitter. These developments not only present grave threats to the long-term physical health of children but also deprive them of social experiences with others.

We need to support both governmental and workplace policies that provide for after-school and summer programs that include individual and group physical recreation. Such programs could also include art, music, dance, and theater in order to stimulate creative interests and the sharing that these activities engender. Retired people and adolescents might be trained to supervise and teach. Parents could attend with their children, and if hours were expanded, working parents might come as well.

We need to look with fresh eyes at the special needs of adolescents—our young citizens who have had the most exposure to sensational media distortions of themselves and their society. Perhaps programs like Vista and the Peace Corps or other forms of national service might be discussed seriously as a means of bringing youth into civic life. The comments of Jane Addams retain their power:

> To insist that young people shall forecast their rose-colored future only in
> a house of dreams is to deprive the real world of that warmth and reassur-

ance which it so sorely needs and to which it is justly entitled; furthermore we are left outside with a sense of dreariness, in company with that shadow which already lurks only around the corner for most of us—a skepticism of life's value.[83]

2. Bring to the attention of the public the concentration and corporate structure of the mass media.

The threat of consolidated control over the mass media must be brought to public attention. In 1977, Representative Morris Udall introduced a bill to study the degree of concentration in important industries, including the media; "it died in committee without a whisper."[84]

Although it may be difficult to find political leaders courageous enough to suggest investigation of the corporations that control their public image, we must try to find those leaders. A careful investigation could bring to public scrutiny the monopolistic structure that has evolved. A listing of major owners and principal outside interests of each newspaper, broadcasting station, film company, and cable enterprise might arouse considerable public interest. Bagdikian argues that even though it may be politically unrealistic to expect divestiture by giants, we still should try to study and influence the mass-media companies:

> There is a chance to reverse the tide. It lies in public awareness of the danger. But because the media are not going to make an issue of their own power, the initiative must come from others. A serious, sophisticated public commission, supported by foundations or other private money, could produce a comprehensive picture of the extent to which diversity and accountability of the marketplace has been lost, and of the financial excesses that threaten the long-term strength of the mass media. But the study cannot be dominated by those who are the problem.[85]

3. Take steps to realize the potential of public television.

Fred Rogers, creator of *Mister Rogers' Neighborhood*, commented that it is "only as we human beings give meaning to science or technology that they will have a positive or negative thrust."[86] It has become clear that the "meaning" given to commercial television in the United States does not enhance the lives of people as children, parents, or citizens. Accordingly, we must isolate some entertainment and news from the economic market altogether if we are to achieve an environment in which diversity, complexity, and creativity may flourish.

We need to fund public television at a higher level. Currently, per-capita government spending on all public broadcasting is 57 cents. In the United Kingdom, it is $18; in Canada, $22; and in Japan, $10. Even adjusting for population differences, the spending in other countries is of a different order of magnitude. Currently two bills in Congress call for $2.5 million to create an endowment for children's television. This is a good and long-overdue idea, but the funding is paltry. Moreover, isolating the young children's educational issue from the larger issue of sensation-driven entertainment and news is like putting a Band-Aid on a hemorrhaging wound.

In 1984 President Reagan vetoed a public broadcasting authorization bill that would have increased federal funding of public television and radio to $270 million by 1989. Federal support in the intervening years has dwindled. Warned in the early years of the Reagan administration to wean itself from government subsidies, PBS began offering corporate underwriters "enhanced underwriting" or additional leeway to promote themselves on programs. Charges of commercialism have led to attempts to refine those rules.[87] Moreover, the meagerness of economic news and public-affairs coverage on public television is blamed by some on corporate financial support.[88] At the same time, public television faces stiff competition from cable networks that also offer quality programming.

Some members of Congress are interested in how public television might be revitalized and expanded into a real network with real resources. But the issue of how to fund a significant, secure public television network is sure to raise the ire of the powerful broadcast industry. In 1978, for example, broadcasters, advertisers, and targeted manufacturers raised a $30 million "war chest" to fight attempts to limit or ban certain kinds of advertising to children.[89] An industry that receives some $21 billion in advertising revenue each year[90] and also faces declining audience shares is sure to react with fury to any idea that smacks of subsidized competition.

Foreign precedents that might be least offensive to the broadcast industry would be a receiver fee, as in the United Kingdom, or the Australian plan that allows individuals to deduct $1.33 from taxes for every $1.00 donation they make to the Australian Children's Television Foundation.[91] In the United States, The Working Group for Public Broadcasting recommends a 2% levy on consumer and broadcast electronic equipment. It estimates that $600 million would have been raised in this way in 1986. Robert Entman suggests funding for public television on the order of $250 million or $1 per capita.[92]

Other means of supporting public television are likely to be highly controversial, for they recognize explicitly the responsibilities of the broadcast industry to the public interest. We are almost unique among industrialized countries in providing private broadcasters with a free, five-year license—with no requirements for performance to benefit citizens. The United Kingdom imposes a license fee to fund public television. British commercial licensees must also provide special news programs, entertainment, preschool education, and "in-school programs"—about 20% of total transmission. Australia's commercial networks must meet rigorous programming requirements in order to have licenses renewed.[93]

Professor Bagdikian's proposal is also likely to face stiff opposition: he recommends imposing a progressive tax on advertising. He argues that such a tax would reduce the volume of advertising on commercial networks and elevate the public's needs in the selection of nonadvertising content.[94] Moreover, those revenues could be used to fund public television. A similar proposal would involve taxing the commercial station revenues.

We expect commercial networks to make a profit. However, we need to rein in what has become an unlimited desire for profit that crushes any meaningful conception of the public interest. We need to give broadcasting a deeper meaning if it is to meet the diverse needs of all people and truly enrich our lives. To achieve this goal is a daunting task. Our challenge, as families and citizens, is nothing less than the reclamation of the moral territory that once was ours but increasingly is ours no longer.

NOTES

1. Laurence A. Cremin, *The Transformation of the School* (New York: Random House, 1961); Merle Curti, *The Growth of American Thought* (New York: Harper and Brothers, 1943).

2. John Dewey, *The School and Society* (Chicago: University of Chicago Press, 1899), pp. 43–44.

3. Garth Jowett, *Film: The Democratic Art* (Boston: Focal Press, 1976).

4. Jane Addams, *The Spirit of Youth and City Streets* (New York: Macmillan, 1909, 1939), p. 76.

5. Ibid., p. 83.

6. Ibid., p. 86.

7. Ibid., p. 84.

8. Joel Williamson, *The Crucible of Race* (New York: Oxford University Press, 1984).

9. See Claude Bowers, *The Tragic Era* (Cambridge, MA: Riverside Press, 1929).

10. Richard D. Schickel, *D. W. Griffith* (New York: Simon and Schuster, 1984), p. 269.

11. Terry Ramsaye, *A Million and One Nights* (New York: Simon and Schuster, 1926, 1964), p. 643.

12. Jowett, op. cit.

13. Ibid., p. 120.

14. Lewis Jacobs, *The Rise of the American Film* (New York: Teacher's College Press, 1939), p. 275.

15. Margaret Thorp, *America at the Movies* (New Haven, CT: Yale University Press, 1939).

16. Robert S. Lynd and Helen M. Lynd, *Middletown* (New York: Harcourt, Brace and World, 1929), p. 266.

17. Ibid., p. 266.

18. Ibid., p. 268.

19. Ibid., p. 265.

20. Edgar Dale, *The Content of Motion Pictures* (New York: Macmillan, 1933); Edgar Dale, *Children's Attendance at Motion Pictures*, (New York: Macmillan, 1935).

21. W. W. Charters, *Motion Pictures and Youth: A Summary* (New York: Macmillan, 1933).

22. Herbert Blumer, *Movies and Conduct* (New York: Macmillan, 1933).

23. Herbert Blumer and P. Hauser, *Movies, Delinquency, and Crime* (New York: Macmillan, 1933), p. 202.

24. Charters, op. cit., p. 54.

25. Ibid., p. 63.

26. Jowett, op. cit.

27. Ibid.

28. Thorp, op. cit.

29. Jowett, op. cit.

30. Thomas Doherty, *Teenagers & Teenpics: The Juvenilization of the Movies in the 1950's* (Boston: Unwin Hyman, 1988).

31. Ibid.

32. Ibid.

33. Cited in ibid., p. 184.

34. William H. Melody, *Children's Television: The Economics of Exploitation* (New Haven, CT: Yale University Press, 1973).

35. Robert M. Liebert and Joyce Sprafkin, *The Early Window: Effects of Television on Children and Youth*, 3rd ed. (New York: Pergamon Press, 1988).

36. Melody, op. cit.

37. Ibid.

38. Robert M. Liebert, John M. Neale, and Emily S. Davidson, *The Early Window: Effects of Television on Children and Youth* (New York: Pergamon Press, 1973).

39. Communications Act of 1934, P. L. 426, 73d Congress, June 19, 1934.

40. U.S. Senate, Committee on the Judiciary, Subcommittee to Investigate Juvenile Delinquency, "Television Programs," *Hearings* 84 (No. 1, April 1955), pp. 91–92.

41. Willard D. Rowland, *The Politics of TV Violence* (Beverly Hills, CA: Sage Publications, 1983).

42. Cited in ibid., p. 131.

43. Ibid.

44. F. Andison, "TV Violence and Viewer Aggression: A Cumulation of Study Results, 1956–1976," *Public Opinion Quarterly* 41 (1977), pp. 314–331; Lynette Friedrich-Cofer and Aletha Huston, "Television Violence and Aggression: The Debate Continues," *Psychological Bulletin* 100 (1986), pp. 364–371; Aletha Stein and Lynette Friedrich, "Impact of Television on Children and Youth," in E. M. Hetherington, ed., *Review of Child Development Research*, Volume 5 (Chicago: University of Chicago Press, 1975), pp. 183–256.

45. Rowland, op. cit., p. 178.

46. Kathryn C. Montgomery, *Target: Prime Time. Advocacy Groups and the Struggle over Entertainment Television* (New York: Oxford University Press, 1989).

47. Ibid.

48. Ibid., p. 12.

49. Aletha C. Huston, Bruce A. Watkins, and Dale Kunkel, "Public Policy and Children's Television," *American Psychologist* 44 (1989), pp. 424–433.

50. Dale Kunkel and Bruce Watkins, *Children and Television, Washington Report* (Bulletin of the Society for Research in Child Development, December 1985).

51. Cited in Dennis D. Kerkman, Dale Kunkel, Aletha C. Huston, John C. Wright, and M. F. Pinon, "Children's Television Programming and the 'Free Market Solution,'" *Journalism Quarterly* (in press, 1990).

52. Huston, Watkins, and Kunkel, op. cit.

53. Kerkman et al., op. cit.

54. Aimee Dorr and Dale Kunkel, "Children and the Media Environment: Change and Constancy amidst Change," *Communication Research* 17 (1990), p. 21.

55. See *Broadcasting*, January 15, 1990.

56. Dale Kunkel, "From a Raised Eyebrow to a Turned Back: Regulatory Factors Influencing the Growth of Children's Product-related Programming," *Journal of Communication* 38 (1988), pp. 90–108.

57. See *Connoisseur*, September 1989.

58. Montgomery, op. cit.

59. Ibid., p. 222.

60. Bill Carter, "The Man Who Owns Prime Time," *New York Times Sunday Magazine*, March 4, 1990, p. 24.

61. Neil Postman, *The Disappearance of Childhood* (New York: Delacorte Press, 1982).

62. Bradley S. Greenberg, Michael Siemicki, Sandra Dorfman, Sandra Heeter, Cynthia Stanley, Anne Soderman, and Renata Linsangan, *Sex Content in R-rated Films Viewed by Adolescents*, Technical Report No. 3 (East Lansing, MI: Michigan State University, Department of Telecommunication, 1986).

63. Bradley S. Greenberg, Renata Linsangan, Anne Soderman, Sandra Heeter, Carrie Lin, Carolyn Stanley, and Michael Siemicki, *Adolescents and Their Exposure to Television and Movie Sex*, Technical Report No. 4 (East Lansing, MI: Michigan State University, Communication Technology Laboratory, 1987).

64. P. R. Abramson and M. B. Mechanic, "Sex and the Media: Three Decades of Best-Selling Books and Major Motion Pictures," *Archives of Sexual Behavior* 12 (1983), pp. 185–206.

65. Jane D. Brown, K. W. Childers, and C. S. Waszak, "Television and Adolescent Sexuality," Paper presented at the Conference on Television and Teens: Health Implications, Manhattan Beach, CA, June 22–24, 1988.

66. Ibid.

67. Jane D. Brown and K. Campbell, "Race and Gender in Music Videos: The Same Beat but a Different Drummer," *Journal of Communication* 36 (1986), pp. 94–106.

68. Mary P. Koss, C. A. Gidycz, and N. Wisniewski, "The Scope of Rape: Incidence and Prevalence of Sexual Aggression and Victimization in a National Sample of Higher Education Students," *Journal of Consulting and Clinical Psychology* 55 (1985), pp. 162–170.

69. David Blankenhorn, "Cosby for President?" *Family Affairs* (Institute for American Values Newsletter, Winter 1988), p. 1.

70. Brown et al., op. cit.

71. Jane D. Brown, K. W. Childers, K. E. Bauman, and G. G. Koch, "The Influence of New Media and Family Structure on Young Adolescents' Television and Radio Use," *Communication Research* 17 (No. 1, 1990), pp. 65–82.

72. John Kelly, "Economic and International Perspectives on Promoting Children's Television in the USA" (Unpublished manuscript, Duke University, Institute of Public Policy, 1989).

73. Ben Bagdikian, *The Media Monopoly* (Boston: Beacon Press, 1987).

74. David L. Paletz and Robert M. Entman, *Media Power Politics* (New York: Free Press, 1981).

75. Bagdikian, op. cit.

76. Ibid., p. 137.

77. Robert Entman, *Democracy without Citizens* (New York: Oxford University Press, 1989).

78. Ibid.

79. Lynette Friedrich-Cofer, Unpublished manuscript, Duke University, 1989.

80. Bagdikian, op. cit., p. 230.

81. Ibid.

82. Lynette Friedrich-Cofer, "Body, Mind and Morals in the Framing of Social Policy," in Lynette K. Friedrich-Cofer, Ed., *Human Nature and Public Policy: Scientific Views of Women, Children and Families* (New York: Praeger, 1986), pp. 97–174.

83. Addams, op. cit., p. 103.

84. Bagdikian, op. cit., p. 225.

85. Ibid., p. 236.

86. 1973 Press Release, Family Communications, Inc. Fred Rogers continues: "Television to me was a challenging new instrument. I wanted to use it the way I had used the piano and drama as a child to communicate some things that I felt were positive—and important—in our world. Since one can't be a communicator with equal impact on all segments of society my early decision was clearly one to communicate with children. I wanted to help as many as I could to feel good about themselves and what they could become. I wanted to show them a wide range of artistry and feeling that make up a varied culture like ours. I wanted to help children to learn to discover worth in little things, in things that had no price tag—in people who might have outer handicaps and great inner strengths. I wanted every child to know that he or she had something lovable and worth expressing, that everyone has limits as well as possibilities. I wanted to engender feelings of responsibility toward the care of oneself as well as others. . . . Public television has been an instrument for me to be a professional worker for families with young children. It must always be an expression of our highest idealism as well as an instrument for our positive creative powers."
    If PBS were to become a well-funded network, one could imagine that other creative and idealistic people might be able to enrich the lives of families with older children, adolescents, the elderly. There could be programs that would address the concerns of children and families in single-parent households, in poverty, of ethnic minorities, and of immigrants. We have a great need for many programs that mean something in the lives of particular and specific people that do not depend for their continued financial support on mass audiences and ratings.

87. See *New York Times*, November 7, 1988.

88. Cf. *Connoisseur*, op. cit.

89. Liebert and Sprafkin, op. cit.

90. See *Connoisseur*, op. cit.

91. Kelly, op. cit.

92. Entman, op. cit.

93. Kelly, op. cit.

94. Bagdikian, op. cit.

Part III

Solutions:
What Is the
Family Agenda
For the 1990s?

═12═
Good News?
The Private Sector and
Win–Win Scenarios

Sylvia Ann Hewlett

W
e are witnessing a profound change in corporate attitudes and behavior—a change driven primarily by the new demographics of the American workplace. The 1990s will clearly be a decade of labor shortages. From now until the end of the century, the population and work force will grow more slowly than it has at any time since the 1930s. Population growth, which was climbing at 1.9% a year in the 1950s, will slump to only 0.7% a year by the late 1990s.[1] The labor force, which exploded by 2.9% a year in the 1970s, will expand by only 1.2% a year in the 1990s. Overall, the labor force is projected to grow 19 million between 1988 and the year 2000, compared with 25 million in the 1976–1988 period.[2]

Behind this slowdown in the rate of growth of the work force is a dramatic demographic shift—from the high birth rates of the baby-boom years (1946–1965) to the low birth rates of the baby-bust years (1965–1980). One thing seems clear: we will have to live with these low growth rates for quite a while, since the baby boom's echo—the babies of the boomers—won't reach working age in large numbers until the first few years of the next century.

Two consequences of these demographic trends are obvious. First, the average age of the work force will rise. Second, the pool of young workers entering the labor market will shrink. The number of young workers age 16–24 will drop by almost 2 million a year during the 1990s. The result? Companies that previously have grown by adding large numbers of lower-paid young workers will increasingly find such workers in short supply.[3]

Sylvia Ann Hewlett, economist and writer, was Executive Director of the Economic Policy Council. Her forthcoming book examines the well-being of children in the United States. Dr. Hewlett lives in Bronxville, New York.

The problems posed by the looming shortage of young workers are compounded by the changing face and form of the work force. In the words of one expert, "New workers will increasingly come from backgrounds not traditionally associated with productive skills."[4] Indeed, white men, who now make up 44% of the labor force, are expected to contribute only 12 out of every 100 new workers between now and the year 2000.[5] Blacks, Hispanics, and women—demographic groups that have traditionally had either weak educational backgrounds or relatively unstable attachment to work—will provide the bulk of the new entrants.

Sixty-three percent of the new recruits to the work force during the 1990s will be women, and minorities will be a much larger share of the new entrants to the labor force in the 1990s than was true in the 1980s or 1970s. Indeed, nonwhites will make up 29% of new workers between now and the year 2000—twice their current share.[6] Although being a larger share of a more slowly growing work force might improve employment opportunities for minorities, realizing this potential will depend on massive new investment in education and other types of social infrastructure because minority youngsters tend to be deficient in the skills needed in the modern workplace.

But the skills shortfall is not confined to minority groups. Underachievement and educational failure reach deep into the white middle class. One 1988 study found that only 6% of high school seniors could solve a two-step arithmetic problem and only 5% could understand a short, complex article.[7] In international math and science proficiency tests, U.S. students consistently finish last or near the bottom when measured against other developed countries.[8]

Ill-prepared young people with major learning deficits are unlikely to find employment in the economy of the 1990s. Global competitive pressures and the rapid pace of technological change are producing a restructuring of U.S. occupational opportunities so as to give much more weight to education and other types of "human capital."

According to projections prepared by the Hudson Institute, during the 1990s job prospects for professional, managerial, technical, sales, and service personnel will far outstrip opportunities in other fields. For example, jobs for scientists and lawyers will grow two or three times faster than the average. In contrast, jobs for machine tenders, assemblers, miners, and farmers will actually decline.[9] Of all the new jobs that will be created in the 1990–2000 period, more than half will require some education beyond high school, and almost one-third will require a college degree. Today, only one-fourth of all occupations are filled by college graduates.[10] Given the deficiencies of our educational system, most higher-range and many middle-range jobs of the 1990s will simply be outside the reach of a large proportion of American youngsters.

THE FAMILY AND THE CORPORATE BOTTOM LINE

Once upon a time, women anchored a domestic and familial support system that enabled male breadwinners to focus on their jobs for at least 40 hours a week. They raised the children, looked after the house, took the clothes to the dry cleaner, and visited Grandma in the hospital. This home-based support system began to recede a generation ago and is now more the exception than the rule. Seventy percent of women with children between the ages of 6 and 17 are now in the labor force, either full or part time, as are more than half of women with children younger than one year old.[11]

This new reality has produced enormous stress in family life. Almost every day, working parents are faced with wrenching dilemmas: Who will take care of the three-year-old who is running a temperature? Can the seven-year-old be trusted to look after herself between 3:30 and 6:00 P.M.? Who will let the plumber in so that the leak in the bathroom can finally be fixed?

For employers, these stresses translate into lower productivity, poor concentration on the job, high rates of absenteeism, and increased labor turnover. It is very easy for worries about a latchkey child or a bedridden parent to get in the way of an employee giving his or her best energy to the job. For individual working parents, particularly women, these strains translate into costly career interruptions and lower lifetime earnings.

These are the demographic facts of life of the 1990s: prospective labor shortages with burgeoning numbers of overburdened working parents. It should come as no surprise that the evidence is mounting that an employer's family-support policies directly affect the corporate bottom line. One of the best-documented studies is the National Employer Supported Childcare Project, a nationwide study of 415 industrial, service-sector, and governmental organizations. In this report employers highlight the following "payoffs" to family benefits: improved recruitment (cited by 85% of the respondents in this project and ranked as the most important benefit in virtually all studies); reduced turnover (65%); reduced absenteeism (53%); increased productivity (49%); and enhanced company image (85%).[12] Harder-to-quantify improvements were also reported in such areas as morale, loyalty to firm, and reduced tardiness. To illustrate, consider a few of the companies that have analyzed in detail the costs and benefits of specific family-support policies.

Merck & Company

Merck & Company has demonstrated impressive returns to its parenting-leave policy. The price tag attached to replacing an employee at this large pharmaceutical firm is $50,000. But by permitting a new parent to take a generous six-month child-care leave—at a cost of $38,000, which includes partial pay, benefits, and other indirect costs—the company succeeds in retaining almost all of its new-mother employees and, in so doing, achieves a net savings of $12,000 per employee.[13] In addition to its parent-ing-leave policy, Merck offers a child-care center, child-care referral services, and a flexible time option that has increased productivity up to 20% in some departments.[14]

J. Douglas Phillips, Senior Director of Corporate Planning at Merck, stresses the large cost savings inherent in bringing attrition rates down. In a rigorous analysis of turnover costs in several industries, he shows that turnover costs average 1.5 times annual salary. He includes direct costs such as agency search fees, but he also includes indirect costs such as incoming employee productivity losses. It takes approximately 13 months for a new employee to achieve maximum efficiency.[15]

According to Phillips, very few companies understand the true costs of replacing workers. But in most firms, "avoiding turnover for just a few employees will yield excellent paybacks."[16] In his research, while other programs are capable of reducing attrition rates, parenting leave and other types of family support have the biggest impact on turnover. Phillips believes that the Merck family-benefit package is a large part of the reason why the company has such a low annual turnover rate, 6% against an American average of more than 14% a year.[17]

Sunbeam Appliance Company

Sunbeam Appliance Company found out the hard way about prenatal care. Four premature babies born in 1984 to women working at the company's Coushatta, Louisiana, plant accounted for fully half of the company's $1 million health care bill that year for 530 employees. One of the babies required the maximum $250,000 in covered major medical expenses.

Shocked by these numbers, the company did some research. It discovered that pregnant workers—and its labor force is 80% female—were waiting too long to see a doctor. In 1986 Sunbeam started a prenatal program. Pregnant employees were allowed to take an hour of company time every other week to attend classes taught by specialists in prenatal nursing. The plant nurse weighed the women weekly, checked blood pressure and urine, and even got them started on prenatal care by setting up appointments with obstetricians.

The program paid quick dividends. Since it started, approximately 65 people have taken part. There has been only one premature birth, which didn't entail severe problems. Average medical costs for childbirth have taken a nosedive, falling to $3,792 in 1987 from $27,243 three years earlier. The program has since been extended to another Sunbeam plant in Mississippi and is now available not only to employees but to their spouses as well. The total cost of the program at the two plants is less than $20,000 a year.[18]

Johnson & Johnson

In early 1989, Johnson & Johnson announced an extremely broad work-and-family initiative that builds upon earlier, more modest company programs in this area. The expanded program includes family-care leave (up to one year of unpaid leave with benefits and job-back guarantees), resource and referral services for child and eldercare, dependent-care accounts (to make it possible for employees to pay for child care on a pretax basis), adoption benefits, flexible benefits programs (to allow individualized family coverage), flexible hours, a compressed work week, and on-site child care.

The enhanced program at Johnson & Johnson was prompted by an in-house study that showed the proportion of women workers at the company rising from 51% in 1989 to 60% at the turn of the century. According to this study, prepared by a task force of senior managers, family supports are increasingly needed if the company is "to attract and retain the top-quality employees it needs to remain competitive."[19]

International Business Machines

For more than a decade, IBM has steadily increased its efforts to adapt to family needs. In the early 1980s it pioneered child-care and eldercare assistance programs. A national resource and referral network put together by IBM in 1984 now serves 900,000 employees in more than 25 companies. Today, most employees have the option of beginning or ending their working day an hour earlier or later.

In addition, IBM employees, 30% of whom are women, can take a three-year break from full-time employment—with part-time work available in the second and third year—to care for young children or elderly relatives. With the exception of the part-time component, this "career break" is unpaid, but health and retirement benefits continue while workers are on leave and IBM guarantees a full-time job at the end of the three-year period. More recently the company has added work-at-home options and has also introduced family-issues sensitivity training for more than 25,000 managers and supervisors.[20]

Other Corporate Initiatives

AT&T recently negotiated a contract with two of its unions that establishes a dependent-care referral service and provides for leaves of up to one year, with job-back guarantees, for new parents and for workers with seriously ill dependents.[21] Apple Computer operates its own employee-staffed child-care center and gives "baby bonuses" of $500 to new parents.[22] In 1989 Allstate Insurance Company created a new package of family-support policies called "Work and Family Connections." The package includes special (pretax) employee spending accounts for dependent care, family-illness allowances, and options for job sharing, part-time, and flexible work schedules.[23] DuPont has helped to establish child-care centers in Delaware with contributions of money and space.[24] Eastman Kodak has adopted new rules permitting part-time work, job sharing, and informal, situational flextime.[25] For reasons that are economic and strategic, "these and scores of other businesses are building work environments that let people give their best to their jobs without giving up the pleasures and responsibilities of family life."[26]

Family-support policies can boost productivity for working dads as well as working moms. Both DuPont and AT&T report that male workers are experiencing significant and increasing child-care problems that affect job performance.[27] Surveys at the Los Angeles Department of Water and Power have uncovered the fact that male employees have even more problems with child care than do female employees. According to this company, these "father-oriented" child-care problems are expensive, costing more than $1 million in absenteeism during 1987.[28]

Prospects for the 1990s

Given this kind of data, it comes as no surprise that the "profamily workplace" is gaining ground in boardrooms around the nation. According to the Conference Board, as of January 1990, close to 5,000 employers had some kind of systematic child-care and parenting assistance as part of their benefits package, up from 600 in 1982.[29] Dana Friedman, Co-President of the Families and Work Institute, describes recent progress as "phenomenal, particularly since the new initiatives comprise a complete package rather than a token policy or two."[30] Companies are increasingly offering a range of family supports: parenting leave, child care, eldercare, at-home and part-time work, flexible hours, and job sharing. As one analyst has put it, "Enlightened executives see family-sensitive policies as giving them a competitive edge in the tight labor markets of the 1990s. . . . Firms slower to react will pay a price"[31] in that they will fail to attract or keep high-quality workers, thus creating built-in obstacles to profits and growth.

In sum, as we move into the 1990s, the pressure on firms is building. Employees' demand for a family-friendly workplace is clearly growing as working parents are empowered by labor shortages. It now makes economic sense for business to recognize that their employees are also family members.

During the past several years, the Roper organization has polled American workers to determine what benefits they expect from employers. The key finding in recent years is a rapidly rising demand for family supports for working parents. Forty percent of all adults now consider it the "definite responsibility" of an employer to provide company-supported child care, up 15 percentage points since the early 1980s.[32]

We can look forward, therefore, to a decade in which corporate America will get into the business of helping dual-paycheck families. The driving force will be enlightened self-interest, not altruism.

One additional point: in many cases, family-support policies will enable women to avoid those costly career interruptions that have so severely limited female earning power. A study by the Rand Corporation shows that a two- to four-year break in employment lowers lifetime income by 13%, whereas a five-year break in employment lowers lifetime income by 19%.[33] Economist Eli Ginsberg goes so far as to say that "a continuous work history is almost a prerequisite for high or even good achievement" in the labor market.[34] If better parenting-leave policies and subsidized child care enable more women to hang on to their jobs during their childbearing years, we can be sure that the gap between male and female earnings will narrow dramatically in the 1990s.

CORPORATIONS AND THE FAMILY BOTTOM LINE

From the perspective of family well-being, what does all of this corporate activity amount to? The corporate bottom line and the family bottom line are two distinctive notions of what is ultimately important. They may at times overlap, but they are not identical. For example, if the new corporate policies will enhance both corporate productivity and female earning power, will they also contribute to the well-being of children and the quality of family life? Can the new workplace flexibilities actually ease the strain that permeates the lives of so many employed parents and their children? Some concrete examples may help unpack these complexities.

Kathy's Story

When Kathy Cruise Murphy talks about Mondays and Tuesdays at home, this efficient, down-to-earth business executive can sound quite lyrical.

> It is a precious time. My little girl can get up whenever she wants—no need to bundle her up in a snowsuit, no need to rush off to the day-care center. We often go out to a long lazy 10 o'clock breakfast or just fool around in bed and watch *The Lady and the Tramp* on the VCR. It seems to be such a wonderful gift—two whole days of totally discretionary time. Of course, by the time Wednesday rolls around I am quite ready to get dressed up in a suit, go into the office and be with grown-ups, and Caroline is equally ready to be with playmates of her own age. But changing the balance of my life so that I have four days at home and three in the office instead of the standard 2 and 5, is quite simply the best thing I ever did.

Kathy works three days a week, sharing a middle-management job in the card division of American Express in New York City. Job sharing was not something she had in mind when she started out at American Express 11 years ago. Kathy is ambitious and capable. But becoming a mother changed her priorities in unexpected ways.

> When Caroline was born three and a half years ago, I just took the standard leave and was back at work full-time when my baby was eight weeks old. . . . I guess I just assumed that we modern women can "have it all" and should "do it all."

For a while things worked out—more or less. After a bad experience with an *au pair* girl who stayed only two months, Kathy put Caroline into a day-care center near their home. Caroline was there 10 hours a day, five days a week. The baby seemed to do well, but Kathy began to feel that her life was unbalanced.

> If you figure in the commute, my job was consuming 55 hours a week. Many evening hours and much of the weekend seemed to be filled with household chores and errands. I felt I was on a treadmill: tired, harrassed, and unhappy. I resented the fact that there was no time to enjoy my child, my husband, my family.

As Kathy was having these second thoughts, she met Jean Gol, another middle-level manager at American Express who had just had her second child and wanted to work part time. (Indeed, Jean had already resigned from AMEX and was looking for a part-time niche elsewhere.) So Kathy and Jean put together a proposal and applied for a middle-management job in human resources. They landed the job and for the last two years Jean has worked two-fifths time (at 40% of her former salary) while Kathy has worked three-fifths time (at 60% of her former salary). Both are entitled to full benefits for themselves, though not for their dependents.

Before Kathy goes home on Friday night she leaves a file folder of pending work for Jean. When Jean comes into the office on Monday, she spends half an hour on the phone with Kathy going over these materials. The same routine is followed Tuesday evening and Wednesday morning when Jean leaves and Kathy takes over. The two women rarely find they need to talk outside of these two half-hour slots. The work gets done efficiently and smoothly. According to a senior colleague, "Jean and Kathy really know how to get this job done; by tapping the experience of both of these women in this one job, the company gets a good deal." Kathy and Jean's job share has proved to be so successful that there are now nine other job shares in the same division of AMEX, one involving a male employee.

According to Kathy, when they broached their plan in 1988, AMEX was surprisingly open to the idea. Moreover, social attitudes were also beginning to change. "The image of the 'supermom' was becoming a little tarnished. For the first time in a while it was O.K. to admit that you wanted to spend time with your baby, that your worth was not solely wrapped up in working a 55-hour week. This change in perspective helped me get together the courage to change the rhythm of my life."

Reflecting on her decision, Kathy says,

> If you're ambitious, or if your identity is mixed up with being a professional, becoming a part-timer is kind of scary. It's easy to imagine that you will become a second-class citizen, that no one will give you responsibility or take you seriously. I don't feel that has happened to me—at least not yet. My work is valued by the company.

How does Kathy see the future?

> We need a whole new career track for part-timers. I know that I would feel better about my future at AMEX if I could identify the next rung on

the ladder. With creativity and imagination it should be possible to create part-time or job-sharing positions up to the vice-presidential level.[35]

Family Time: The Ultimate Win–Win Scenario

Job sharing clearly involves sacrificing some income. Thus it might not work for a parent who needs to maximize earning power, such as a single mother. However, for many dual-worker households, which today account for 24.9 million children, job sharing would seem to be the ultimate win–win situation. The working parent is able to achieve real balance in his or her life. The company retains highly productive employees who might otherwise be forced to leave. The child gets to see more of Mom or Dad.

It also can be more than a one-shot or temporary solution. Ten years down the road a job-sharing arrangement would allow Kathy (or her husband) to spend extended time with Caroline in her early teenage years—a time when youngsters often benefit from lots of parental attention. As Kathy correctly points out, there is no reason why companies can't build entire career ladders for part-time or job-sharing employees. Most hourly work, and a great deal of middle-management work, is susceptible to being organized this way. There is nothing inherently efficient in 9-to-5 workdays, or 40- to 50-hour work weeks. Things were set up this way to fit the needs of male breadwinners in an earlier period. Why can't we reorganize the rhythm of work so that contemporary parents can give more time to their children?

Which brings us to a central question. What does a family-friendly workplace mean for the well-being of children?

Most corporate supports for working parents do promote the interests of the child. The generous parenting-leave policies of companies such as Merck and Johnson & Johnson make an important difference in the critical first months of life. Job sharing, part-time work, compressed work weeks, staggered hours—all those flexible options now offered by companies such as American Express and IBM—are clearly good for children in that they free parents to spend more and better time with their children. Mothers working full time can experience so much stress in their daily lives that "quality time" for the children seems like a bad joke.

Finally, on-site child care, or subsidies that permit a parent to opt for higher-quality child care, can upgrade the quality of out-of-home care available to children. This is clearly a step in the right direction. Today, many parents are forced to put their infants or toddlers in third-rate, unlicensed, and even dangerous day care because they simply cannot afford anything better.

But we shouldn't fool ourselves that the interests of the working parent—or the interests of the corporation—are identical to those of the child. Some working parents may be more interested in getting promoted than spending time with little Johnny. Moreover, companies are mostly interested in easing the lives of working parents so that these employees can devote more "quality time" to the firm. For quite understandable reasons, corporate America is more interested in better workers than it is in better spouses or parents.

Because of this divergence of interest, at least some of the new corporate policies, even those labeled "family supports," are not particularly good for children. A few may actually harm them. For example, out-of-home emergency or sick care for children might reduce absenteeism for the firm and boost earning power for the individual working parent, but such a solution may seem singularly unattractive to a child who wants to be home with Mom or Dad.

Last year Wilmer, Cutler & Pickering, a prominent Washington law firm, set up an on-site child-care center for emergencies—times when a child is sick or a regular babysitter fails to turn up. Despite the fact that this facility proved to be expensive (start-up costs were in the $300,000 range), the law firm expects the center to more than pay for itself.[36] The reason is that (high-priced) female lawyers are now much more available to work late into the night and on weekends.

This idea makes sense for Wilmer, Cutler & Pickering. It may even make sense for individual women lawyers, who are freer to work toward partnerships by logging 14-hour workdays, just like their male colleagues. But even if the center has a cute name and is described as a "family support," is it actually good for the children, who now spend even less time with their mothers?

Edward Zigler, Professor of Psychology at Yale University and longtime children's advocate, has problems with these kinds of emergency arrangements. He points out that children who are ill often want to be with their parents, not with strangers. "Over the long term," Zigler says, "we need a solution like the one in Sweden where mothers have a certain number of days off when their children are sick."[37]

Time is the crucial issue here—or more specifically, what one analyst calls "the family time famine." Parents today are working more and spending less time with their children and with each other. According to one estimate, the amount of total contact parents have with their children has dropped 40% since 1965.[38] According to a recent survey commissioned by Massachusetts Mutual Life Insurance Company, Americans today believe that "parents having less time to spend with their families" is the most important cause of fragmentation and stress in contemporary family life.[39]

Accordingly, new corporate policies that empower parents to spend more time with their families are truly "pro-family" and in the best interests of children. The same cannot be said, however, of those new policies—sick-child care being one example—that seek solely to free parents from parental obligations so that they can spend more, not less, of their time and energy at work.

Yet despite this important qualification, it does seem that most of the new policies, such as the one that benefits Kathy Cruise Murphy and her family, are genuinely win–win scenarios: good for the company, good for the worker, good for family life. By the end of the century it is very likely that business will be reaching out to help up to half of all working parents in this country, and in most cases this help will also improve the life prospects for children. The looming labor shortage has tilted the balance of power in society toward skilled labor. Working parents, particularly mothers, are prime beneficiaries of this shift.

A CORPORATE WAR ON POVERTY?

If close to 5,000 corporations have created family-support policies for their employees, a smaller but significant group is reaching beyond working parents to intervene directly in the lives of disadvantaged children. Business leaders are concerned that in the 1990s companies will be unable to grow and compete because an expanding educational underclass will be unable to meet the demands of jobs generated by an increasingly sophisticated economy.

This concern is relatively recent. Historically, poor children have always been less likely to complete their education (until the 1950s, fewer than 50% of all students graduated from high school). But in earlier periods our nation could tolerate a sink-or-swim attitude toward those in school. The reason? American industry could absorb massive numbers of unskilled laborers. A strong back and a pair of deft hands would always secure a decently paid factory job or help run a farm.

But today the industrial and service sectors rely less and less on unskilled manual labor. Production processes increasingly depend on computers. Most manufacturing jobs demand greater intellectual ability. Likewise, jobs in the growing service industries require more literate workers with good problem-solving skills. Peter Drucker calls the employees of the 1990s "knowledge workers" and points out that at least half of American youth are unprepared for knowledge work.[40]

Concern over this "human resource deficit" is fueling corporate support of primary and secondary education, particularly in the inner cities. In recent years, General Electric, American Express, Xerox, AT&T, General Motors, and scores of other corporations have all gotten into the business of education. The new interest in children is largely a response to twin phemomena: the deteriorating quality of American schools and a tightening labor market.

"We read the gloomy education reports and decided that if we were going to make any increases in giving, it should be in precollege education for minorities as a matter of company interest and our national interest," says Edward Bligh of AT&T.[41] Business leaders look at the changing work force between now and the year 2000 and see that almost a third of the new entrants to the labor market will be ill-prepared minorities. Many are attempting to reach out and improve the life chances of these disadvantaged youngsters.

Into the Family

A great deal of corporate effort is now focused on reforming and improving the educational system. But for at least some business leaders the problems of America's children are so profound and pervasive that solutions to educational failure must reach beyond the traditional boundaries of the school into the family and the community.

In the mid-1980s, the Committee for Economic Development (CED), a Washington-based research organization comprised of more than 200 high-level executives, published a study on business and the public schools.[42] In preparing their report, the corporate leaders at CED came to believe that very little can be achieved within the formal educational system.

To senior executives such as Owen Butler, retired chairman of Proctor & Gamble, it seemed increasingly clear that "the seeds of educational failure are planted early. Children who are born into poverty or overly stressful family circumstances often suffer from a wide variety of physical and emotional problems . . . that impair their ability to function effectively in the typical public school setting."[43] In other words, no matter how much money we pump into schools, no matter how well we pay the teachers, fine-tune the curricula, or enrich the programs, we do not address the critical needs of a substantial segment of students unless we also concern ourselves with nutrition, health care, housing, family functioning—all those things that determine the early development of the child. If children are hungry or abused, if their minds are paralyzed by fear, if they live in cramped, squalid tenements, or if they come from dysfunctional single-parent families, it is unlikely they will do well in school.

In 1987, CED published *Children in Need: Investment Strategies for the Educationally Disadvantaged.* A startling document that created a stir in corporate America, it called upon the nation to spend billions of dollars and "give highest priority to early and sustained intervention in the lives of disadvantaged children."[44]

Janine's Story

It is 11 o'clock on a Monday morning and nine-year-old Janine Rios is sitting on the stoop of a dilapidated apartment house on East 124th Street in Manhattan, throwing stones into the gutter and watching hookers ply their trade on the other side of the street.

"I ain't going to school today," she tells me. I asked her why. "I've got these nits in my hair and the school nurse sent me home so that my mom could get this special stuff and wash the nits out." Janine ducked her mop of curly hair so that I could take a look if I felt so inclined. A minute later she came up for air and explained, "that was last month, my mom hasn't gotten 'round to getting the stuff yet so I guess I'll be out of school for a while." Janine sounded philosophical; she didn't mind missing school.

Janine attends P.S. 146, a school in East Harlem that has put in place an elaborate program aimed at preventing students from dropping out of school. With funds provided by the city and a variety of private donors, this school offers remedial math and reading, after-school enrichment activities, and big "brothers" and "sisters" who act as mentors to the children. But no one has thought to deal with the head-lice problem. During the 1988–1989 school year, Janine was out of school for a total of seven weeks because her dysfunctional family was incapable of buying the shampoo or producing the level of hygiene that, together, would have gotten rid of the head lice.[45]

Sandra's Story

In the entrance hall of the George Washington Preparatory High School in Los Angeles is a handmade plaque bearing the names of 500 students, friends, and relatives who have died violently since the early 1980s, most of them victims of the ferocious gangs that rule the local streets.

This high school is a gang-war demilitarized zone—a magnet school offering enhanced math and science. Under the guidance of Principal Larry Higgins, 2,700 youngsters are supposed to be concentrating on getting into college. Most students are grateful. They are acutely aware that they are being given a chance for a very different kind of life.

But for a while last year, Sandra Deas, 17, was afraid even to go to school. Three kids were gunned down in front of homes nearby, and several more were caught in crossfire between two gangs. For weeks, says Sandra, "I was so scared." Now, her mother forbids her to walk to school. Some days Sandra gets rides from family members or friends; other days she is forced to skip school.[46]

The Cost of Inaction

If a child's mind is filled with fear or her hair is full of head lice, it is hard to take advantage of available educational opportunities. The CED estimates that today 30% of all American children are coping with severe problems on the family or community front, and many of these problems are linked to poverty.[47]

More than 20% of all children younger than 18 and 23% of children younger than 6 currently live in families whose incomes fall below the poverty line. Children in poverty suffer more frequently from almost every form of childhood deficiency, including infant mortality, malnutrition, recurrent and untreated health problems, psychological and physical stress, child abuse, and learning disabilities.

Not surprisingly, poverty correlates closely with school failure—especially when the family has disintegrated as well. Poor students are three times more likely to become dropouts than are students from more economically advantaged homes. The patterns of behavior that lead to school failure begin to appear in early childhood. Teenagers rarely make a sudden, conscious decision to leave school at age 15 or 16; the act of dropping out is the culmination of years of frustration and failure.

In *Children in Need* the CED recommends that the U.S. government intervene directly in the lives of poor families and spend much more money on programs such as prenatal and postnatal care for pregnant teens and other high-risk mothers, parenting education for both mothers and fathers, family health care, and quality preschool programs for all disadvantaged three- and four-year-olds.

Although family intervention can be useful at any point during childhood, the earlier the intervention, the less costly and the less risky it is. Prenatal care is especially cost effective. Prenatal care for a pregnant teen can cost as little as $600 per patient, whereas intensive care for low-birth-weight, premature babies can easily cost $1,000 a day.

The CED report is particularly eloquent in presenting the cost–benefit arguments for early intervention in the lives of children. Improving the prospects for infants and toddlers is an investment that can be postponed only at much greater cost to society. Every $1 spent today to prevent educational failure can save $4.75 in remedial education, welfare, and crime further down the road. In the words of these corporate executives, "the price of corrective action may be high, but the cost of inaction is far higher."[48] According to *Children in Need*, the private sector can play an important "pacesetting" role in improving the early environment of the child, and it cites the Beethoven Project as a model program that might well be worth copying nationwide.

Victoria's Story

In early 1987 Victoria Brown was a frightened teenager expecting her first child, worrying about caring for an infant, and without plans for the future. Today, her baby, Constance, has grown into a healthy, alert toddler. The 19-year-old mother exudes new confidence: "I graduate from high school in June. I want a job working with computers and I want to leave Robert Taylor and live in a house. I'm happy with the baby, but I don't want more kids."[49]

The turn-around in Victoria's life and the improved prospects for her daughter are due to the vision of businessman Irving B. Harris and his "Beethoven Project," an innovative cradle-to-kindergarten program he helped launch at the Robert Taylor Housing Project in Chicago.

The goal of the Beethoven Project is to improve—by means of a range of social, medical, and educational services—the life chances of children born into the nation's largest public housing project. The context is grim. The shabby 16-story concrete towers known as the Robert Taylor Homes are situated in a desolate, crime-ridden neighborhood on Chicago's South Side. The majority of the 20,000 residents in this housing complex are single women with children who survive on public assistance. Like Victoria, most mothers are young; virtually all are black. One community leader calls the Robert Taylor homes a "breeding ground of despair." Infant mortality, teenage pregnancy, and illiteracy are rampant.

The program targets the kindergarten classes that will enter the nearby Beethoven elementary school in 1993 and 1994, providing an array of services that have not been available to these children before: comprehensive prenatal care, nutrition and health education, a family drop-in center, parent education, developmental screening, a toddler school, and Head Start. All of these services are designed to prepare these disadvantaged children so that they will enter school "primed for success."

The initial impetus for this program came from Irving Harris, a Chicago entrepreneur and philanthropist. Since the early 1960s, Harris has devoted some of his best energy (and substantial amounts of money) to disadvantaged children. In 1982, Harris joined with the Illinois Department of Children and Family Services to create the Ounce of Prevention Fund (based on the premise that an ounce of prevention is worth at least a pound of cure). This fund sparked the Beethoven Project in late 1987. Harris believes strongly that the enormous human and societal cost of a lifetime in poverty can be greatly reduced by early and sustained intervention in the lives of poor children. He is impressed by the cost of wasted lives and estimates that one child's "failure" as a member of society costs the taxpayer approximately $300,000.

That figure represents the cost of *not* preventing problems that are, in many cases, preventable: intensive hospital care for premature babies, special education for children who are developmentally delayed or handicapped, AFDC and Medicaid for families in the welfare system, truant officers, and corrections services. According to Harris, the only way to avoid these huge costs is to invest a much more modest amount of money in the early development of the child. The Beethoven Project is not cheap: estimates are in the $50,000 range per child from before birth to kindergarten. But if this money is not spent, the costs are certain to be much greater in the long run.[50]

Efficiency and Compassion

Overall, it is not clear how much of a difference corporations are able to make when they reach out to disadvantaged youngsters. The initiatives described in this chapter are clearly laudable, but so far they are a drop in the bucket. American Express now contributes $3 million a year to the Academy of Finance, which currently enrolls 2,000 students.[51] This is better than nothing, but it only skims the surface of our problems. The dimensions of our educational deficit are gigantic. In 1989, New York City alone spent $6 billion on education; yet this was a long way from being enough: the city still generates 45,000 dropouts a year.[52]

Business executives know that they face a huge problem. David Kearns, chairman of Xerox, talks about the lack of qualifications among U.S. workers, "putting this country at a terrible competitive disadvantage,"[53] while Owen B. Butler, retired chairman of Proctor and Gamble, describes "a Third World within our own country."[54] Despite anxiety and concern, there is one very important reason why corporate America will not devote massive resources to the problems of underprivileged youth: *it is impossible for an individual company to reap the rewards of this type of investment in any direct way.*

General Electric spends a few million dollars preparing Aiken High School students for college.[55] Eastman Kodak devotes some resources and energy to reforming the Rochester school system.[56] But both companies know that although their efforts may "improve" the pool of labor from which they draw, they cannot expect to employ very many of the graduates of these programs and therefore reap the benefits of their largesse, which is precisely why they are spending millions rather than billions on these programs. An executive at American Express reports that only a handful of the graduates of the Academy of Finance are now with the firm; these well-qualified young people are now "scattered all over Wall Street." Unlike family-support policy, from which companies can expect to see an immediate return on their investment (attrition rates go down, productivity goes up), high school enrichment programs or early childhood education cannot be counted on to pay off for the firm, even in the long run.

These investments clearly pay off for the community and for the nation. However, business executives are not paid to promote the national good. Some companies will still choose to undertake these programs: they improve the general business environment and are good for company image. But in the aggregate, rather few companies will get involved with schools and with children, and when they do, it will be on a modest scale. In other words, we cannot look to the private sector to provide the bulk of the resources necessary to upgrade the life prospects of disadvantaged children. Government cannot pass the buck and pretend that business can somehow "fix" the problem of underachievement and failure among poor children. The public sector is uniquely qualified to undertake this mammoth task.

But if the private sector cannot be expected to bankroll educational reform or other types of intervention in the lives of children, business can play a central role in identifying what should be done and in telling us why we should do it. Corporate leaders have an accurate and urgent sense of what is at stake. In the ringing words of *Children in Need*,

> The United States is creating a permanent underclass of young people for whom poverty and despair are life's daily companions. . . . The nation can ill-afford such an egregious waste of human resources. Allowing this to continue will not only impoverish our children, it will impoverish our nation—culturally, politically and economically.[57]

Corporations are rarely in the vanguard of social policy, but in this area the statistics and trends speak with an urgency that hard-boiled executives find utterly convincing.

There is real clarity to the corporate point of view. Precisely because business is ruled by the need to make a profit, it is well suited to hitting upon the efficient solution to a problem. When Irving Harris founded the Ounce of Prevention Foundation and initiated "Project Beethoven," he was driven by the commonsensical notion that in the Chicago slums relatively small investments in young children yield handsome returns.

We should not be afraid of cost-driven, efficient solutions to the problems of our children. In the waning years of the 20th century, doing what is right for our kids and what is necessary to save our collective skins may finally converge. In the 1990s efficiency and compassion must go hand in hand.

NOTES

1. William B. Johnston and Arnold H. Packer, *Workforce 2000: Work and Workers for the 21st Century* (Indianapolis, IN: Hudson Institute, June 1987), p. xix. Their projected expansion of 1% annually in the 1990s was updated using the following report: Howard B. Fullerton, Jr., "New Labor Force Projections, Spanning 1988 to 2000," *Monthly Labor Review*, 112 (No. 11, November 1989), p. 3 (published by the U.S. Department of Labor Bureau of Labor Statistics).

2. Fullerton, loc. cit.

3. Johnston and Packer, op. cit., pp. xix–xx.

4. David E. Bloom and Neil G. Bennett, "Future Shock: America's Dismal Demographic Future," *The New Republic* (June 19, 1989), p. 20.

5. Ibid., p. 20.

6. Johnston and Packer, op. cit., p. 89.

7. *New York Times*, April 23, 1989.

8. National Assessment of Educational Progress, "The Mathematics Report Card," Executive Summary, *Mathematics: Are We Measuring Up?* Report (Princeton, NJ: Educational Testing Service, 1988).

9. Johnston and Packer, op. cit., pp. 96–97.

10. Ibid., p. 97.

11. Fran Sussner Rodgers and Charles Rodgers, "Business and the Facts of Family Life," *Harvard Business Review*, 67 (No. 6, November–December 1989), p. 121.

12. Sandra L. Burud, Pamela R. Aschbacher, and Jacquelyn McCroskey, *Employer Supported Child Care: Investing in Human Resources* (Dover, MA: Auburn House, 1984), pp. 22–26.

13. *The Christian Science Monitor*, June 30, 1988.

14. *New York Times*, July 20, 1988.

15. J. Douglas Phillips, "Employee Turnover and the Bottom Line," Working paper in presentation format, Merck & Company, Rahway, NJ (last revised February 1989), p. 2.

16. Ibid., p. 6.

17. *New York Times*, July 20, 1988.

18. Verbal communication with David Adams, Health Services Administrator, Registered Nurse, and Assistant Personnel Administrator at Sunbeam Appliance Company's Coushatta, Louisiana, plant. See also *New York Times*, December 28, 1988.

19. Johnson & Johnson, *Work and Family Program Overview*, Report (New Brunswick, NJ: October 1988).

20. Verbal communication with James E. Smith, IBM spokesperson; IBM, "IBM Work and Personal Life Balance Programs," Booklet. See also Rodgers and Rodgers, op. cit., p. 127.

21. *Newsday*, May 31, 1989; *New York Times*, May 30, 1989.

22. Press information (dated July 1989) from Apple Computer, Inc., Cupertino, CA.

23. Allstate Insurance Company, Corporate Human Resources, *Work & Family Connections*, Corporate Brochure (Northbrook, IL: Allstate Insurance Company, 1989).

24. Work/Family Program information from E. I. du Pont de Nemours & Company Incorporated, Wilmington, DE.

25. Rodgers and Rodgers, op. cit., p. 127; see also *Business Week*, September 19, 1988.

26. Rodgers and Rodgers, op. cit., p. 127.

27. Ibid., p. 123; see also *Redbook*, March 1990.

28. *Wall Street Journal*, March 18, 1988.

29. Telephone interview with with Arlene Johnson of The Conference Board, May 21, 1990.

30. Sylvia Hewlett, "Family Support Policy? Consult the Bottom Line," *Management Review* (January 1989), p. 57.

31. Ibid., p. 57.

32. National Council of Jewish Women, Center for the Child, "Employer Supports for Child Care," Report, in NCJW, *Mothers in the Workplace*, Study (August 1988), p. 2.

33. Cited in Sylvia Ann Hewlett, *A Lesser Life: The Myth of Women's Liberation in America* (New York: William Morrow, 1986), p. 82, and footnote no. 41, p. 418.

34. Cited in ibid., p. 82, and footnote no. 42, p. 418.

35. Interview, May 18, 1990.

36. *Wall Street Journal*, March 18, 1988.

37. *New York Times*, September 7, 1989.

38. William R. Mattox, "The Family Time Famine," *Family Policy*, 3 (No. 1, 1990), p. 2.

39. Mellman & Lazarus, Inc., *Mass Mutual American Family Values Study* (Washington, DC: Mellman & Lazarus, Inc., 1989).

40. Peter F. Drucker, *The New Realities* (New York: Harper & Row, 1989), p. 190.

41. *New York Times*, December 4, 1988.

42. Committee for Economic Development (CED), *Investing in Our Children: Business and the Public Schools* (New York: Committee for Economic Development, 1985).

43. Committee for Economic Development, Research and Policy Committee, *Children in Need: Investment Strategies for the Educationally Disadvantaged* (New York: Committee for Economic Development, 1987), p. 21.

44. Ibid., p. 3.

45. Interview, November 12, 1988.

46. *U.S. News & World Report*, November 7, 1988, p. 36.

47. Committee for Economic Development, op. cit., pp. ix, 5–8, 21.

48. Ibid., p. 15.

49. *New York Times*, April 10, 1988.

50. Material on the Beethoven Project obtained from Judy Langford Carter, Acting Executive Director, The Ounce of Prevention Fund, Chicago, Illinois, Testimony before the National Commission on Infant Mortality, Atlanta, Georgia, January 11, 1988; Irving B. Harris, "What Can We Do to Prevent the Cycle of Poverty?" 1987 Clifford Beers Lecture, Child Study Center, Yale University, March 24, 1987; Barbara Vobejda, "From Cradle to Grades: A Chicago Program Starts before Birth to Help the Neediest Children," *Washington Post National Weekly Edition*, February 17, 1988, pp. 10–11.

51. "Philanthropy at American Express," American Express, 1990.

52. Interview with spokesperson Frank Sobrino, New York City Department of Education, May 16, 1990.

53. David T. Kearns, "Help to Restructure Public Education from the Bottom Up," *Harvard Business Review* 66 (November–December 1988), p. 70.

54. Ibid., p. 70.

55. GE Foundations Annual Report 1988; see also Kathleen Teltsch, *New York Times*, December 4, 1988.

56. Steven A. Holmes, "School Reform: Business Moves In," *New York Times*, February 1, 1990, p. D1.

57. Committee for Economic Development, op. cit., pp. 2–3.

=13=
The Invasion of the
Money World

Robert N. Bellah

A *New Yorker* cartoon illustrates some of the tensions of contemporary family life. The cartoon shows a toddler walking into a room, holding a ball. His father is stretched out on the couch, holding a can of beer and potato chips and watching a football game. He says to the child, "Not now, this is when Daddy has some quality time for himself." We could take this simply as a comment on "me-ism." But to give this father the benefit of the doubt, perhaps he was so stressed out from a long week of overwork that he simply lacks the psychic energy to play with the child. He might explain to us, if we asked, that he "needs" to work so hard to make money to support his family. He might even tell us that he has worked so hard in order to buy a house in a pleasant, crime-free suburb with good schools—for the sake of his children!—but that living there adds three hours of commuting time to an already overbusy day so that he has less and less time and energy to spend with his children.

VALUES AND NORMS

Developing the story this way might help us understand the distinction between values and norms raised by Dennis Orthner in chapter 6. Orthner has argued that it is not so much values that have changed as norms. Perhaps the father in the cartoon, as we have explained his story, is devoted to some very long-term family values, but is finding that incorporating those values into the behavioral norms that govern daily life is increasingly difficult.

We thus discover a tension between the capacity to make long-standing commitments to the family, based on the ideal of indissolubility of marriage and a profound sense of responsibility toward children—

Robert N. Bellah is Elliott Professor of Sociology at the University of California at Berkeley.

toward intergenerational solidarity—and the actual conditions of American life. In spite of all the social changes, however, the basic commitments have survived at some level. They remain cultural resources for us. People still respond to that older understanding of the family, an image that touches something very deep that is still there in us and is more than some lingering "traditional" residue.

On the other hand, I think that Professor Orthner's point that norms have undergone a revolution needs to be taken seriously. Norms have to do with the way in which values are institutionalized—specified in operative social institutions. It has become increasingly difficult to act out institutionally things that we believe deeply at the value level. In the face of many kinds of pressures, we have altered (partially legally and partially due to mores) our normative understanding of marriage and the family much more rapidly and much more drastically than we have at the value level.

I would push Professor Orthner's emphasis a little farther by insisting that you can't go on revolutionizing norms forever without changing values. So I don't think we should be overly optimistic about continuities at the value level, although the continuities are there and are a sign of hope for all who believe that a strong family is a necessity for a decent society.

LIFEWORLD AND SYSTEM

Whatever may be the case with values, why have the norms been changing so rapidly? In general, the essays in this volume do not address themselves as much as I would have liked to that issue. I would answer the question very succinctly: the "systems" have invaded the "lifeworld." I have found helpful the distinction, taken from Jurgen Habermas, between "lifeworld" and "systems."[1] The lifeworld is the sphere of human action that is oriented by language about the right way to act. It includes the family, the church, and the public as a realm of discussion about the common good. The systems, by contrast, are primarily oriented to maximizing means, above all money and power, rather than ends, and are exemplified in our society by the market economy and the administrative state.

These systems have invaded the "lifeworld" more and more systematically and distorted it in the modern era. Czeslaw Milosz, the eloquent Polish poet, talked about the ways in which the state, rather than withering away in Eastern Europe in the early 1980s, was, in fact, eating up society. I want to suggest that the economy can also eat up society, including the family.

So I take the unpopular position that the "triumph of capitalism," which Americans have congratulated themselves about recently, should lead us not to triumphalism but to self-reflection. Indeed, I believe that the greatest threat to our genuine human happiness, to real community and to the creation of strong families and a good society, does not come solely from a state whose power becomes too coercive (though we can never underestimate that danger). The threat also comes from an economy that becomes too coercive, that invades our private and group lives and tempts us to a shallow, competitive individualism that undermines all our connections to other people.

Of course, we need a good government and a good economy. It is not a question of abolishing them, but of putting the proper limits on them. We know that we need to limit the state. I want to argue that we need to limit the economy as well when it becomes imperialistic and threatens to dominate our lives. Indeed, I would argue that there is such a thing as market totalitarianism that parallels state totalitarianism and is a real threat to us in America today.

THE IDEOLOGY OF MARKET TOTALITARIANISM

Adam Smith taught moral philosophy for many years at Edinburgh University. He believed in the importance of what he called civil society, based on sympathy and enduring moral commitments—what I am calling the lifeworld. Civil society, according to Adam Smith, provides the essential context within which the market can operate. Indeed, Smith never speaks of "the market" in a single unified sense at all. Only specific, particular markets exist, each hedged in by a set of moral relationships. Smith never imagined the possibility of a society that could run on self-interest alone. Nor could the founders of the American republic. Such a society would self-destruct, they thought. And today, as the ideology of radical self-interest, the principle of the market, spreads, we see more than a few destructive symptoms.

In the hands of Milton Friedman's successors, the so-called Chicago school, economics becomes a total science that explains everything. As so-called "rational choice theory," it has invaded all the social sciences—especially political science and sociology. Alan Wolfe, in his recent book *Whose Keeper?*, criticizes this school of thought, protesting especially its imperious demand that economics should replace the humanities and thus become our new moral philosophy or even our new religion:

> When neither religion, tradition, nor literature is capable of serving as a common moral language, it may be that the one moral code all modern people can understand is self-interest. If social scientists are secular priests, Chicago school economists have become missionaries. They have an idea about how the world works. This idea seems to apply in some areas of life. It therefore follows, they believe, that it ought to apply in all. . . .
>
> Chicago school theorists insist that the tools of economic analysis can be used not just to decide whether production should be increased or wages decreased, but in every kind of decision-making situation. Thus we have been told . . . that marriage is not so much about love as about supply and demand as regulated through markets for spouses; . . . and a man commits suicide "when the total discounted lifetime utility remaining to him reaches zero." From the perspective of the Chicago school, there is

no behavior that is not interpretable as economic, however altruistic, emotional, disinterested, and compassionate it may seem to others. . . .

How far Chicago theorists are willing to take their arguments . . . can be illustrated by Elizabeth Landes and Richard Posner's argument for a free market in babies. At the present time, they suggest, revulsion against the buying and selling of babies, combined with ineffective legal efforts to regulate such activities, has caused a massive number of social problems. . . . If women were allowed to sell their babies on the market [these problems would decrease]. Problems of racial discrimination would be taken care of by the market, for blacks would buy black babies and whites would buy white ones: Were baby prices quoted as prices of soybean futures were quoted, a racial ranking of these prices would be evident, with white baby prices higher than nonwhite baby prices.[2]

"Were baby prices quoted as prices of soybean futures . . ." These bizarre ideas are not, unfortunately, just theoretical. Especially during the past decade, they have in many ways shaped our society. They have led some in France to speak of American capitalism as *le capitalisme sauvage*, savage capitalism.

THE MONEY ECONOMY INVADES THE FAMILY

Robert Heilbroner suggests how the market invades our private lives when he speaks of "the implosion of capitalism":

From this point of view, "economic growth" means the introduction of capitalist social relations into new social terrain. . . . For example, the enlargement of the proportion of the population engaged in wage labor, dramatically evidenced in the case of women in all capitalist nations, testifies to the implosion of capitalism, just as the imperialist extension of power during the late nineteenth century testified to its explosion. No less important is the "commodification" of life, the extension of commodity production to areas previously outside the ambit of the market. The rise of prepared foods, laundry services, home entertainment, and the pharmaceutical industry are instances of how the accumulation implodes capitalist relations, just as the transformation of peasant agriculture into plantation agriculture is an example of its explosion.[3]

As an example of what Heilbroner is talking about, we might notice a poll that showed that the one thing affluent Americans said they could least do without was—not their BMW or their vacation in Europe—but their microwave oven. We know that an increasing proportion of American families never have a meal together. One by one, family members drift into the kitchen and stick something in the microwave. (This is called grazing rather than having a meal.) Then it's "So long, I gotta go," as each family member departs for his or her separate pursuits.

One newer manifestation of this trend is the marketing by food companies of microwave meals for children: special products that now make it possible for children, quite literally, to feed themselves. If, as I believe, the family meal is the family sacrament and if it is also the place where children learn the terms of civil discourse, what happens to the family when commodification, the colonization of the family by the economy, reaches this extent?

Arlie Hochschild, in an important study of two-earner families, puts the issues bluntly:

> For all the talk about the importance of children, the cultural climate has become subtly less hospitable to parents who put children first. This is not because parents love children less, but because a "job culture" has expanded at the expense of a "family culture."[4]

And she goes on to point out,

> Corporations have done little to accommodate the needs of working parents, and the government has done little to prod them. The nuclear family is still the overwhelming choice as a setting in which to rear children. Yet we have not invented the outside supports the nuclear family will need to do this job well.[5]

Hochschild suggests a variety of policy changes, some well established in other, advanced, industrial societies, such as family leaves, flextime, job-sharing, and nonexploitative part-time work. Other chapters in this book consider these policies; I believe the specific policies we should adopt will become clear only after an extended national discussion of what we expect from the family and how we might better achieve those expectations. In the meantime, the pressures to make ends meet that have driven more Americans than ever into the work force, and into working longer hours as well, cannot help but be profoundly destructive to family life.

The job culture is indeed crowding out the family culture, given the economic pressures of our era. The invasion of the "lifeworld" by the market economy is complex and multilayered. Many women have had to go to work just to keep things level, given a variety of economic pressures. But the amount of time people work is due to more than necessity. It is also due in part to the commodification of family life in light of expanding consumer goods that quickly become defined as "needs."

The question of whether a mother goes to work because she "needs" to, for example, must be evaluated with reference to needs and wants that are culturally very problematic. I don't want to target women alone, however, because I believe men are responsible for child care from day one and that men, too, are responsible for balancing job and family pressures. Both parents have to carry economic and family responsibilities.

But the question remains of somebody being at home for a sufficient amount of time. Day care is certainly essential today, but the quality of much day care is doubtful and even the best day care cannot make up for lack of parental attention. If both parents are working, and perhaps working for excessive hours, not to meet the basic necessities of life but to pay for what they think is a preferred style of life because of the pressures of consumerism, family life can suffer as a consequence. This is an example of the invasion of the lifeworld by the systems, in this case, the money economy.

Another aspect of the present situation that worries me very much as a teacher is the appalling illiteracy of undergraduates at first-rate institutions. Why? In part, at least, because here, too, economic pressures are at work. Young people are already starting in junior high school to work after school, not for necessities—their parents can pay for their food and clothing—but because they are buying stereos and fancy cars. They are working at meaningless jobs that don't further their moral or intellectual development—all in order to buy these things. In the meantime, they are not reading anything. A recent *Harvard Alumni Journal* has a scathing article by a writing instructor about the illiteracy of Harvard undergraduates. I see the same thing in my own undergraduates at Berkeley. The Harvard writing teacher's essential argument is that the students come to college without having read anything. If they have read anything at all, it's Stephen King. How can you teach people to write who haven't read? Certainly, this situation cannot be totally explained by the many hours they spend working to buy designer jeans, but that is part of it. The chapter in this volume on the media reminds us of the amount of time spent on television, and television, also, gives images of life built around consumerism.

The way in which the economy invades the "lifeworld" is very complex. But in our society, at the moment at least, it is a clear threat to family and community life. I wish we in America had an equivalent of Poland's Solidarity or Czechoslovakia's Civic Forum, which have done so much to dismantle the totalitarian state, to help get the totalitarian market economy off our backs and let us live human lives in families and other so-called "backward" institutions. But it looks now as though both we and the East Europeans will be facing the problem of controlling consumerism for quite some time to come.

THE IMPORTANCE OF BEING SOMEWHERE

The current difficulties of the family have a great deal to do with how isolated it is, both geographically and socially. There is much talk about the increasing variety of forms the family takes these days. We hear much about the family's "experimental" character—two-earner households, single-parent households, same-sex couples with children, as well as "traditional" families in which husbands work and wives stay at home. But in spite of their diversity, these families have a great deal in common. And it is precisely what they have in common, moreover, that makes it difficult for any of them to sustain family life. As John Snow puts it:

> In all these cases the absence of generational rootedness in a certain place with a long-term commitment to its community and economic life makes money—cash flow—the primary source of security.

> With professional people there is the added security of insurance, health insurance and pensions. For the rest there are welfare, Social Security and Medicare. In all cases the bottom line of security is money, not extended family and community.
>
> For some families there is no bottom line at all. They may be found in shelters, and some of them are healthy young people with small children and no addiction to drugs or alcohol, sometimes with jobs, yet unable to afford rent in such cities as Boston or New York. They lack even an address.[6]

What Snow is suggesting is that stable and warm families may depend on commitment to place. To create conditions today that respect and foster these commitments, in turn, would require more locally and regionally coherent economies. Certainly, many of the things that make childhood enjoyable, such as extended family celebrations, get-togethers, and reunions, have become rare in our society. Snow is almost certainly right that the cause of our present condition is the pressures from our current form of market economy rather than the desires of people. Indeed, in our present world, with its ever-accelerating international economy, Snow's proposed solution may seem nostalgic, utopian, or both.

In our present form of society, money is essential. The first obligation of public policy is to provide the resources to meet the most obvious needs of those who are hurting most. But as David Popenoe points out in this volume, the example of the successful welfare states such as Sweden suggests that money and bureaucratic assistance alone do not halt the decline of the family, even though they do halt the obvious symptoms of homelessness and disease. What the family most needs is a context of relationships and institutions that foster adequate attention—not just money.

Remedies for our plight, such as the decentralization of the economy and other institutions, would seem to go against the whole trend of modernity. But it just may be that new developments in high technology could provide the basis for a reversal of long-standing trends. With heavy equipment no longer the basis of our economy, bringing training and jobs to where people are rather than the reverse may be more possible than it has been for a very long time. Some of the new experiments in private/public initiative at the local level might provide models that could be generalized.

FLEXIBILITY IN ROLES

In the increasingly frequent two-earner families, a more equitable sharing of household tasks becomes essential for basic fairness and even for the survival of marriage itself. But the fact that roles must change does not mean we can abandon the idea of roles altogether. I affirm Gilbert Meilaender's unhappiness, in his chapter in this volume, with the widespread tendency today to think of roles as something alien from our personhood. Role expectations contribute to the structure of relationships and must be taken seriously. Roles are, moreover, constitutive of ourselves as persons.

The notion of some deep, private self, wholly separable from life relationships, is a profoundly bizarre idea. If you strip me of my roles as husband and father and Christian and teacher and friend, there isn't any wonderful, profound "self" left to consult or to discover. My "self" is composed of my relationships and commitments, my "roles," if you will. That doesn't mean I lack autonomy. Indeed, only because of my relationships and commitments can I be autonomous at all. If I were isolated, I would be helpless.

I do find a problem in Meilaender's reaffirmation of traditional parental roles and use of Carol Gilligan's position to argue the difference between mother and father and to express an anxiety about unisex parenthood. I am more worried that parental roles are still too stereotypically different. One of the reasons that roles have gotten a bad name is that they are too often talked about as fixed entities rather than as in continuous change and reformulation. If roles never changed, they would indeed be coercive.

Of course, it is also true that roles require continuity. But I am constantly learning something new about even my most central roles. For example, my role as father goes on changing. I have grown children who talk to me almost every day, which is not at all what I did at their ages. I am learning that being the father of children who have left home is full of new challenges. I have a grandchild for the first time; that is a whole new experience and a new role to learn and to learn to change. A certain core comes from tradition, but that core has to be applied, and the world to which it is applied is changing, and, therefore, the definition of the role has to change.

In respect to the family, men and women need to experience a larger range of potentiality rather than restrict themselves to separate boxes. My sense is that men still need to learn a great deal about the relational side of life and women need to understand justice as something that they have a share in. In that sense, although I basically support the notion that we realize ourselves in roles, I do want to keep things open. My preference for flexibility is not simply because it is the only practical position, though I think it is, but because it is the right one.

With respect to roles, it is important whether we take a "hard" position or a "soft" position. The hard position—forcing men and women into boxes—has been used for too many centuries to justify too many injustices. No one would want to go back to the family of 150 years ago, when women had no property rights and no opportunity for higher education. We must recognize that certain features of our present situation, problematic as they are, represent significant moral advance.

I also agree with Jean Elshtain in arguing that we must affirm the primacy of the intergenerational family of parents, grandparents, and children. But we do not have to deny other kinds of committed relationships. My sense, for example, is that recognition of commitment in same-sex relationships is not a danger to the family; it supports the family insofar as it counters the lack of commitment so common in our culture that creates chaotic individual exploitation of other human beings and so undermines the family. Here again, I am concerned with ending centuries of oppression of people who, for reasons not of their own choosing, cannot meet certain social expectations. I don't think we have to glorify or glamorize something that is, validly or not, called "the gay community." But when people of the same sex sustain deep, lasting, faithful commitments—if that's what's possible for them and a heterosexual marriage isn't—I believe in affirming that relationship. At the same time, without denigrating alternative forms, especially those alternative forms that express norms of fidelity and commitment, I think we can make it clear that primacy in our society belongs to the two-parent family with children.

THE FAMILY IN THE LARGER SOCIAL WORLD

Finally, I strongly believe that strengthening not only the family but the larger "lifeworld"—what is often called civil society—is critical. The destructiveness that comes from the economy can be mitigated in part by state action, but only in part. The most powerful intermediate organizations in America are religious organizations; they are where people's charitable giving mainly goes, where people's donated time mainly goes, where their commitments are. If we are going to get through this crisis of the family, we have to strengthen these institutions. The fact that they, like all lifeworld institutions, have been undermined by many current trends is a serious problem.

Churches and synagogues need to regain their teaching authority. They must support parents and strengthen parental self-confidence, especially when parents are saying things different from the dominant culture. One of the most obvious tensions between the secular and the religious culture is the issue of love. Romantic love is fundamentally different from Christian love. There is some overlap, but not much. Romantic love lasts in its full intensity for about 90 days. You can't build a marriage on that. The Christian commandment to love God and our neighbor, and even to love our enemies, makes it clear that love in this sense is not the same as being swept away by emotional passion.

Christian love is oriented toward the good of the other. It is based on the intention to stand by that imperative, recognizing that we are fallible and may not be able to sustain all our commitments. In marriage, that is expressed in the intention that the relationship be indissoluble. We may not be able to keep that intention, but that is the ideal; falling short of it is a failure. But because, in this religious perspective, we are all sinners and failure is part of human life, having had a divorce does not mean that we are bad persons or that we can't do better next time. But understanding marriage as in principle indissoluble does mean that divorce is a failure. We should work to avoid it if we possibly can. This understanding of marriage could and I believe ought to be reasserted by the religious community. But so far that community hasn't done a very good job of reasserting it, partly because the local congregation is under the same pressure as the family to go along with the cultural climate.

Finally, though I believe that most of our problems in America come from the market economy, I don't believe the family and religious institutions can together create a little island of survival in the midst of a sea of consumerism. Christian discipleship includes the obligation of citizenship. It includes being a witness to the whole society and a willingness to take responsibility in and for that larger society and to recognize that we are a part of it. Both family and religion need to nurture citizenship. In 1989 and 1990, religious groups have made an enormous contribution to the reassertion of democracy in other nations. We can learn from the Catholic Church in Poland and the Lutheran Church in East Germany that there are times when religious institutions can say to the secular society, "Change your ways!" In America, where the political parties are afraid to jeopardize their incumbents by taking a vigorous stand on any of our serious problems, including the decline of family life, religious bodies have a special obligation to raise the unpopular issues and to help our society to recognize faults and challenges that we might otherwise ignore.

NOTES

1. Jurgen Habermas, *The Theory of Communicative Action*, Vol. 2: *Lifeworld and System: A Critique of Functionalist Reason* (Boston: Beacon Press, 1987).

2. Alan Wolfe, *Whose Keeper?* (Berkeley, CA: University of California Press, 1989), pp. 36, 32, 37–38.

3. Robert Heilbroner, "The Coming Meltdown of Capitalism," *Ethics and International Affairs*, 2 (1988), p. 74.

4. Arlie Hochschild, *Second Shift: Working Parents and the Revolution at Home* (New York: Viking, 1989), p. 231.

5. Ibid., p. 267.

6. John Snow, "Families in Fast Lane to Nowhere," *Episcopal Life* (May 1990), p. 18.

=14=
An Agenda for the 1990s: Supporting Families

Edward F. Zigler & Elizabeth P. Gilman

F amilies today are struggling to cope with rapid and startling social change. Profound changes in the daily lives of American families—even in the definition of "family"—have inflicted tremendous stress as we are dragged, often without our consent, into another world. As Alvin Toffler's *Future Shock* suggests, we are a people who've not caught up with ourselves.[1] Yes, families are besieged, and family structure is changing.[2] No, we cannot go back. We can, however, benefit from research into what is essential in family life and what leads to the healthy development of individuals.

Given our current knowledge of factors that tend to foster optimal development, we should be able to formulate an enlightened social policy, one that gives families genuine alternatives for dealing with the realities of raising children in the 1990s. Should we choose to ignore the clear findings of social scientists and the undisputed facts of family change and resultant family needs, the human casualties will not be so easily ignored: they will seek us out in crime and delinquency, in drug use, in unemployability, in social waste and personal desolation.

Two points should guide our family agenda for the 1990s. First, our knowledge of child development informs us that each child needs to follow a certain trajectory to achieve optimal growth. Our task is to enhance the factors that foster optimal development, while minimizing the influence of factors known to undermine the growth of the child. Second, as today's families struggle to raise healthy children in a society that offers them little tangible support, our task is to formulate and implement an enlightened

Edward F. Zigler is Sterling Professor of Psychology at Yale University, where he also directs the Bush Center in Child Development and Social Policy. Elizabeth P. Gilman is a Postdoctoral Associate in the Department of Psychology at Yale University and a Fellow of the Bush Center in Child Development and Social Policy.

social policy that gives families a choice among realistic alternatives to assist them in carrying out the important work of parenthood.

In this dual agenda, we do not align ourselves with any ideology beyond that of pragmatic conservatism. Along with Edmund Burke, we ask that someone offering a social proposal "show it to be common sense; show it to be the means of attaining some useful end."[3] If we create policies that support families in their essential work, we will, as a society, realize the developmental promise of our children. Much lip service is accorded this promise. It is time the promissory note was paid. To recall Burke again, "A state without the means of some change is without the means of its conservation."[4]

CHANGES IN FAMILY LIFE

The experience of growing up in America has changed for a large number of our nation's children. The most dramatic change stems from the rapid increase of women in the out-of-home work force, itself due in part to the economic need for two incomes in most families and in part to the rise of women-headed, single-parent households.

Approximately 60% of mothers of preschool children work outside the home, and 51% of mothers of infants under one year of age are now in the out-of-home work force.[5] According to one major study, three-fourths of the mothers of school-age children and two-thirds of the mothers of preschool children will be in the out-of-home work force by 1995.[6] Moreover, potential parental time—the time a parent is able to spend with a child—fell approximately 10–12 hours per week between 1960 and 1986.[7]

The numbers are staggering. By 1995, given current trends, 14.6 million preschool children and 37.4 million school-age children will have mothers who work outside the home.[8] The divorce rate contributes to this trend. Although this rate has leveled off, it has done so at a very high level: approximately 50% of marriages that take place this year will end in divorce.[9]

The unmarried teen pregnancy rate is equally disturbing. Teenage pregnancy in our society remains endemic; it has leveled off at about a million pregnancies, including about 500,000 to 600,000 live births, per year. Approximately 22% of children born today are born to mothers who have never married. Approximately one-third of these children are born to teenage mothers. Since 1960, the proportion of teen births occurring outside marriage has risen from 15% to 61%.[10] Of these pregnancies, it has been reported that 80% are unplanned and unwanted.[11]

Because of high incidence of unmarried motherhood and divorce, we see what is probably the second most important demographic change in family life: the single-parent family. This term is really a euphemism for a woman-headed family, in that more than 90% of single-parent families are headed by a woman. Today in the United States, 25% of all children are being raised in single-parent homes; among our black children that number is more than 50%. Of the children born in 1980, 70% are expected to spend part of their lives in single-parent homes.[12]

The burgeoning number of children who are alone after school has been studied as well. A recent study reported in *Pediatrics* found that "latchkey" children are twice as likely to engage in substance abuse as are children who have adult supervision after school.[13]

These are daunting demographics. Yet we recite them not to lay blame. They are bare facts with which we must deal. Our economy does not permit a return to the "typical" family of the 1950s, in which only one parent worked outside the home. David Blankenhorn has observed that for many families, even then, this "ideal" was never a reality (see chapter 1). Now it is less so. The blame is not to be laid at women's doors, or at men's. If there is a failure of ethos, perhaps it derives from a waning of the sense of community—a declining sense of the responsibilities that made up some of the meaning of family life for Americans.

As the Mass Mutual American Family Values Study (reviewed in chapter 12) indicates, 81% of Americans polled stated that the family was a primary source of pleasure in life, although for 51% of the parents it was also one of the greatest sources of worry.[14]

Nevertheless, familism seems to be dying out as a way of life for many people. A 1977 survey of American families conducted by General Mills found a dichotomy of parental values: attitudes attributed to a "traditional" family model stood in sharp contrast to those characteristic of an emerging style of family called the "new breed," which represented 43% of those polled. When compared with adults of previous generations, new-breed adults were less child-oriented and more self-oriented; children were not the most important aspect of their lives.

For example, 46% of the new-breed parents questioned the idea of sacrificing to give their children the best, as contrasted with 16% of the traditionalist parents.[15] In keeping with the individualistic orientation of these "new" parents, they also did not expect their children to assume any future obligation to them, nor did these parents espouse the belief that unhappy parents should remain together for the sake of children. As David Popenoe has correctly observed in chapter 3, we may be seeing a weakening of the once widespread "assumption that children are to be loved and valued at the highest level of priority."

Against this background, it is not difficult to perceive how attitudinal shifts have contributed to changes in family functioning, to what David Blankenhorn has described in chapter 1 as our culture's "conspicuous tilt away from children's needs" and society's failure to frame policy based upon what children need for optimal development.

These developmental requirements have been delineated in our own work and in that of several colleagues, notably Urie Bronfenbrenner and Jay Belsky.[16] We researchers have found that four systems largely determine the growth and development of the child: health, family, school, and child care. Yet, as Bronfenbrenner notes in chapter 2, the more we learn about the conditions that "foster the development of human competence and character, the more we see these same conditions being eroded" in our social environment.

The first system that underpins social competence is health. If the child is not healthy and well, the other systems are almost irrelevant. Poor prenatal health and nutrition on the part of the mother can lead to congenital defects and low birth weight in infants. Once born, a child's poor general health often leads to a failure to benefit optimally from schooling and other learning environments.

After the health system, the most important system for the child is the family. To paraphrase Bronfenbrenner, every child, in order to develop optimally, needs increasingly complex "reciprocal activity." Through this interaction with another, usually a parent, the child develops a strong, sustained mutual attachment. For healthy growth, this manner of relating should be regularized over the child's life and ideally is undertaken by one or more persons committed to the child's well-being.

Instability and inconsistency undermine the wholesome effects of such attachment bonds. We are converts to family systems theory. The family is a dynamic system in which an impact anywhere redounds in other parts of that system. The family is crucial for the child because through the medium of the family other important institutions reach and influence the child. When we speak about variance in children's behavior or growth outcomes, family factors account for the largest part of the variance. Evidence suggests that the quality of the early attachment bond between the child and the caregiver forms the basis for later attachments to other adults and to peers.

Thus differences in the psychosocial environment in which a child is nurtured cause wide variation in outcomes such as the predisposition to delinquency.[17] Among the most important precursors to delinquency, for example, are factors such as poor supervision by parents and poor child-rearing techniques. Also contributory is a parental lack of belief in or commitment to the value system of the larger society.[18] This fact is especially relevant because the value systems embraced by parents are changing; the larger society no longer has a unified code of values.

The school environment is another very important determinant of growth and development for the child. The school is a place where the child spends many thousands of hours and that provides the occasion for continuing socialization and further development of cognitive skills. The child's family environment lays the groundwork for the subsequent psychosocial development that occurs in school. Should the school environment be inadequate or, at worst, destructive to the child, then it follows that optimal development will be impaired.

The final system that profoundly affects the child is child care. Growing numbers of children will spend years of their lives in some form of child care and they are entering that system at an increasingly young age. We are now seeing children placed in out-of-home care at six weeks or even three weeks of age.[19] It is no solution to argue that mothers should remain at home; mothers today are in the labor force because of economic necessity.[20]

As developmental psychologists, we track the social indicators surrounding each of the four systems discussed above. The news is very bad, and it is worsening daily.[21] Julius Richmond, Director of Health Policy Research and Education at Harvard, recently convened a group of advocates and organizations concerned about children and families. The conclusion of that meeting? In the past 30 years of monitoring the indicators of child well-being, never have the indicators looked so negative across all four systems essential to the growth of the child.[22]

The Declining Quality of Life for America's Children

First, the state of health care for families is a disgrace. Although the United States remains the world's wealthiest nation, its infant mortality rate ranks 20th in the world, roughly comparable to that of Hong Kong. This rate places us behind Japan, Ireland, Australia, and Canada. Infant mortality is a benchmark social indicator, and ours is twice as high for blacks as it is for whites. Today an estimated 25% of women now carrying children receive no prenatal care and will not receive such care before the birth of their children. The inevitable results are infant mortality, low birth weight, and physical defects.[23]

After infancy, 30% of our children receive inadequate medical care; 25% do not receive physical examinations over the course of a year. Half of the children in this country younger than 15 and 90% younger than five have never visited a dentist. Two of every five preschool children are not immunized against childhood diseases.

Economic factors clearly affect the health of children. Among families with annual incomes greater than $35,000, approximately 62% are in excellent health. Only 38% of families with incomes less than $10,000 enjoy that status.[24] Victor Fuchs points out in chapter 4 that the 21% poverty rate among children in this country is nearly twice that of adults.

The family system also lacks the assistance it needs to fulfill its role in the development of children. The changes in family life are not being addressed by structural supports within the society. One main reason for this failure may be the individualist orientation of American society. Even the practices that can make a workplace "family friendly," such as employer-assisted day care and flexible time schedules, are not widespread enough to make a difference to the majority of parents.

On the other hand, the boundary between the home and the workplace is becoming more permeable. We are recognizing that the quality of home life is influenced by workplace practices, just as productivity at work is

affected by the functioning of the home. Yet we are still struggling to institute a national infant-care leave policy. Perhaps Bruce Hafen, in his chapter
on individualism and family law, is correct in observing that our society
increasingly stresses individual autonomy rather than any larger conception
of social good. Yet this very emphasis on individual autonomy, when played
out in the policy arena, may result in the paradox of an environment that
helps prevent positive autonomy for family members. The paradox, therefore, is that genuine autonomy—understood as mature independence rather
than simply isolation from others—is best achieved within the context of a
well-functioning family, not in its absence. Thus our failure to assist families,
particularly disadvantaged families, will continue to reap harrowing consequences, most dramatically in the numbers of abused children and other victims who are unlikely to achieve the kind of "autonomy" that we often seem
to celebrate.

An article by Edward Zigler in 1979 questioned whether we would
ever control child abuse in the absence of a unified policy effort to help
families.[25] Since then, annual reported cases of child abuse have increased
from one million to two million; these cases tripled between 1976 and
1985. The debate continues as to whether these figures reflect higher rates
of reporting or an actual increase in incidence. Our best judgment is that
it is some of both. Despite public outcry regarding abused children, our
national ambivalence about child abuse is best exemplified by the fact
that corporal punishment in the schools, which may be seen as an institutionalized form of child abuse, remains legal in many states.

Across the many analyses of abuse, a few conclusions emerge: the
child abuser is typically isolated and without a social support system,
stresses on the family increase the likelihood that abuse will occur, and
programs that focus on improvement of child health and that include
home visitation tend to diminish the likelihood of abuse.[26]

Education is a troubled system as well. Despite the rise in per-capita
expenditure in public education, SAT scores declined during the 1960s
and 1970s and have stabilized somewhat only in the 1980s. Many have
studied and criticized American education; the outcry began with the publication of A Nation at Risk and was followed by numerous other horrific
accounts.[27] Thirty percent of children fail to complete high school; for
nonwhites, the rate is 40%.[28] Many businesses find their young employees
lack basic reading and reasoning skills.

Moreover, these difficulties are compounded by the growing problem
of homelessness. Despite national concern about this problem, prevention
of homelessness by assisting low-income persons with housing remains
unaddressed. Today, nationwide, 500,000 of the homeless are children, the
majority of whom receive neither health care nor education.

Finally, there is the disaster of child care. When parents are forced
into the out-of-home work force for economic reasons, it is not a matter of
choice whether they place their child in care; it is a necessity. In 1989, the

House Select Committee on Children, Youth and Families reported that in two-parent homes, 60% of employed mothers had husbands who earned $15,000 to $19,000 annually.[29] For economic survival, it is clear that both spouses must now work in many families.

A two-tiered child-care system has emerged in our country. The affluent are finding very good care. However, the working class, the lower middle class, and the poor are receiving care that without question is compromising the development of children. In 1989, the most significant child-care study of the decade was published: the National Day Care Staffing Study.[30] It provides justification for the statement that we are cannibalizing our own children through the state of child care in America. The inconsistency and quality of care documented in the study are appalling.

WHAT IS TO BE DONE?

Although it is a cliché in America to refer to children as "our greatest resource," they are a resource in which we may have grossly underinvested. In some cases, as Victor Fuchs argues persuasively in his investment analysis of children, we may have misinvested our programmatic dollar. As a nation, we have failed repeatedly to utilize the collective wisdom of our developmental experts in formulating enlightened social policy. Such policy recommendations are made by Dennis Orthner in chapter 6. He properly concludes that our social goal must be to buffer the impact of change on our families, especially by supporting programs that assist parents in reducing the effects of social instability.

Despite the magnitude of the problems we face, we do not lack solutions. We know what works. It is not a question of knowledge; it is one of commitment and will. A number of national child health initiatives, such as Medicaid and the Women, Infants, and Children (WIC) program, have been demonstrated to be effective. The WIC program has proven successful in reducing infant and maternal mortality, low birth weight, and congenital defects. It has also proven to be cost-effective. Prenatal care today costs an average of $900. Placement of a premature baby in intensive care costs an average of $10,000. Our best cost–benefit analyses indicate that a dollar investment in prenatal care can save more than three dollars in the costs associated with low birth weight infants. Because of inadequate funding, WIC serves less than one half of the families eligible for the program. Similarly, the child immunization initiative launched by the Public Health Service in 1977 has increased the number of children protected from seven major childhood diseases. One dollar invested in the childhood immunization program saves an average of ten dollars in later medical costs.

Comprehensive family-support models also work. One such model, the Yale Child Welfare Research Program, proved very successful in assisting disadvantaged young parents. The goals of the program were to help the parents deal successfully with the arrival of their first child and generally to improve family life for the participants. This project, conducted in the early 1970s by Sally Provence and Audrey Naylor of the Yale Child Study Center, consisted of several components, including health care, monthly home visits, and child care as required.[31]

The families were assisted by an interdisciplinary team of physicians, clinical social workers, nurses, and psychologists. Lengthy developmental and medical examinations provided parents the opportunity to learn about the developmental needs of their children. Home visitors helped parents to solve immediate problems, such as inadequate food or housing, and also linked the family with additional services in the community to address larger issues, such as education and employment. The services ended when the first-born children reached the age of 30 months. Control children were matched with the experimental group.

Although the significant gains of the intervention group at 30 months were limited to language development, a ten-year follow-up showed broader differences. The intervention children demonstrated better adjustment to school and higher school attendance. In addition, the intervention mothers showed a greater employment and self-support rate at the ten-year mark. They had also acquired more education than the control mothers and had chosen to bear fewer children. On measures of social adjustment, the intervention children showed significant positive differences.[32]

The Provence and Naylor project, in essence, taught two important lessons: Services to the family as a whole can bring significant, long-term social benefits to children; and such services must be sustained and comprehensive in order to achieve long-lasting effectiveness. Significantly, such a program addresses all four of the systems basic to the child's opportunities for optimal growth. If we have learned anything over decades of child study, it is the need to be broad based and family centered; there are no instant, one-shot solutions.

Another successful intervention model that includes family support components has been the Head Start Program. Head Start began in 1965 on the wave of enthusiasm accompanying President Johnson's "War on Poverty." The program sought to eradicate social-class inequities in the United States by giving preschool children an inoculation against the ill effects of poverty. What began as an eight-week crash course in social skills the summer before kindergarten soon expanded to a year-long preschool program for low-income four-year-olds. Fortunately, the planners of Head Start—who included developmental psychologists and pediatricians—shared the broad goal of improving the children's social competence, in contrast with previous models that focused on increasing cognitive functioning.

To accomplish their broad goal, the founders of Head Start included the following program elements:

● A health component including a medical and dental evaluation of each child, referral for needed treatment, and one nutritious hot meal per day
● A social service component to inform parents of existing services in their community
● An early childhood education component, using a developmentally appropriate curriculum to help children learn to work and play with others and to interact with adult teachers
● Parent involvement, to encourage active parent interest and participation in all aspects of the program in order to reinforce at home the experiences the children were having at the centers
● A volunteer effort, to draw on the considerable interest expressed in the communities
● Community participation in the governance of the program, to engender a sense of ownership in the local communities
● Career ladders and in-service training, to help Head Start assistants gain training and education to qualify as Head Start teachers

Head Start has had mixed reviews from evaluators over the years. From the beginning, participating families were pleased when they saw their children happier, better nourished and healthier. After four years, however, reports showed that IQ gains made by children faded over time. Because of its popularity, the program survived despite criticism. Later, researchers developed more sophisticated assessment techniques and discovered that Head Start does in fact have significant, long-lasting, positive effects on social adjustment and quality of life.[33] The jury is still out on exactly why these positive effects occur, but we suspect the key is in the involvement of the parents. Through their participation, parents are able to become better socializers of their children, permitting the beneficial effects of Head Start to spill over into the home environment.

In the past 25 years, millions of children have participated in Head Start, at the rate of more than 400,000 per year. Still, only 18% of the children eligible for the program are enrolled. President Bush's recent move to add $500 million to Head Start's budget will help reach a significant new portion of the disadvantaged population. The challenge to Head Start in the 1990s is to maintain high quality as it attempts to reach more children and to expand its hours to accommodate the child-care needs of low-income working mothers.

SUPPORTING WHAT FAMILIES DO

Of all the intervention approaches designed to help children, those based on a family-support model show the most promise. The best interventions, in short, are those that help parents do a better job. Many of these programs are not very expensive. One successful element of such programs is home visitation, a component that has proven valuable in reducing the impact and incidence of many family problems, including child abuse.[34] Such projects could easily employ senior citizens as home visitors. We have to discover ways to avert the possibility of children and the elderly becoming foes in the policy process. An exploration of inter-generational activities looks like a simple and inexpensive way to enhance the lives of all participants.

Another positive step would be the institution of a national infant-care leave policy. At long last a vigorous national debate focuses on this issue. Among all industrialized nations, the United States stands alone in its lack of a statutory infant-care leave policy. Seventy-five other countries offer an average of four to five months of paid leave and grant average benefits of from 60% to 90% of a woman's wage.[35] In many other nations, fathers are provided with leaves as well. But in the United States, women have no fed-erally mandated right to a furlough from work to care for a newborn. Should they take such a leave, they must forgo income and benefits; they also have no job protection when they want to return to work.

The lack of an infant-care leave has potentially damaging effects. In a survey of 181 American women who had recently given birth, researchers found that many of the mothers felt that they were compelled to return to work before they were physically and emotionally ready to do so.[36] Moreover, infants themselves may be unready for their mothers' departure for work.

The arrival of a new infant signals many changes within the life of the family, and the way the family unit adjusts to those changes may have developmental consequences for the infant.[37] During their first months, infants have special needs and are extremely sensitive to the interpersonal climate in which they are reared. A number of experts have documented the precise nature of this sensitivity.[38] An infant's first experiences with a caregiver influence not only the parent–child bond but also subsequent relations with other adults and with peers. If allowed to develop, feelings of acceptance and effectiveness gained in early infancy can positively affect the entire developmental course.

For all the above reasons, statutory parental leave is essential now that so many parents are in the out-of-home work force. Those of us in the field of child development have recommended a six-month leave, with pay at 75% of salary for three months.

Statutory parental leave would serve at least three purposes. First, it establishes some entitlement for parents and renders the workplace a bit more family friendly. Second, health benefits are continued during absence from work. Third, it guarantees mothers a job when they return to work. At present, many parents effectively must choose between having a child and having an income. The absence of adequate child care com-pounds this problem.

At the 1970 White House Conference on Children, child care was voted the primary problem faced by American families. Not only do we as a nation lack minimal physical standards for child-care settings, we also fail to recognize the need for skilled, adequately compensated staff who will remain in their positions and provide children with continuity of care.

Too many Americans see child care as a service that permits parents to work. It is far more than that. In purchasing child care, parents are buying an environment that will influence significantly the development of their child. Child-care environments can be placed on a continuum from good to bad. If the quality of care falls below a certain threshold, the child's optimal development will be compromised.

The standards that we have been working to establish in this country at the national level since 1969 represent the attempts of experts to define that threshold. Experts agree that for optimal care, no adult should care for more than three infants. Today in the United States it is common to find a ratio of six to one and eight to one. Only three states have a three-to-one standard.

Meanwhile, the child-care debate rages at the federal level. Not only standards are at issue; funding is an additional thorny problem. Because of pressure from special-interest groups, notably large, for-profit child-care chains and smaller, home-based facilities, we are unlikely to see adequate national standards in the near future. We may have to address the problem state by state, but address it we must, and soon, before another generation of children suffers the grave consequences of undependable and inadequate child care.

One promising solution to the child-care crisis is the School of the 21st Century, a proposal for a national system of child care and parent support based in neighborhood schools.[39] Several states have taken the initiative in establishing model projects. A school district in Missouri heard of the plan and asked for assistance in setting up the entire program, which includes three outreach elements in addition to day care for three- to five-year-olds year-round in school buildings and care for school-aged children before school, after school, and during school vacations.

Outreach consists of parent education, screening of children, and guidance for parents of children up to age three; a support network for registered neighborhood family day-care homes; and information and referral services. The State of Connecticut has passed a bill funding demonstration projects of the School of the 21st Century; these are now under way in three schools. Similar legislation has been introduced in Florida. Programs are already under way in Wyoming and Colorado and are in the planning stages in Iowa, Wisconsin, and Ohio. The Bush Center in Child Development and Social Policy at Yale has held a training institute for school administrators interested in establishing programs in their districts and the Bush Center will continue to offer assistance to fledgling programs.

The future looks promising for comprehensive family-support programs such as the School of the 21st Century. Despite the individualistic cast of much of American social thought, recognition is growing that family support fosters the growth and development of the individual and thus protects the individual. Given the current state of our society, some broad forms of family support are necessary if our children are to reach their developmental potential. Although some view family support as an intrusion on family and individual rights, children will not be able to assume such rights without the opportunity to grow up in an environment that meets their basic needs.

Our agenda is not to place families in mandatory programs. Rather, our goal is to make attractive options available to parents. As a nation, we must confront the massive structural problems that plague family life. If we continue to ignore the relation between social policy reform and the quality of life for children and families, we will do so at our peril.

NOTES

1. Alvin Toffler, *Future Shock* (New York: Random House, 1970).

2. Sar A. Levitan, Richard S. Belous, and Frank Gallo, *What Is Happening to the American Family?* (rev. ed.) (Baltimore: Johns Hopkins, 1988).

3. Edmund Burke, *Reflections on the Revolution in France* (1760; rpt. Harmondsworth, England: Penguin Books, 1984), p. 103.

4. Ibid, p. 106.

5. Bureau of Labor Statistics, U.S. Department of Labor, *Employment in Perspective: Women in the Labor Force*, Fourth Quarter, Report 749 (Washington, DC: U.S. Government Printing Office, 1987).

6. Sandra Hofferth and Deborah A. Phillips, "Child Care in the United States, 1970 to 1995," *Journal of Marriage and the Family* 49 (August 1987), pp. 559–571.

7. "The 21st Century Family," *Newsweek*, Special Edition, (Winter–Spring, 1990).

8. Hofferth and Phillips, op. cit.

9. "The 21st Century Family," op. cit., p. 16.

10. Joy D. Osofsky, "Risk and Protective Factors for Teenage Mothers and Their Infants," *SRCD Newsletter* (Winter 1990).

11. Ibid.

12. Hofferth and Phillips, op. cit.

13. Jean L. Richardson, Kathleen Dwyer, Kimberly McGuigan, et al., "Substance

Abuse among Eighth Grade Students Who Take Care of Themselves after School," *Pediatrics* 84 (No. 3, 1989), pp. 556–566.

14. Mellman & Lazarus, Inc., *Mass Mutual American Family Values Study* (Washington, DC: Mellman & Lazarus, Inc., 1989).

15. Yankelovich, Skelly & White, Inc., *The General Mills Family Report, 1976–1977: Raising Children in a Changing Society* (Minneapolis: General Mills, Inc., 1977).

16. Jay Belsky, "Early Human Experience: A Family Perspective," *Developmental Psychology* 17 (1981), pp. 3–23; Urie Bronfenbrenner, *The Ecology of Human Development: Experiments by Nature and Design* (Cambridge, MA: Harvard University Press, 1979); Edward Zigler and Winnie Berman, "Discerning the Future of Early Childhood Intervention," *American Psychologist* 38 (No. 8, 1983), pp. 894–906; Edward Zigler and Matia Finn-Stevenson, *Children: Development and Social Issues* (Lexington, MA: D. C. Heath, 1987).

17. Edward Zigler and Nancy W. Hall, "The Implications of Early Intervention Efforts for the Primary Prevention of Juvenile Delinquency," in James Q. Wilson and Glenn C. Loury, eds., *From Children to Citizens, Vol. 3: Families, Schools and Delinquency Prevention* (New York: Springer-Verlag, 1987).

18. David P. Farrington, "Early Precursors of Frequent Offending," in James Q. Wilson and Glenn C. Loury, eds., *From Children to Citizens, Vol. 1: Families, Schools, and Delinquency Prevention* (New York: Springer-Verlag, l987).

19. Jay Belsky, "Infant Day Care: A Cause for Concern?" *Zero to Three* 6 (No. 5, 1986), pp. 1–7.

20. Patricia Schroeder, "Parental Leave: The Need for a Federal Policy," in Edward Zigler and Meryl Frank, eds., *The Parental Leave Crisis: Toward a National Policy* (New Haven, CT: Yale University Press, l988).

21. Daniel Goleman, "New Measure Finds Growing Hardship for Youth," *New York Times*, October 19, l989.

22. Meeting of child and family advocates and organizations convened by Julius Richmond, Cosmos Club, Washington, DC, March, 1989.

23. Eleanor Szanton, *Infants Can't Wait: The Numbers* (Washington, DC: National Center for Clinical Infant Programs, 1986).

24. "The 21st Century Family," op. cit.

25. Edward Zigler, "Controlling Child Abuse in America: An Effort Doomed to Failure?" in Richard Bourne and Eli Newberger, eds., *Critical Perspectives on Child Abuse* (Lexington, MA: Lexington Books, l979).

26. Julius B. Richmond and Juel Janis, "Child Health Policy and Child Abuse," in George Gerbner, Catherine J. Ross, and Edward Zigler, eds., *Child Abuse: An Agenda for Action* (New York: Oxford University Press, 1980); David L. Olds, "The Prenatal/Early Infancy Project," in Richard H. Price, Emory L. Cowen, Raymond P. Lorion, and Julia Ramos-McKay, eds., *Fourteen Ounces of Prevention: A Casebook for Practitioners* (Washington, DC: American Psychological Association, 1988).

27. National Commission on Excellence in Education, *A Nation at Risk: The Imperative for Educational Reform* (Washington, DC: U.S. Government Printing Office, 1983).

28. Ibid.

29. Edward Zigler, "Addressing the Nation's Child Care Crisis: The School of the Twenty-First Century," *American Journal of Orthopsychiatry* 59 (No. 4, October 1989), pp. 484–491.

30. Child Care Employee Project, *Who Cares: Child Care Teachers and the Quality of Care in America*, Executive Summary, National Child Care Staffing Study (Oakland, CA: Child Care Employee Project, 1989).

31. Sally Provence and Audrey Naylor, *Working with Disadvantaged Parents and Their Children: Scientific and Practical Issues* (New Haven, CT: Yale University Press, 1983).

32. Ibid.

33. Edward Zigler, Willa A. Abelson, Penelope K. Trickett, and Victoria Seitz, "Is an Intervention Program Necessary in Order to Improve Economically Disadvantaged Children's IQ Scores?" *Child Development* 53 (1982), pp. 340–348.

34. Ronald J. Lally, Peter L. Mangione, and Alice S. Honig, "The Syracuse University Family Development Research Program: Long-range Impact on an Early Intervention with Low-income Children and Their Families," in Douglas R. Powell, ed., *Parent Education as Early Childhood Intervention: Emerging Directions in Theory, Research, and Practice* (Norwood, NJ: Ablex Publishing Company, 1988), pp. 79–104.

35. Sheila Kamerman, Alfred J. Kahn, and Paul Kinston, *Maternity Leave Policies and Working Women* (New York: Columbia University Press, 1983).

36. Ellen A. Farber, Marguerite Alejandro-Wright, and Susan Muenchow, "Managing Work and Family: Hopes and Realities," in Edward Zigler and Meryl Frank, eds., *The Parental Leave Crisis: Toward a National Policy* (New Haven, CT: Yale University Press, 1988).

37. Pauline Hopper and Edward Zigler, "The Medical and Social Science Basis for a National Infant Care Leave Policy," *American Journal of Orthopsychiatry* 58 (No. 3, 1988), pp. 324–337.

38. T. Berry Brazelton, Barbara Kozlowski, and Mary Main, "The Origins of Reciprocity: The Early Mother-Infant Interaction," in Michael Lewis and Leonard Rosenblum, eds., *The Effect of the Infant on the Caregiver* (New York: John Wiley, 1974); Daniel N. Stern, *The First Relationship: Infant and Mother* (Cambridge, MA: Harvard University Press, 1977); James Sorce, Robert Emde, Joseph Campos, and Mary Klinnert, "Maternal Emotional Signaling: Its Effect on the Visual Cliff Behavior of One-Year-Olds," Paper presented at the meeting of the Society for Research in Child Development, Boston, April 1981.

39. Zigler, "Addressing the Nation's Child Care Crisis: The School of the Twenty-First Century," op. cit., pp. 484–490.

═══15═══
Conclusion:
Family Values and
Policies in the 1990s

I. THE SMITH FAMILY AGENDA

Searching through this book for final conclusions—some transcendent meaning, some call to action—two simple images stand out. The first, drawn from Jean Elshtain's chapter, is the fictional Smith family of Fremont, Nebraska. Like millions of real families across the nation, the Smiths are a strong, successful family whose members live out, every day, the idea of "family values." Although the Smiths, Elshtain tells us, may not match "the romantic bohemian or rebel" in achieving "those creations of self that enhance an aesthetic contruction of life and sensibility," they do undertand the moral meaning of "sitting up all night with a sick child."

The second image is from G. K. Chesterton, who is quoted by Gilbert Meilaender in chapter 8 on the subject of a little girl's hair:

> That I know is a good thing. . . . If other things are against it, other things must go down. . . . All around her the social fabric shall sway and split and fall; the pillars of society shall be shaken, and the roofs of ages come rushing down; and not one hair of her head shall be harmed.

I have never visited Fremont, Nebraska, but I feel certain, somehow, that the Smith family would endorse this sentiment.

One basic conclusion from these essays, however, is that the Smith family is in trouble. Their ideal of family life—"if other things are against it, other things must go down"—is not fashionable in today's society. Especially within elite culture, the Smiths come across as a bit quaint, almost anachronistic.

Today's social institutions—the workplace, the schools, the media, the courts, the government—demonstrate very little support for or even understanding of the Smith family. At times, these institutions even seem hostile to the Smiths. With each passing year, moreover, fewer and fewer children in America live in families like the Smith family: two parents, married for life, strongly devoted to each other and to raising their children.

Yet, oddly enough, not many policy experts, when pressed for answers to today's family dilemma, would risk the naive-sounding reply: "We need more Smiths!" Indeed, for most legislators and students of family policy, the Smiths amount to pretty thin gruel. They provide no easy handles, no obvious "policy implications." Certainly they are rarely the standard by which current policy is crafted or evaluated. As a result, most of today's conferences or Congressional hearings on family issues would strike the Smiths, correctly, as largely irrelevant to their lives. Current family policy, in short, focuses on casualties and crises—what's broken—rather than on what seems to work in Nebraska.

This fact is both tragic and ironic. The Smiths, from society's perspective, function as highly successful unpaid social workers. They are precisely the reverse of a problem: their life-style works to prevent a whole range of family problems analyzed in this volume. The irony, therefore, is that the Smiths constitute a demonstrably effective social program. The tragedy is that our society is slowly dismantling this particular type of social program.

Perhaps it is no wonder, then, that family life in our society is deteriorating and that, as Edward Zigler and Elizabeth Gilman forcefully point out in chapter 14, the quality of life for America's children is declining. For the family as a social institution, the evolutionary process seems to be going in the wrong direction. Both public policy and cultural fashion, especially elite fashion, encourage adaptation to what is dysfunctional rather than emulation of what is functional. Our society, to put it more simply, is becoming an increasingly less friendly place for the Smith family of Fremont, Nebraska.

If this is the nub of the problem, what is the solution? If the Smith family were to read these essays and discuss them at the family dinner table, I imagine them—perhaps with my help—picking out several proposals that, taken together, constitute what might be called the "Smith Family Agenda."

The Smith Seal of Approval

Doubtless, for example, the Smiths would concur with Urie Bronfenbrenner in chapter 2 that the "development of human character and competence" is shaped primarily by the quality of the child–parent bond—what he describes as the "escalating psychological ping-pong game between two people who are crazy about each other." Yet Bronfenbrenner warns that the "conditions that undergird" those relationships are "being eroded and destroyed in contemporary societies," particularly by "the increasing instability, inconsistency, and hectic character of daily family life."

Accordingly, as a new tool of policy analysis, the Smiths might favor what could be called the "Bronfenbrenner Test." Under this plan, our society would pose a challenge to every program, both governmental and private sector, that affects children: Does this program strengthen the parent–child bond? Or does it contribute to family fragmentation? In evaluating programs, the Bronfenbrenner Test would not be the only question. But it would be the first and most important question.

Some other ideas might also merit the Smith seal of approval:

● David Popenoe's call for a new social movement to "reinvigorate the cultural ideals of family, parents, and children within the changed circumstances of our time."

● Victor Fuchs' proposal for larger tax credits for families with children. Such credits would constitute an incentive for greater investment in children as well as a means for a more equitable distribution of income. In describing the phenomenon of Americans underinvesting in children, Fuchs also suggests that "in some ways the simplest reallocation would be for parents to spend more time with their children." I see the Smiths nodding in approval.

● Mark Mellman, Edward Lazarus, and Allan Rivlin's finding that, in all of the challenges facing contemporary families, the theme running through and uniting them is that of time—or more precisely, the decreasing amount of time that family members spend together. Accordingly, the Smiths might well agree with Sylvia Hewlett that, for employed parents, workplace policies that give them more time with their children are often preferable to policies that simply free them to spend more time on the job.

● Edward Zigler and Elizabeth Gilman's call, echoed by Dennis Orthner and others, for expanded parental-leave policies and also their assertion that the best policy interventions are simply those that help parents do a better job.

● Gilbert Meilaender's plea that religious leaders reclaim their ability and authority to speak normatively about family life—to teach family values—as part of the larger mission of faith.

● Bruce Hafen's argument that family law should become more supportive of the family as a social institution and less preoccupied with the enshrinement of personal autonomy as our reigning legal norm.

● Lynette Friedrich Cofer and Robin Smith Jacobvitz's conclusion that we need "disaster relief " from the impact of movies and television on family life—much more funding for quality public television, a national debate about the concentration of media power in the hands of a few giant corporations, and a requirement that patently trashy and offensive television shows be restricted to late-night time slots during which fewer children will be watching.

● Jean Bethke Elshtain's view of strong families as the enemy of political tyranny and the guardian of political pluralism—fundamental cornerstones of free societies and democratic institutions.

Smith for President?

Elshtain stubbornly refuses to say, but I suspect that among these Smiths—perhaps a grandfather or great uncle—we might discover one Jefferson Smith, the hero of Frank Capra's 1939 movie, *Mr. Smith Goes to Washington*. In the film, the naive Mr. Smith tangles with cynical big shots—and wins—over his belief in American ideals and his determination to create a new social program to help children (in this case, a camp for boys). Perhaps one of those Smiths—maybe Mrs. Smith this time—ought to get busy in the 1990s. David Popenoe and company will need many friends in order to launch a "new social movement" to strengthen family life.

Perhaps she could even run for political office. In contemporary political terms, the Smith Family Agenda, taken as a whole, is neither conservative nor liberal, neither Republican nor Democratic. Because it focuses on the quality of family life, it stands in sharp contrast with the symbols, slogans, and polarizations of both left and right in today's political debate. At bottom, it recognizes that strong values and new policies can work together, not against one another in some false political antagonism. Perhaps Mrs. Smith, or someone like her, could fill an astonishing political void in our nation. She could become our electoral equivalent of Bill Cosby—the pro-family candidate. She would certainly have my vote.

David Blankenhorn

II. STRENGTHENING THE TWO-PARENT HOME

The family debate in America has entered a critical stage. Liberals and conservatives both proclaim the centrality of the family in society, but differ over the policy implications of that proclamation. Political leaders advocate differing solutions to controversial questions of child care, parental leave, teen pregnancy, and abortion. Others look to the private sector, particularly the workplace, to become "family friendly" through policies that will enable parents to be effective as both workers and parents. Recommended employment policies include greater availability of part-time employment opportunities, flex-time, job sharing, and child-care assistance. Still others argue that "family policy begins at home"—that is, ultimate responsibility resides not with the government or the employer, but rather with parents themselves. In this view, families can be no stronger than the family environment that parents create.

These contrasting positions have often led to political paralysis concerning family policy. Liberals desire greater governmental activism. They cite the measures that Scandinavian countries have taken to support families and decry the fact that America is the only advanced nation that does not have a national policy of family supports.

Economic conservatives worry about the budgetary impact of family-support programs. They cite the tax rates of Sweden and Israel as the price Americans would have to pay for a national family policy. Instead, many of these analysts look to the private sector to help, claiming that when employers recognize the demographic realities of the 1990s, especially the role of working women in a generally shrinking labor force, they will take measures—out of self-interest, not altruism—to help working parents.

Social conservatives claim that the family is undermined by policies that encourage mothers of young children to leave the home or that foster "social parenting" in child-care settings. These thinkers desire clear statements upholding the moral value of the family as a social institution and rejecting the widely heralded "alternatives to the family" so popular in the 1960s and 1970s.

This political polarization produces, in turn, a polarized cultural climate. Liberals perceive the social conservatives as nostalgic for an image of the nuclear family more mythical than real and perhaps also as moral absolutists so convinced of the righteousness of their positions that they blame and stigmatize those who do not fit the traditional family model. Conversely, conservatives decry the permissiveness of the liberal ethic, which, they claim, has promoted a culture of hedonistic individualism that is antithetical to family life. Contemporary liberalism, they claim, is rooted in a moral relativism that harms family life by insisting that all lifestyles are morally, and therefore socially, equal.

Yet this polarization is by no means inevitable. Here is the basic point for the coming period: *the concern for preserving family values can be combined with new public and private sector policies to strengthen family life.* Such a centrist consensus is not only politically useful; it is intellectually compelling. We need not choose between governmental intervention and greater emphasis on family values. Both are important. Each, by itself, is necessary but not sufficient.

Nor must we choose between a moral absolutism that suggests intolerance and a moral relativism that denies clear articulation of norms and preferred models. In other words, we require policy instrumentalities—child care, parental leave, and others—because they will assist parents. However, these instrumentalities will be effective only within an overall culture supportive of family as a basic value. In short, we have the opportunity to seize the moral high ground, to fuse the vision of cultural values with family-support policies.

Until now the family-support movement, rooted in the demand for more and better government programs, has not succeeded. More than two decades of public advocacy on behalf of family supports have yet to produce a political breakthrough. One reason for that failure is that the liberal sector is widely perceived in our society as undermining the family, primarily because of its endorsement of moral relativism. This perception is unlikely to change unless policy advocates themselves change. In the future, then, those policy advocates who are committed to the family as a basic value—who are willing to stand up for norms rather than simply endorse an ethos of permissivism—are far more likely to capture the attention and support of the American people for their policy ideas.

Work and Family

What would such a new program—call it "policy initiatives and cultural education"—look like? One issue clearly relates to balancing work and family responsibilities. Employers need to recognize that employees have family responsibilities and that workers are not deficient if they take those responsibilities seriously. The workplace, in short, must be made "family friendly." It should assist workers in securing quality child care, provide parental leave for parents of newborn infants, and offer flexible work hours through flextime, job sharing, and part-time employment.

As Sylvia Hewlett points out in this volume, some of these developments are already taking place in the corporate sector. As employers examine the demographic projections for the 1990s and beyond, which suggest that quality employees will be at a premium, they will seek to create an environment that will attract and retain employees who wish to be both responsible parents and responsible workers.

Yet instrumentalities such as day care and flextime may assist only those already committed to preserving families. Much more basic than these instrumentalities are the values—the family philosophy—that people actually live out in their family lives. In this sense, to strengthen today's families requires a program of cultural education to combat the ethos of unbridled individualism and the culture of narcissism that inhibit the commitment and sacrifice so crucial to successful marriages and effective parenting.

Marriage and Family Life Education

Curricula and programs must be developed to help couples to grow together, to accommodate each other, and thereby lessen our society's rate of divorce. To be sure, divorce need not be stigmatized. Often it is not only a personal tragedy but also a necessary solution to an irreparable marriage. But divorce also should not be viewed simply as one good way to solve marital problems—one "viable option" whenever difficulties arise—but rather as a course of last resort, after all efforts to save the marriage have failed.

Programs are needed that will train young people in the art of healthy marital communication and family relationships. Premarital counseling, family life programs, and high school and college courses on the family provide excellent opportunities to sensitize individuals to the heavy demands of marriage, to the need for mutual respect and accommodation, and to the necessity of the commitment to one another and to the relationship that is so crucial for successful marriages.

Mass Media Makeovers

Moreover, we need to change the image of marriage and family conveyed in the popular culture and media. In 1983, an American Jewish Committee report on situation comedies on prime-time television pointed out that all marital difficulties were portrayed as solvable within 22 minutes or less of program time.[1] In contrast, we require—and should advocate for—television programming that portrays realistic role models and suggests that conflicts can be resolved only if the family members are committed to working together to iron out difficulties. Greater consultation with media personnel are necessary to encourage development of realistic portraits of marriage and broader dissemination of successful role models for contemporary families.

Cultural Education and Building Strong Communities

Public and private sectors alike ought to consider developing programs to strengthen marriage by providing greater training for marriage and promoting realistic expectations of what marriage entails. Author Francine Klagsbrun, in her recent book *Married People*, urges such a bias in favor of marriage.[2] If we consider marriage and family as desirable ends in themselves and vital to the health of society in general, that pro-marriage bias should be strongly encouraged.

The "delivery system" for such a program of cultural education might best be channeled through the network of mediating structures that serve as a buffer between the family and society. These churches, synagogues, and volunteer associations may best inculcate family values by building strong communities that can serve as peer-group support for the idea and value of family and that can assist families in crisis, functioning as a surrogate for the older model of the extended family.

A model for such groups may be drawn from the Orthodox Jewish community. Orthodox Jewish families generally have three or more children, invest heavily in quality Jewish education, and maintain very low rates of divorce. These facts should not be attributed to religious prohibitions against birth control or divorce, which are minimal to nonexistent in traditional Judaism. Rather, the successes of Orthodox families testify to the close interrelationship between family and community. Strong families build strong Jewish communities. Conversely, vital Jewish communities create a public climate conducive to healthy family life. Traditional Jewish families that celebrate Jewish holidays and life-cycle events are expressing the relationship between strong families and strong communities. They are expressing how the public realm can strengthen the private realm of family life through public norms valued by the community, combined with programs that help parents to be better parents.

This overall proposal—developing a consensus uniting advocates of policy instrumentalities with advocates of cultural values supporting family life—will certainly not be easy to achieve. In 1980, the White House Conference on the Family, unable to agree even on a definition of the family, changed its name to the White House Conference on Families. A coalition that included both the right-to-life movement and the National Association of Non-Parents could hardly have agreed on the ideological issue of what constitutes a family. Thus the conference abandoned any attempt at normative discourse in favor of a celebration of pluralism in which virtually all types of living patterns might be considered a family.

Yet family issues do not disappear by redefining terminology. In New York City alone, 37% of all births in 1983 were out of wedlock. In Baltimore, the figure that year was 60%. One may hardly claim that children born to teenage unwed mothers mature in a privileged environment. Absent fathers, inadequate finances, adolescent parents—all promote an atmosphere unconducive to nurturing and personal growth. Surely both liberals and conservatives, policy advocates and moral philosophers, can agree on this point as we approach the new century.

Stable families, in turn, both provide opportunities for personal growth and hold the key to society's future through the socialization of children. For these reasons, we should be willing to assert our cultural preferences for traditional norms such as marriage and the two-parent home while at the same time accommodating and reaching out to those who have chosen to lead their lives within alternative settings. We need have no nostalgia for the mythical nuclear family of the 1950s. Conversely, we have no need to redefine the family so as to recognize all possible living arrangements as being equally preferable. Rather, we need to advocate programs that encourage responsible preparation for marriage and parenthood and that communicate that if society acknowledges family cohesion as a desirable personal and communal goal, it is the responsibility of society to support families.

Steven Bayme

III. THE FAMILY IN A TIME OF TROUBLE

Every known form of human existence includes not only the family, but also family norms—a cluster of core moral ideas, including both calls to action and barriers to action, regarding sexuality and family obligations. Every way of life must by definition embody some such set of basic notions.

My hope for our society is that we value a particular ideal of family life that does not repeat earlier forms of female oppression and is based in equality, on the ideal of husband and wife as helpmates, and on children, not as property, but as a gift and a responsibility.

Children should be reared in a setting where they are loved in a manner that establishes basic trust. This requires the presence of specific beloved others. Today, as a society, we are faring poorly in our treatment of children.

Most of us affirm children's needs for primary, long-term ties with others. But the wider society often fails miserably in efforts to help sustain those ties.

Consider this paradox: Despite the massive changes of the past three decades, most people in our society still desire strong families and remain devoted to an idealized picture of family life. Yet we make it more and more difficult for families to survive as intact, intimate units. Family imagery figures prominently in our political symbols and slogans. It permeates our deepest aspirations, fears, resentments, and hopes. It runs like a strong river through American fiction. But we have made it almost impossible for families to flourish. Exploring this paradox has been, in some ways, the central mission of this book. I offer only three concluding thoughts. One is a small quarrel over a word; the second is a plea for disenthrallment; and the last, perhaps fittingly, is a story about grandmothers.

Family "Functions" and Ideals

My small quarrel is with the word "functions." It is a word from sociology that, alas, pops up in most discussions of the family. It has even crept frequently into this book. Many analysts study the family primarily because it performs, or has performed, various "functions" for the wider society. Today, they argue, many social functions previously performed by the family have been reassigned elsewhere. In the past, the typical family functioned as an economic cooperative, a kindergarten, a school, a welfare department, a Sunday school, a house of correction, and a vocational training institute—all under one roof.

Today, with these previous functions dispersed to a variety of other social institutions, all that's left to the family is the private psychological well-being of its members and something called the "nurturant socialization of the young." Families, in short, become primarily emotional or affective institutions. Some even argue that these modern, trimmed-down families, no longer burdened by so many functions, are now better equipped to succeed at the psychological and nurturing tasks that remain.

There is, of course, much truth to this "functionalist" approach. But there is a problem as well, as several essays in this volume demonstrate. This framework, which dominates contemporary social science treatments of the family, cannot help us to understand the inner realities of family life. It ignores the nuances and textures of those human relations that make up the heart of the family's existence. All too few specialists attempt to see the family whole, on its own terms: first, as a set of powerful social relations with their own vital integrity and meaning to participants; and second, as one dimension of a wider community conceived not in functionalist terms but as a normative ideal of social and political life.

Disenthrallment

The family debate typically splits into two camps. One conveys a doomsday mentality and foresees the end of Western civilization if something isn't done, and soon, about the crisis of the family. The other lapses into cozy assurances that things are not really that bad, that reports of family fragmentation are exaggerated, and that people still, most of the time, grow up in families, create new families, and live out their lives in families.

Together with several contributors to this volume, I reject these either–or polarities. Certainly millions of individual families show great resilience, good humor, and strength of character when confronted with the possibilities and the pitfalls of modern life. There are both individual and family survivors; some families seem to grow stronger with each passing year.

But finally, we must acknowledge the signs of danger. Great and serious obstacles block our human paths. These obstacles stem in part from the economic and political trends of our time. But above all, they stem from fears and dislocations that are essentially moral and cultural. The evidence of human sorrow, confusion, and tragedy created by these combined forces is simply too ominous to ignore. America is an innately optimistic society, but sometimes we indulge that optimism at our peril.

In the dark days of the Civil War, Abraham Lincoln insisted that the time had come to think and act anew, to disenthrall ourselves. The essays in this volume ought to help disenthrall us from tired ways of thinking about the family and from threadbare approaches to family policy. Disenthrallment is never pleasant or easy. Accordingly, this volume may generate controversies. We hope it does.

Controversy, it seems, is inevitable when the subject is family. For we are, first and foremost, familial beings. We all have a stake in what happens to family values. Nothing less than our most precious and vulnerable human ties are at stake.

Grandmothers

My co-editor, David Blankenhorn, sometimes suggests that we can learn more about the family from 10 grandmothers than we can from 10 family experts. He may be serious. He may be right. During a trip to Argentina in 1986, I met a group of women known as the *Abuelas*, the Grandmothers of the Plaza de Mayo. These grandmothers organized to find their missing grandchildren, who may have been abducted by an out-of-control military junta that had kidnapped, tortured, and murdered thousands of civilians in its campaign against "subversives." The logo of this organization features a happy child, grinning ear to ear, arms outstretched, hands opened wide, framed by three words: *Identidad, Familia, Libertad*—identity, family, liberty.

For these grandmothers—who, in many cases, have spent a decade or more trying to recover their lost grandchildren—personal identity, family ties, and liberty are one and inseparable: the basis of their existence. Yet in contemporary America, we seem to have constructed a cultural ethos that defines personal identity as that of a sovereign, untrammeled self. Family ties become a drag on the freedom of that sovereign self: something to get out of, reduce in importance, or redefine as simply one choice among many. Liberty, in this view, is defined as self-assertion and mobility—not, as the grandmothers understand it, as a celebration of the interdependencies of family, friends, comrades.

To the Grandmothers of Plaza de Mayo, who have lost family in horrible ways, this modern American ethos, which tends to see freedom and commitment as opposites, must seem inexplicable and even cruel. Perhaps we could learn from the horrors they suffer and the hopes they cherish.

Jean Bethke Elshtain

NOTES

1. Harry Kovsky, *Family: The Missing Ingredient in TV Family Fare*, Report of the American Jewish Committee (New York: American Jewish Committee, June 1984). This report was based on 1983 data.

2. Francine Klagsbrun, *Married People* (New York: Bantam Books, 1985).

About the Editors

David Blankenhorn is President of the Institute for American Values, a New York City-based organization devoted to research, publication, and public education on issues of family well-being and family policy. Prior to founding the Institute in 1987, he worked as a community organizer in Virginia and Massachusetts. He is a graduate of Harvard University and received an M.A. in history from Warwick University in Coventry, England. His essays on family issues have appeared in many publications.

Steven Bayme is Director of Jewish Communal Affairs at the American Jewish Committee in New York City. He is a graduate of Yeshiva University and received his Ph.D. in Jewish history from Columbia University. He is the editor of *Facing the Future: Essays on Contemporary Jewish Life* and has published numerous articles on family well-being, family policy, parenting, Jewish religious movements, and Jewish responses to modernity.

Jean Bethke Elshtain is Centennial Professor of Political Science at Vanderbilt University in Nashville, Tennessee. She is a graduate of the University of Colorado and received her Ph.D. in politics from Brandeis University. She is the author of *Public Man, Private Woman* and *Women and War*. She has also written many articles on politics, women, and the family for both scholarly and popular publications.

Next Steps: How to Help

This book is one part of a larger effort to create new opportunities for a national conversation about the status and future of the family as a social institution. This effort seeks to involve scholars, opinion leaders, and concerned citizens from a diversity of disciplines and perspectives and will include conferences, research, publications, and public education. If you are interested in contributing to that conversation, contact one or more of these organizations:

Institute for American Values
250 West 57th Street, Suite 2415
New York, New York 10107
(212) 246-3942
David Blankenhorn, President

The American Jewish Committee
165 East 56th Street
New York, New York 10022
(212) 751-4000
Dr. Steven Bayme, Director of Jewish Communal Affairs

Family Service America
11700 West Lake Park Drive
Milwaukee, Wisconsin 53224
(414) 359-1040
Dr. Robert M. Rice, Executive Vice President